Moving Lessons

Frontispiece. A 1920s photograph of one of Margaret H'Doubler's University of Wisconsin dance students posing lakeside in Madison, Wisconsin. She holds a giant hoop, one of many devices H'Doubler used to facilitate students' movement explorations. (Courtesy University of Wisconsin–Madison Archives)

Moving Lessons

MARGARET H'DOUBLER
AND THE BEGINNING OF DANCE
IN AMERICAN EDUCATION

Janice Ross

The University of Wisconsin Press

The University of Wisconsin Press
2537 Daniels Street
Madison, Wisconsin 53718

3 Henrietta Street
London WC2E 8LU, England

1   3   5   4   2

Printed in the United States of America

Library of Congress Cataloging-in-Publication Data
Ross, Janice.
Moving lessons : Margaret H'Doubler and the beginning
of dance in American education / Janice Ross.
298 pp.   cm.
Includes bibliographical references and index.
ISBN 0-299-16930-8 (cloth: alk. paper)
ISBN 0-299-16934-0 (pbk.: alk. paper)
1. H'Doubler, Margaret Newell, b. 1889.   2. Dance teachers—United
States—Biography.   3. Dance—Study and teaching (Higher)—United
States—History—20th century.   4. Feminism and dance—United
States—History—20 century.   I. Title
GV1785.H37 R68   2000
792.8'0973—dc21   00-008344

Contents

v

Contents

Illustrations

Foreword

In 1926, the University of Wisconsin's Physical Education Department, after ten years of offering dance courses to college women, created the first university dance degree program in the world. Also in 1926, Martha Graham gave her first group dance concert in New York City. American modern dance and dance in American higher education crystallized in the same year, and both were deeply connected to the incursion of women into new spheres of public life since the turn of the century.

The story of how dance entered the twentieth-century university and flourished there—and of how American academia helped to shape the distinctive, powerful genre of American modern dance and, later, postmodern dance—is a complex one. It encompasses threads from diverse histories: the history of women's health, sexuality, education, and political status; the history of dance as art, as entertainment, as recreation, as a form of heterosexual courtship, as psycho-physical expression, and as ethical training; the history of Progressive social reform; and the history of American higher education.

This is the story that Janice Ross tells, in rich and fascinating detail, in *Moving Lessons*. Ross argues that Margaret H'Doubler—a young basketball teacher who, on orders from her (female) boss, single-handedly launched the pioneering dance program at the University of Wisconsin—was a figure who both emblematized her time and also left deep new imprints in American culture. A "New Woman" who, like many in her generation, emerged from a sheltered female Victorian world to take dynamic action in the public sphere, she changed the way Americans thought about not only dance and female physicality but also higher education for women. She was an athlete and an innovator, and yet H'Doubler was not a radical. She was engaged, as Ross puts it, in a "moderate discourse of new womanhood," finding ways that were palatable to administrators and to the public (and thus extremely effective) to advance her innovations. She was a reformer, making changes from within the culture's dominant institutions; as Ross explains, H'Doubler was a pioneer who was also a strategic peacemaker. But the changes she made were lasting and profound.

Ross shows how, like Isadora Duncan, Ruth St. Denis, and other forerunners of modern dance in the early part of the twentieth century, H'Doubler helped to raise the status of dance in the eyes of the American middle class from its despised footing—as either a tawdry lower-class entertainment or a decadent, elitist European art form, and also as a "dangerous" social/sexual interaction between young people—to a serious intellectual and creative enterprise. At a time when the dancing female body became a battleground for cultural anxieties about public morality, these women created forms of dance that simultaneously asserted the dignity and the freedom of dancing women. And that was a feminist issue.

Yet Ross also demonstrates how, although they had much in common, the projects of the art dancers (like Duncan) and the dance educators (especially H'Doubler, but also her lesser-known peers and her disciples) diverged in significant ways. For H'Doubler, dance was of value not primarily as an art form in performance but as a personal form of human expression and mind-body integration in daily practice. Indeed, Ross observes, H'Doubler was "never really a fan of dance as an art form," and when she took her students to see Graham's company perform in Chicago, she remarked disparagingly that she found the spectacle "too professional." H'Doubler instigated a different way of thinking about and doing dance—as a form of democratic "creative art experience" that trained the whole person for civic life. H'Doubler wrote, in *The Dance, and Its Place in Education*, that dance was a means toward "developing a free and full individual" and "a resource for happy living that can be done anywhere and without special equipment." Indeed, she thought it could supply "a philosophy of life" (xi, 31).

For H'Doubler's supervisor and mentor, Blanche Trilling (the director of physical education for women at the University of Wisconsin), for H'Doubler, and for their contemporaries in the field of women's physical culture, issues of women's health were intricately tied up with women's intellectual growth and training—with their success in higher education and in the rest of their lives, whether as wives and mothers or as (largely) unmarried teachers. In the face of a tradition of powerful rhetoric against women's education advanced by men of prestige—such as Harvard University Medical School's Dr. Edward H. Clarke, who worried in 1887 that women might become sterile if they studied too hard (and thus implied that women's enlightenment could lead to the extinction of the human race)—women like Trilling and H'Doubler fought for a partnership of physical *and* intellectual liberation for women. Indeed, Ross argues that the battle for women's health and for the freedom of female bodily movement (both of which were also goals of the dress reform movement that would free the body from crippling corsets and immobilizing heavy layers of clothing) was a direct physical parallel to the contemporaneous battle for women's suffrage.

If in late nineteenth-century iconography in painting, photography, and fashion ideal women were shown as physically *inactive,* these early twentieth-century reformers created spaces where women could learn to be active, even vigorous—athletically but gracefully—and where they could enjoy the community of other women in a noncompetitive ambiance of confidence and self-reliance. H'Doubler's program also created possibilities for women's financial independence from men, since she trained teachers who were quite successful in finding employment; by 1936, alumnae from her dance courses taught at twenty-five colleges and universities and numerous public schools. And these women passed along to new generations of women and girls the values they had learned through dance.

What H'Doubler taught these women was how to explore, cherish, and mold the self through the body—how to unite mind and body in analytic, inventive physical action. Her dance classes, Ross argues, were an early form of assertiveness training for women. Here young women learned not only about anatomy—a liberating study, safely distanced from living bodies by the use of a heuristic skeleton that would become H'Doubler's teaching trademark—but about scientific method, about systematic problem-solving, about disciplined self-expression, and, importantly, about their own capacity for inventiveness and imagination, harnessed to physical realities. This was liberal education at its best, placing a pre-Foucauldian emphasis on taking care of the self in an ethics construed as far broader than morality.

Although women college students had been given programmatic physical education to improve their health since the 1830s—and it had been required of women at the University of Wisconsin since the 1890s—H'Doubler's breakthrough was different from those offered by previous women's exercise programs in academia: it introduced the elements of creativity, guided self-discovery, and student-centered learning. Further, H'Doubler's introduction of dance into the physical education curriculum was paradoxically twofold: on the one hand, she feminized physical education, offering, as an alternative to competitive male sports and mechanical calisthenics, a distinctively female, graceful activity framed as harmonious and natural as well as healthful; on the other hand, she masculinized dance, bringing it into the realm of science and the intellectual public sphere, into the laboratory and the academic classroom.

Thus she raised the social and intellectual status of dance by situating it firmly in a male institutional world, while still preserving its features as an aestheticized, noncompetitive feminine activity that was "safe" for women students.

It is telling that H'Doubler (who began college in 1906) originally wanted to study medicine. Although some women did successfully pursue medical careers at that time (and in fact, Ross tells us, for a long time women doctors were a sine qua non on women's physical education faculties), H'Doubler rechanneled her interest in the human body as a domain of scientific inquiry in a different direction. Her undergraduate degrees in biology and philosophy ultimately informed her analytic studies of the social, scientific, and creative potentialities of the dancing body, rather than of the pathologies of the medical body.

In her teaching and in her own highly influential writings, H'Doubler, like so many progressive twentieth-century educators, closely followed the tenets of John Dewey, with whom she studied as a graduate student at Columbia University in 1916–17. Dewey reinforced H'Doubler's own antipathy toward mind/body dualisms. From him she learned that action precedes ideas—that experience informs knowledge. And from him she absorbed the idea of educating the student as a whole person—not in a narrow vocational way, but for life. Calling him "the father of dance in American higher education," Ross reminds us that Dewey himself had worked with body therapist F. M. Alexander and had earlier introduced dance into the curriculum for children at the University of Chicago Laboratory School. Dewey wrote, in *John Dewey and F. M. Alexander*, that without knowledge of the "psycho-physical life," education is "miseducation" (19). Ross shows that H'Doubler's books *The Dance, and Its Place in Education* (1925) and *Dance: A Creative Art Experience* (1940) directly applied Dewey's ideas to dance, setting forth enduring models for dance education.

Although the founding of Bennington College in 1932 and the summer Bennington School of the Dance in 1934 soon established a different model—an academic dance curriculum that stressed the training of performing artists—nevertheless H'Doubler's approach to training "the thinking dancer" for life has continued to have an enormous impact on dance education at every level. In fact, in spite of H'Doubler's suspicion of dance as a professional performing art, her methods contributed to the various strands of modern and postmodern dance performance that questioned technical training and valued improvisation and the creative impulse. Anna Halprin, who was H'Doubler's student in the late 1930s and the 1940s, has been a key exponent of dance as the exploration of the self, bringing that aspect of dance into both the ecstatic theater of the 1960s and the therapeutic culture of the 1970s and after.

And in the 1960s and 1970s, an entire generation of postmodern dancers, many of whom studied H'Doublerian methods with Anna Halprin and thus are, in a sense, H'Doubler's artistic grandchildren, sublated distinctions between art and life. They eschewed the polish of dance technique in favor of democratic access to dance for all; they preferred the pleasures of somatic discovery in the dance process over the perfection of an aesthetic dance product. Although they were probably unaware of it, their appreciation of the amateur dancer's body as a refreshing antidote to what they saw as the overprofessionalization of dance had a precedent in H'Doubler's own history: Ross suggests that perhaps it was because H'Doubler never trained as a dancer herself that she was able to teach dance and lobby for dance with revitalizing objectivity.

Through a penetrating analysis of H'Doubler's work, Ross not only chronicles the history of the University of Wisconsin dance program but also traces the vicissitudes of dance in the university curriculum. For this is not simply a local history; H'Doubler's program was the template and the source of personnel for so many other university dance programs, both nationally and internationally. Ross pinpoints both the advantages gained and the conflicts that arose when a discipline that stresses bodily knowledge and that mainly attracts women students became institutionalized in academia. She also assesses accurately the quite different challenges university dance programs have faced since H'Doubler's day, as a new generation of teachers, trained as artists rather than educators, with very different values, has come largely to populate dance faculties—especially after the dance boom of the 1960s and 1970s. The issue of whether art is for life or for a profession—and indeed, the general question of whether education should be broadly liberal or narrowly vocational—has deep contemporary resonances especially now, as we begin the twenty-first century.

H'Doubler's ideal of democracy in dance and education was an ideal of liberal education, and yet, for the first half of the twentieth century, for the most part only the more affluent classes could afford this kind of learning. But ironically, when university education became more widely accessible after World War II, partly due to the GI Bill, and when that generation then sent *its* daughters to college, the dollar democracy of the marketplace asserted different priorities. Increasingly, people expected a college education to prepare them for jobs. In terms of arts education, this often meant that they expected to gain a high level of technical proficiency along with their diploma, in order to gain a competitive edge in the scramble for employment. And as Ross points out, by the 1960s becoming a stage dancer was a thoroughly respectable ambition for a woman. Thus, the postwar democratization of higher education—including the entry of many more women into universities—caused professional training programs in dance to proliferate. Even dance programs that had adopted the H'Doublerian approach, including the original dance program at the University of Wisconsin itself, felt the growing pressure from students (and their parents) to place more emphasis on performance skills. Yet now, for a variety of reasons—including the shrinking professional dance marketplace and a heightened awareness of the dancer's physical and emotional stresses—the wisdom of intensive technical training in university dance programs is once again being questioned, and perhaps as a result many dance educators are returning to a more holistic approach.

H'Doubler was a visionary who served as a guru to many, and it is hard to find scholarship about her pedagogical theories and methods that avoids hagiography. One of the great strengths of *Moving Lessons* is Ross's thorough and objective treatment. On the basis of having gathered an enormous amount of evidence, she presents a judicious balance of respect and even admiration for H'Doubler's very real achievements with candid assessments of her flaws and shortcomings.

In the same way, Ross takes a nuanced critical approach to the history of women's bodies—to their representations and realities—that is very welcome as a corrective to monolithic narratives of female victimhood; she shows how despite certain norms, images, and beliefs, and despite enormous social and political limitations for women, some individuals resisted or manipulated cultural pressures to their own and other women's advantage. Consider, for example, her descriptions of late nineteenth-century spas, to which women went not only as neurasthenic invalids seeking cures but also to escape the household, enjoy the company of other women, and taste the sensual pleasures of water treatments.

Though it is an impressive work of archival scholarship and interpretive history, *Moving Lessons* is anything but sober. It is written in a lively, evocative style that makes for riveting reading, whether in the sections on H'Doubler's biography, the detailed descriptions of her classes, or the more abstract unpacking of philosophical theories of learning. Ross has carried out interviews with many of H'Doubler's students, several of whom went on to be influential artists and teachers in their own right. She dug through H'Doubler's lesson plans and notes, and she literally retraced H'Doubler's steps through Lathrop Hall to the dance studio in which she taught so many generations of dancers. Not only dance history but feminist studies and the history of education in America will be enriched by this meticulous and energetic analysis of how dance emerged as a distinctively female field of inquiry and activity in the modern university. It will be indispensable for dance educators, who, in order to plot where we are going, need to know where we are coming from.

SALLY BANES

A Reminiscence

All great innovators and pioneers have three characteristics in common: a fierce commitment and uncompromising integrity to their ideas; a profound and lasting impact on society and culture; and a grand and eloquent vision. Margaret H'Doubler stands among the pioneers in the world of dance. She was a maverick in the field, a woman of strong integrity, a master teacher, and a deep thinker. I was lucky enough to have been her student, disciple, and good friend throughout her life. Of all the teachers I have encountered, hers was the teaching which lasted, the one which first set me on my path and offered me a way to forge my own work. For this, I will always be grateful.

In 1938, when I graduated from high school, only two schools in the United States offered a dance major. One was Bennington College in Vermont, and the other was the University of Wisconsin. I was primed to go to Bennington. I had studied with the most famous modern dance teachers of the time—Doris Humphrey, Charles Weidman, Martha Graham, and Hanya Holm—who also taught at the American Dance Festival at Bennington College. Doris Humphrey had invited me to join the Humphrey-Weidman company in New York City. I had promised my family I would graduate from college before I became a professional dancer, so I decided to postpone this opportunity until I had finished school. I anticipated working with these professional dancers at Bennington.

However, I was not accepted at Bennington. This left me with little option but to attend the University of Wisconsin. What felt like a bitter disappointment at the time turned into the luckiest mishap of my life. It was at the University of Wisconsin that I met the two people who would most influence my dance career: my future husband, Lawrence Halprin, and my mentor, Margaret H'Doubler.

A Reminiscence

In the early 1940s, there were two separate and distinct paths for a dancer. One was to go to New York City and become a member of a professional dance company. The other was to work as a teacher. Bennington was the training ground for the professional life in New York City; Wisconsin was the training ground for the dancer-as-educator. Although these paths remained separate for many years in the dance world, H'Doubler showed me a way to do both. The expansiveness of her vision encouraged me to redefine dance professionalism to include teaching and performing. As I have been successful as a dancer and teacher, I have been able to pass this idea on to subsequent generations of students. I think this has changed the field, as well as the expectations of young dancers regarding the breadth and depth of their careers.

As I write, I am overwhelmed with many memories of Marge and feel a deep sense of awe and affection for this woman who affected my life so deeply. I want to share with you the exact memories and thoughts to reveal just who she was to me. Here is my first memory of Marge. When I arrived at the Lathrop Hall studio for my first class at the University of Wisconsin, I waited nervously in line with forty other bright-eyed students. I assumed our teacher would begin the class with exercises, the way a dance class usually began. Instead, H'Doubler arrived all breathless and enthusiastic. She greeted us warmly and, instead of taking her place in front of regimented lines of students, she invited us to gather informally around her in front of a skeleton. I was shocked. By the end of the day, I was so intellectually stimulated and creatively engaged that I could not wait for the next class.

After this, I understood on some intuitive level that I was not expected to imitate her dancing but rather to learn about the true nature of movement as applied to the human body. Her knowledge of biology, coupled with her understanding of human nature, led to a balanced and holistic teaching. This was all very new and exciting for me. She encouraged us to take the biological, factual knowledge she had and explore it on our own terms as we explored all the possibilities a movement could yield. This self-discovery evoked qualities, feelings, and images. Out of these personal responses we would then create our own dance experience. She helped us infuse our movement with our own creativity. This understanding of the relationship of the objective and the subjective aspects of movement was a road map which has been essential to me in my work.

The four and a half years I spent as her student were continually challenging, inspiring, and creatively engaging. I loved being her student and continued to stay in touch with her up until the time of her death. I can hear her now as I would tell her about an idea I had. She would say, "Ann, you are so right," and then go on to embellish, deepen, clarify, and broaden my thoughts. I never felt disempowered by her deep thinking, but rather enlightened and curious. She was a great listener and wanted to be sure I understood the "big picture" from many perspectives.

Let me share an example of this from a letter she wrote to me in December 1968: "In life, emotions [feelings] exist to call forth action, i.e., behavior for survival. But in dance as art, movement exists to evoke feeling states. It is in the forms . . . of our survival behavior that we find the source of dance forms. It is nature's principle of time and . . . [rhythm] that exists in all movement and when we understand her principle, and work accordingly, nature is rewarding." These were big thoughts for me to meditate on, experiment with, and use to deepen my understanding of my craft. Her perspective so wonderfully included the human experience in relation to the entire world. I found this deeply inspirational and continue to this day to explore along the lines that she so simply pointed out to me. I would often laugh with her as she would invariably explain the properties of protoplasm while I was talking to her about dance. She never stopped giving, caring, and teaching.

I have so many small memories that shed light on her humanity. I remember visiting her in Door County at her summer home and spontaneously skinny-dipping with her in the lake. I remember her elegant clothes, her capes with the stately verve. She prepared her meals with an eye for color and texture. When I started to pick the white seeds out of a bright yellow squash dish she had made, she stopped me, saying, "The seeds are there for the texture." When we would walk down the campus sidewalk, the college boys seeing her from the back would whistle because she had such a great figure. We did a lot of laughing and giggling together. She had a wonderful sense of humor. She could also be determined, strong, stubborn, and powerful.

She steadfastly resisted the demands from other faculty members to incorporate the contemporary "professional" dance personalities and styles of movement into her teaching. This choice was not made out of personal ego; rather, as a true pioneer, she was committed to her beliefs whether or not they were popular. Dance, she believed, must be a creative experience for everyone, and the imposition of an idiosyncratic technique, such as modern dance, was a betrayal to her approach and to the students themselves. She believed that bringing this element into the Dance Department would prevent the students from focusing on the nature of movement and its basic structural principles.

Listen to her own words on this subject: "Technique and expression really become one and the same thing if we think of technique as the only adequate means of expression. Developing technique means directing and changing the untrained, seemingly natural movement patterns into their related art forms. The word 'natural,' however, is an unfortunate one to have crept into dance parlance. It has come to be almost synonymous with that which is formless and without discipline. The 'natural' should mean the perfect state. In this light, 'correct' might be substituted for 'natural.' So few people have developed, without training, the control necessary for good body motion; consequently the first step is to train back to the natural or correct way of moving. This is the only basis upon which consciousness of art movement can be established." This thought has been consequential in my own work with dancers and nondancers alike.

Rooted in this approach, she encouraged us to develop a movement style based on our own personal mythology. This meant finding our own movements within the context of our life experiences, our feelings, our images, and our beliefs. I never felt a lack of "technique" in the more popular sense of the word, because Marge provided me with the road maps to responsibly develop my physical skills with understanding and efficiency.

My last impressions of Marge came with a telephone call from her husband, Wayne Claxton. Marge had died. He said that on her last day she was sitting in a wheelchair in the rest home waving her arms with gusto as she taught an imaginary dance class to the patients in the room. This was a perfect metaphor for her undying passion for the art of teaching. This passion was rooted in her belief that everyone had the birthright to be a dancer and an artist, even her friends in the rest home. She said, "Of course, not everyone can be an artist in the more limited sense of the word. But, if we recognize that it is the nature of the original impulse that leads to creative activity, and the emotional value of its expression that distinguishes any activity as art, then we shall see that he who approaches his work in a creative spirit and makes it the expression of his own vision of life is an artist."

Perhaps the most important way that H'Doubler has affected my work and life was in her view of dance as a holistic art. Long before ideas about the connection among body, mind, and spirit were in common parlance, H'Doubler conceptualized dance from the perspectives of science, philosophy, and aesthetics. She understood dance to be a physical, emotional, and intellectual art. I believe this holistic viewpoint is very significant, and I am glad to see that it is now getting the kind of attention it deserves. Ironically, a lot of this acknowledgment comes from people who do not necessarily call themselves dancers but who enjoy their capacity as human beings to express themselves in movement. I think H'Doubler would be happy to see that this is so.

H'Doubler is said to have remarked that she would know if she had been a successful teacher if she could see how her teaching had affected her students when they reached fifty. I can safely say, from my perch of seventy-eight, that her approach to dance has affected me deeply. The basic, objective, and fundamental road maps she gave me pointed me toward a path I have followed for the whole of my working life. Here was an open-ended method which enabled me to walk this path *in my own way*. And being so open-ended, it allowed me to be this way with my own students, thereby transferring some of H'Doubler's rigorous objective understanding of the body, and her compassionate understanding of human nature, to the people I have encountered on the path.

At last someone has written extensively about Margaret H'Doubler. Janice Ross, a tireless, meticulous researcher, has captured the true significance of H'Doubler's contribution to the fields of education and dance as a creative, humane experience. As you read through this book, you will be continually reminded of the breadth of H'Doubler's holistic vision. Ross places H'Doubler's work squarely in the cultural context of her time. As I read through this book, I was reminded of what H'Doubler wrote in *Dance: A Creative Art Experience*. She said, "To consider a theory, a philosophy, and a science of dance, as well as its claims to be an art and its justification as a way of education, we must extend our inquiry into the related fields of history, philosophy, science, psychology, sociology, education, aesthetics, and art in general. Any study that will contribute to an understanding of human life and its manifestations is pertinent to dance; for the impulse to engage in expressive movement is embedded in the organic nature of man."

It is true for me that through H'Doubler's influence, my own experience in dance addressed a broad spectrum of human issues reflective of the times. This book stands as a firm tribute to a woman who brought the field of dance to its rightful place among the great philosophical, aesthetic, and scientific inquiries. I am indebted to H'Doubler for her courage, her humor, and her humane approach to an art form which has at its heart the intrinsic and deep expression of the human body in relation to the greater world.

ANNA HALPRIN

Acknowledgments

I would like to thank the extraordinary alumnae of the first years of the University of Wisconsin's dance program. These individuals were the cornerstone of my research with their generous sharing of memories of the early years of Margaret H'Doubler's program. Among these alumnae is Anna Halprin, who was the original inspiration for this study; my research on Margaret H'Doubler began in an effort to trace the roots of Halprin's early training at the University of Wisconsin in the 1940s. The indefatigable Hermine Sauthoff Davidson shared with me, in interviews, telephone conversations, and letters, and over meals with Charles Davidson, her rich stories, her original programs, and the names of many other alumnae. Edith Boys Enos also became a wonderful correspondent, sending photographs, letters, and anecdotes. Marion Bigelow, Julia Brown, Frances Cumbee, Jane Eastham, Nancy Harper, Mary Hinkson, Louise Kloepper, A. A. Leath, Ellen Moore, Margaret Jewell Mullen, Helen M. Neihoff, and especially Mary (Buff) Brennan were also invaluable for their patience with lengthy interviews and questions about the early years of the University of Wisconsin dance program. Dr. Brennan freely shared videos, articles, photographs, and dissertations with me and generously provided access to the Lathrop Hall facilities. Louise H'Doubler Nagel, niece of Margaret H'Doubler, shared memories and photographs. Bernard Schermetzler, archivist at the University of Wisconsin–Madison Archives, was patient and generous in allowing me access to boxes of H'Doubler's and Trilling's materials. David Benjamin, the visual materials archivist at the State Historical Society of Wisconsin, was also helpful.

I am grateful to the members of my dissertation committee, particularly Professors Wanda Corn, David Tyack, and Patricia Gumport, and especially to my principal adviser, Elliot Eisner, for extensive advice and encouragement. The many hours spent in discussion with him have profoundly shaped my thinking, writing, and analysis as well as my methods of critical inquiry and scholarship. The book has also benefited from the reading and advice of Mindy Aloff, Sally Banes, Mary Alice Brennan, Julia Brown, Ellen Moore, Hermine Sauthoff Davidson, and Jill Antonides, who also provided masterful editing expertise. To all of these individuals, and to the staff and associates of the University of Wisconsin Press—Scott Lenz, India Cooper, and above all my editor, Raphael Kadushin—thank you. Finally, my special appreciation to Keith, Josh, and Mimi Bartel for their individual brands of steady faith—in me and this project.

Moving Lessons

Introduction

I believe that an understanding of where schools have been and
of what social forces affect them at present is extraordinarily
useful for interpreting our present state of affairs. Without an
historical perspective our analyses are likely to be naive and
misguided.

Elliot Eisner, keynote address, Pennsylvania State University, 1989

I N THE SUMMER OF 1925, THE NEWLY LAUNCHED AMERICAN THEAT-
rical dance quarterly, *The Denishawn Magazine*, carried a three-page
review of a new book on dance education, *The Dance, and Its Place
in Education*. The *Denishawn Magazine* had been begun a year earlier,
primarily as a vehicle for two of the leading American theatrical dancers
of the time, Ruth St. Denis and her husband and partner, Ted Shawn, and
their own professional schools of dance, Denishawn.[1] The review was
unusual on two counts: first, it presented St. Denis devoting pages to a
book by another dance teacher, and second, St. Denis not only seriously
considered but praised the work of this teacher and author, Margaret
H'Doubler, a physical educator.[2]

Although both the fields of American modern dance and dance in
American higher education were in their infancy in the 1920s, already
there was some tension between the two disciplines.[3] For reasons of terri-
toriality as well as survival, H'Doubler had defined her educational dance
as distinct from the modern dance of the stage. A full rapprochement
would be years in coming, but St. Denis's gesture in reviewing Margaret
H'Doubler's first book was an acknowledgment of her esteem for this
woman who was on her way to becoming the doyenne of American dance

education. St. Denis's "review," therefore, is fascinating for what it reveals of this division between the educational and modern or theatrical arenas of dance and what it coincidentally suggests about the role of a determined individual's sensibility in affecting educational change.

St. Denis begins by situating her review as a platform for disagreement. She objects to an observation H'Doubler makes in the opening of her book, that the stimulation for the emerging curricular field of dance education has come from a scholarly interest in physical education.[4] "Not so!" St. Denis declares. "Nearly all phases of music interpretation and of what is loosely called 'Greek Dancing' [educational dance] in this country, owe their genesis to Isadora Duncan."[5] This question of the provenance of dance education was crucial and, as became apparent over the subsequent seven decades, profoundly divisive. For any art form in education, the context of whether one is training students to be artists or training students for life profoundly shapes the whole enterprise of the classroom. "Let us not forget that art leads, and education follows," St. Denis cautions. "First there is always the new circle drawn by the philosopher, the inventor, the poet, the artist; then education in its orderly classification and practice follows."[6]

In fact, both women were right; they were describing the truths for their respective areas of dance, theater, and academia. H'Doubler's search for and discovery of dance was motivated by her supervisor Blanche Trilling's direction and her own desire to broaden the university's physical education curriculum for women. St. Denis, by contrast, saw herself, along with Isadora Duncan, as introducing an American voice into concert dance. Behind both these innovators lay similar late nineteenth-century systems of physical movement—François Delsarte's methods and the German *turnvereine* gymnasiums, most prominently.

The differences between St. Denis's and H'Doubler's viewpoints on dance played out with particular clarity in their approach to dance teaching. The Denishawn schools were an important part of the major cultural empire known as Denishawn, which, during the period of 1922 to 1925, franchised dance schools in a dozen American cities. As a means of identifying and training performers for the Denishawn company, these schools were also an efficient way to earn money to help support the tours of the performing group.[7] H'Doubler, in contrast, saw herself as giving students the power to link emotional and physical understanding in order to become better adjusted and more efficacious individuals in the world. These were vantage points that would be central to this dialogue for the next eighty years.

Ruth St. Denis and Margaret H'Doubler were both pioneers. St. Denis had turned her back on the popular-culture musical theater of the time in favor of more elite entertainment, and H'Doubler never personally explored musical theater dance before deciding her form of dance would be radically different and significantly more respectable. In their own ways both women would link dance to a new portrait of the American woman. This was not a simplistic image of American women, but rather multifaceted and complex, and dance in American education would figure significantly in it. As a messenger relaying the private studio practice of dance into the university, H'Doubler also invariably brought part of her own personal history as well.

Both the immediate educational context in which H'Doubler worked and the larger social context of the time in which she lived (1889–1982) offered significant challenges as H'Doubler attempted to shape dance educationally. H'Doubler was a "new woman" in the sense that the womanhood she defined for herself encompassed contradictory discourses on gender difference, sexuality, motherhood, work, and the family.[8] H'Doubler was genteel but also staunchly independent: when it was still considered risqué to do so she bobbed her hair, rode horses aggressively, and was a single working woman into her forties, when she entered into a marriage with a man significantly younger than herself. H'Doubler continued to teach at the University of Wisconsin while her husband taught in another city, and they saw each other mostly on weekends in one of the first commuting marriages. H'Doubler never had children.

Like the Gibson Girl prototype made famous by the illustrator Charles Dana Gibson during the 1910s, H'Doubler enjoyed athleticism but was always careful to temper it with grace. "The Gibson girl was a figure of accommodation," feminist art historian Ellen Wiley Todd comments. "She mirrored the aspirations of many young women who wanted both possibilities and limits." H'Doubler, like the Gibson Girl Todd describes, balanced an independent manner with a care not to "radically challenge patriarchal assumptions."[9] To the degree that she was a personification of a Gibson Girl in academia, H'Doubler maintained her status as a charming upper-middle-class woman while also forging ahead as an athlete and, later, an educational innovator. In both arenas she represented a moderate discourse of new womanhood. H'Doubler's simultaneous negotiation of contradictory and moderate discourses of womanhood reflects the social complexity of the time, which left women caught between beckoning possibilities and persistent limitations.

H'Doubler entered the University of Wisconsin at Madison in the fall of 1906 as part of the wave of women from upper-middle-class social groups who found going to college socially acceptable in the transitional era of the late nineteenth and early twentieth centuries. As a college woman herself in this period, H'Doubler understood vividly the paradox of possibilities coupled with limitations encountered by women in higher education. Women were in the university, but they were also restricted to classes, majors, and professions deemed acceptable, by an overwhelmingly male administration, to women. At the very least, education for H'Doubler, as for other women of her time, introduced the possibility of an identity outside the home-and-family model. It also both invited and encouraged women to think of themselves, at least marginally, in opposition to confining norms, since a scant few years earlier even being in college would have been a rarity.[10]

So the social situation in which H'Doubler found herself, caught between two worlds, invited a dramatically altered perspective on society. Historian Rosalind Rosenberg describes the two worlds of this time as "the Victorian world of domesticity with its restrictive view of femininity, and the rapidly expanding commercial world of the late nineteenth and early twentieth century with its beckoning opportunities."[11]

As a woman in higher education, though, H'Doubler was already a step outside the Victorian norm before she ever embarked on teaching her first dance class. As a native-born, middle-class woman, she also belonged to the strongest locus of what Todd calls "the new womanhood."[12] Not only was the Victorian concept of separate existences for men and women being eroded, but the divide between the Victorian and commercial worldviews was slipping as well. The commercial worldview, initially in opposition to the Victorian, would eventually replace it. For H'Doubler this would be crucial, giving her a new social context and model for how she might willfully assume the status of an iconoclast once she began her innovations in women's education.

Yet H'Doubler was never a flamboyant radical. Even when her personal needs prompted her to make what were for the time dramatic changes, she either hid or, if necessary, revoked them. For example, she cut her hair short while studying at Columbia University during a one-year leave of absence from the University of Wisconsin. H'Doubler had yearned for the comfort of short hair for a long time, but once she cut it she kept it hidden by carefully tucking it up as if it were still long. When she returned to the University of Wisconsin she dutifully reported her transgression and offered to resign if the dean of women so chose.[13] Likewise, she stopped the little touring program of dance lecture-demonstrations she initially organized with her students the moment President Birge of the University of Wisconsin chastised her for lending the school the image of a center for dancing.[14]

It is particularly interesting that, contrary to what one would expect of one of the leading pioneers of dance in higher education, H'Doubler was never really a fan of dance as an art form. She considered Martha Graham "a little too professional," as she once remarked to her students after a Graham performance in Chicago.[15] She neither attended concerts with regularity nor followed the great dance artists of the time, with the exception of a brief personal correspondence and friendship with the German dancers Mary Wigman and Harald Kreutzberg.[16] Her interest in dance was unequivocally that of an educator. Her interest in movement was that of a women's physical education instructor and amateur aesthetician. Physical education was a particularly favorable and malleable corner of the university at this time; it was a place where a low-profile innovator like H'Doubler could institute changes with relatively little attention or resistance.

More broadly, H'Doubler's introduction of dance into the curriculum of American higher education represented an important linking of the physical and the intellectual for women in academia. H'Doubler's classes offered a new interpretation of the collegiate push for the education of the whole person. Other college educators at this time were actively instilling ethical purpose and physical, intellectual, and moral values through the more traditional portions of the curriculum in an effort to create the well-rounded college man or woman.[17] H'Doubler, however, worked in the reverse. She, along with other movement reformers, came to believe in a new notion of the expressivity of the body and the tightness of the links joining the emotional, physical, and intellectual aspects of the individual. Her task, then, was to create a place in the curriculum for these concerns to be addressed.

Most important, for late twentieth-century art education, H'Doubler's success demonstrated how a performing art like dance could be opened up to a rich exploration of its myriad educational virtues. Even St. Denis remarked on this, noting, "I should call the working classes of Miss H'Doubler a splendid environment for all the capacities for reaction and invention that a pupil might have, rather than for that intensely individual and solitude-seeking mood of the creative artist."[18]

For the subsequent several decades H'Doubler's *Dance, and Its Place in Education* and its sequel, *Dance: A Creative Art Experience,* were to be looked to as the mission statements for the nation's college and university dance programs.[19] In conceiving of dance so exclusively as the medium of educational discovery about oneself, the mechanics of one's body, and the links between emotions and physical actions, H'Doubler peeled away some of the veneer of mystery from the art of dance. In her classroom, dance became a tool for bodily, kinesthetic, and cognitive discovery.[20] Initiated in part as a way to counter skepticism about women's fitness for mental learning, this model of *thinking* physical activity would in fact help establish a new standard for how education could not only address but enhance the mind/body *union* in its students.

Over the subsequent decades these contours of how H'Doubler initially defined dance have begun to erode. Increasingly, dance's educational virtues have been neglected in favor of an emphasis on its identity as a performing art. Many factors have influenced this shift: a more open social acceptance of dance as a performing art, the increasing numbers of college dance instructors with performing experience rather than training as dance educators, and a certain ossification of models for creating dance educators. Yet even as the emphasis shifts, H'Doubler's fundamental introduction of dance into the American university curriculum stands as a remarkable, and resonant, achievement.

Formally positioning dance in higher education was a far more complicated feat than H'Doubler knew. Viewed from the perspective of the end of the twentieth century rather than the beginning, certain larger themes become apparent, and consistencies and changes come into focus. The arts in American education were and still are marginalized, and dance has for some time been among the least regarded of the arts. Examining how dance emerged in the university and how two individuals, H'Doubler and Blanche Trilling, played key roles in this emergence makes possible new understandings about the position of dance in the university. The larger story here is the extent to which such a history of dance in the university allows us important insights into our culture, our institutions, our conception of education, and the aesthetic thrust of American dance created by generations of artists.

Stylistically H'Doubler's innovations reentered the world of theatrical dance via one of her most illustrious students, Anna Halprin. Reinterpreted by Halprin, who directly influenced the first generation of postmoderns, H'Doubler's antitheatrical bias and her focus on internal feeling became the basis for the 1960s revolution in dance.

1

Early Twentieth-Century Dance Education and the Female Body

Dance has suffered too long from the common use made of it as a means of recreation and amusement.
Margaret H'Doubler, *The Dance, and Its Place in Education*, 1925

ONE SUMMER DAY IN 1917, A YOUNG WOMEN'S BASKETBALL COACH and physical education teacher, Margaret H'Doubler, stepped to the front of her new class of summer session students at the University of Wisconsin and asked the women to lie on the floor. Here, with the pull of gravity at a minimum, with the students' bodies relaxed and their limbs resting easily on the floor, H'Doubler described to the young women a simple series of muscular exercises they were to execute, based on an easy opening of the joints and the body's relaxed play with the force of gravity.[1]

Writing eight years later in *The Dance, and Its Place in Education*, a book dedicated to her students at the University of Wisconsin, H'Doubler set down her vision that had begun that day in 1917:

The dance is peculiarly adapted to the purposes of education. It serves all the ends of education—it helps to develop the body, to cultivate the love and appreciation of beauty, to stimulate the imagination and challenge the intellect, to deepen and refine the emotional life, and to broaden the social capacities of the individual that he may at once profit from and serve the greater world without.[2]

9

These words contained extraordinary claims for dance as well as remarkably ambitious personal goals for H'Doubler herself as a dance educator. Over her subsequent long career, H'Doubler held firmly to this early ambition and standard. When she began teaching educational dance in 1917, H'Doubler was still a young physical education instructor with a penchant for sports and a background in biology, yet she was initiating a practice that would have a profound effect on the American university, the lives of its women students, and the conception of dance in America. In this first class, H'Doubler already revealed an understanding that dance could be uniquely adapted to the purposes of education. Her subsequent instruction would be as much about sharing this discovery with each group of students as it would be about renewing her own beliefs and refuting claims regarding dance's value.

The Dance, and Its Place in Education is a remarkable document for its time. It is filled with passionate rationales for the value of dance in daily life, as well as rich insights about the manner in which dance must be taught in order to realize its educational values.[3] Arguing for the cultural legitimacy of dance as a performing art is one thing, but to insist that it has educational merit and belongs in the curriculum of higher education is yet another. H'Doubler needed ample passion as well as a forceful rationale to succeed in her quest. There were plenty of critics. In 1917, the same year that H'Doubler's class in dance began at the Univeristy of Wisconsin, Matthew S. Hughes, a bishop of the Methodist Episcopal Church, published his own statement on dance in education, *Dancing and the Public Schools.*

Echoing the sentiments of many religious leaders of the time, the group most outspoken against dance, Bishop Hughes systematically analyzed what he referred to as "the moral tendency of the dance." He concluded that "modern dance" (i.e., social dance) was inimical to essentially every value of public education:

Our public schools should conserve the health and vigor of our young people; the modern dance is destructive of health and wasteful of the vital forces. Our public schools are dedicated to intellectual attainment; the modern dance is guiltless of any great demand for intellectual capacity and makes no contribution to intellectual life. Our public schools are supposed to serve the wholesome interests of social life; the modern dance is used as a makeshift to hide the poverty of social resources and to fill a social vacuum. Our public schools are supposed to teach and enforce certain canons of good taste; the modern dance is a gross violation of conventionalities as accepted and observed elsewhere by respectable society. Our public schools are intended to develop and safeguard a fine morality; the modern dance, even with careful chaperonage and under the best auspices, cannot be credited with tendencies in that direction.[4]

H'Doubler was certainly aware of these kinds of objections to dance. The bibliography in *The Dance, and Its Place in Education* lists at least three antidance publications, and H'Doubler's enumeration of the virtues of dance addresses each of the general concerns Bishop Hughes lists, point by point,[5] yet what is most interesting is that rather than rendering dance a neutral force in her claims, H'Doubler goes much further. Although the "modern dance" Bishop Hughes is referring to here is social dance, it was the art form of dance itself that was under indictment, not just its social practice.[6] H'Doubler responds by claiming it is, in fact, richly beneficial.

Part of H'Doubler's rationale was to root dance in antiquity, particularly Hellenic culture, and to note the prominence and high regard the Greeks had for rhythmic movement. H'Doubler may well have done this as a means of gently shaming contemporary skeptics like Bishop Hughes. This was not a novel strategy for the early twentieth century. Other arts advocates and artists were borrowing styles—and by extension status—from antiquity for their works, in particular by evoking the ancient Greeks.[7] Yet H'Doubler, like Isadora Duncan, used this reference pointedly not with the intent of mimicking the Hellenic conception of dance but rather as a way to carry it forward into a form suited for the modern age.

America in the 1920s was in the midst of significant cultural change, much of it spurred, as were H'Doubler's innovations in dance education, by what historian Stanley Coben has labeled a widespread "rebellion against victorianism." H'Doubler was in distinguished intellectual company during this decade of reaction and reform. Traditional Victorian values were being challenged on many fronts. Black leaders like W.E.B. Du Bois and Marcus Garvey, feminists like Alice Paul, politicians like Robert La Follette, social scientists like Franz Boas and Margaret Mead, and dancers like Isadora Duncan and Ruth St. Denis all challenged nineteenth-century standards and inequities in their respective fields.[8]

H'Doubler, however, tended to frame her change more as reform than rebellion. This is a wise posture for a revisionist, for it implies that all that H'Doubler is doing is dusting off a forgotten treasure for humanity and reestablishing it where it belongs, at the heart of cultural transmission, in education. H'Doubler's entire second chapter in *The Dance, and Its Place in Education*, in fact, focuses on this idea of the cultural longevity and utility of dance:[9]

About 1900 the reaction against artificial and sterile forms set in, and soon after that time the movement was started to lead the people back to the Greek ideal of dancing—that is to movement founded on the laws of natural motion and rhythm. It began in private studios, but it is gradually finding its way into the colleges and public schools of the country. . . . From the Greeks the leaders of the movement have learned again the educational value of dancing, and a technique which is based on natural rather than unnatural positions of the body.[10]

These claims echo through H'Doubler's teaching as well. Her classroom exercises suggest a reclaiming of innocent childhood play experience. Toward the end of her book H'Doubler expands her claim for dance to include its capacity to affect social change. "The dance, freeing the body from needless inhibitions, and breaking down some of the unessential reserves, frees the real man for a wider and more satisfying life," she writes in the conclusion.[11] Despite the prescience and originality of what she is saying, H'Doubler's posture throughout *Dance* is usually that of a mere conduit for self-evident truths. Her outlook was forged in the just-concluded Victorian era, and she is, along with other activist women of the time, transitioning into being a New Woman. Her agenda may be rebellious, but her means are subtle and genteel. (The phrase *New Woman* came into being in the 1890s to denote a woman of progressive views and conduct. The term came from Sydney Grundy's play *The New Woman*, which opened at the Comedy Theatre in London on September 1, 1894, and included a portrait of this new type.[12])

It is this anchoring of the dance as historically indispensable, and yet retooled for the new America, that H'Doubler would use to win its acceptance. With each argument H'Doubler makes for the importance of dance as she describes it, she neatly ties it into a contemporary social value, in the process refuting the major common objections that Bishop Hughes and other antidance clerics were raising. The dances to which they were objecting, H'Doubler suggests, were ballet and tawdry theatrical forms that descended from seventeenth- and eighteenth-century aristocratic practices, which she criticizes as contributing to a decline in the personally expressive qualities of dance. This happened, H'Doubler reasons, because the nobility, wealthy and bored, tended to value technical tricks, thus contributing to a lessening of the noble and pure nature of dance and its ultimate degeneration.[13] It is not difficult to read a class critique into her comment. The "good" kind of dance thus becomes equated with egalitarian, middle-class, Hellenic, democratic ideals of the individual, and the critics of dance are gently told that their objections have legitimacy—but for a different time and a different type of dance than those for which H'Doubler is advocating.

For all of her embracing of new ideals, however, one area in dance where H'Doubler reflected an unchanged Victorian sensibility was in regard to race. She echoes what Coben calls the "Victorian color caste system." During the 1920s there were major migrations of urban blacks to the North, particularly Chicago, and this shift made for a sudden release of black speech, jazz, blues, and dances into white American society.[14] However, H'Doubler, like the other preeminent dance pioneer, Isadora Duncan, initially had an implicit vision of America as white, Europeanized, and without significant social, racial, or economic diversity.[15]

In carefully selecting her dance values, H'Doubler, like Duncan, aligned her dancing with middle-class WASP America, excluding the black forms of jazz dance and music, as well as popular social dance forms, from her models.[16] In her 1925 book H'Doubler speaks openly about how dance progresses along the lines of its "racial development," that is, the more "sophisticated" a culture, the more developed the dance. "The United States has no dances of its own, no dances which are expressive of the race which is an amalgamation of all races, no dances which are truly American. Each race has its dance, but there has been no dance to express the spirit of the race to which all these others have together given birth," she writes, singling out jazz, the dance form of black Americans, for special criticism. "For many years, however, especially since the introduction of jazz from South America, there has been no popular form of dancing that is in any sense artistic."[17] The jazz from South America that H'Doubler is referring to was a hybrid result of African influence in Brazil and other South American countries with large populations of African slaves.

Here again H'Doubler's values unknowingly echo Duncan's, by equating the African aesthetic with a "wild" and "unartistic" dancing body. Ideologically this also aligned H'Doubler and Duncan on this issue with spokesmen like Bishop Hughes, whose antidance tract similarly singled out "Negroid and South American" dance forms for special criticism. "These groups of dances, the negroid onesteps and the Spanish-American varieties, have had the dancing floors of the United States since that time, and represent the latest offering of Terpsichore to a civilized people," Hughes noted sarcastically, suggesting that the very cultural origins of these dance forms revealed why they were "provocations to immorality."[18]

Implicitly, the dancing female American body was being constituted as counter to the Africanist presence.[19] H'Doubler's notion of dance as a glorious means of heralding democracy and egalitarianism avoided the topic of class conflict and racial sterotyping. In the 1940s H'Doubler would number among her students Matt Turney and Mary Hinkson, two young African American women who would go on to become leading dancers in Martha Graham's dance company and women emblematic of the racial openness of Graham's troupe. However, with both H'Doubler and Graham, Turney and Hinkson were not dancing African-based movement forms, nor was jazz music the accompaniment.[20]

Behind H'Doubler's first dance class, then, lay a complex tale of the acceptance of middle-class white women, their intellects and their bodies, into American higher education. Eventually, in the 1940s, this would extend to African American women too, as the choreographers Katherine

Dunham and Pearl Primus began to create dances expressive of their culture and lives.

The emergence of the American woman's identity in dance is linked with women's reclamation of their physical health, through movement, in a post-Victorian world in which vestiges of the anorexia nervosa, hysteria, and neurasthenia so common in the late nineteenth century were evident.[21] This story of the transition of the malady-ridden nineteenth-century woman into the physically active, twentieth-century New Woman is intentionally complex, for it involves the refutation of systems of belief about gender roles, the body, and the linkage of physicality, education, and culture. Once one begins to look for connections, however, they are everywhere apparent. During the decades from 1870 to 1910, when middle-class women in America were beginning to organize on behalf of higher education, entrance into the professions, and political rights, women's symptoms and doctors' vigilance in identifying and treating their complaints boomed to an all-time high.[22] The body became the de facto battleground for the unfolding redefinition of women's place in society.

The social stakes were at least as significant as the educational and medical challenges. Ahead lay a new terrain of the American woman's role in society, in the family, in education, and in dance as both an artistic and educational discipline. Although it was unforeseen at the time, the university would become a key forum for this transformation of women's place from the private to the public sphere. It would also support the transition of the subject of dance from a disreputable social practice to a valued educational medium.

ISADORA DUNCAN

As already mentioned, the leading theatrical dance iconoclast of the time, California native Isadora Duncan, represented a magnificent amplification of the ideals of new physical health and sanctioned pleasure in bodily movement. During this turn-of-the-century period, Duncan's uncorseted body, what she called a symbol "of the freedom of woman and her emancipation from the hidebound conventions that are the warp and woof of New England Puritanism,"[23] was a theatricalization of the new model for American womanhood (figure 1). Duncan "performed" this model in her interpretive solo dances, but what made it such a vital image was that she also lived the part.[24] Duncan shunned many social conventions by being an expatriate, taking numerous lovers outside the bonds of marriage, refusing to wear corsets and confining garments, and bearing two children out of wedlock. These were major lifestyle innovations that echoed the boldness of her artistic choices. Duncan's presentation of herself as a majestic woman moving alone on a bare stage hung with

Figure 1. Isadora Duncan photographed by Arnold Genthe, 1916 (Jerome Robbins Dance Division, the New York Public Library for the Performing Arts)

15

dark velvet curtains and dancing expressively to great music—Beethoven, Brahms—offered unfettered (and to some, frightening) images of what American women might become.

Literary historian Amy Koritz contends that "Duncan attempted to convey a spiritual state, making her stage presence, or 'personality,' at best a medium rather than an end in itself, and ideally something to be forgotten altogether at the height of the aesthetic experience."[25] It was as if she became spirit rather than flesh. It was the idealism her art suggested rather than the reality of her flesh under her dancing tunic that she wanted audiences to attend to. In opposition to the long-standing theatrical notion of a woman onstage always being an eroticized figure, Duncan opened the possibility for the female dancing body to carry other meanings and for it to be a medium for other values and aspirations. For her audiences, however, this may have ironically been all the more threatening, because there is a certain safe element of unattainability to the eroticized woman onstage; Duncan's teaming of spirituality with this image complicated things. It confused the eroticism of the woman onstage with the purity of a devotional one.

H'Doubler's classes at the University of Wisconsin would be the first comprehensive efforts to institutionalize in higher education this general redefinition of the American woman as a robust and spiritual presence through dance. In New York Gertrude Colby was also experimenting with a form of what she called "natural dance" in classes at Columbia's Teachers College beginning in 1917. Colby, however, favored a more dramatic, pantomimic approach to dance, and her efforts largely concluded in the mid-1930s without ever becoming institutionalized, as H'Doubler's did, into an academic major.[26] H'Doubler's work, however, would prove to be about systematizing dance teaching as well as institutionalizing dance. Like Duncan, H'Doubler worked in the territory of interpretive dance, but her classroom exercises were designed to foster her students' own well-being and capacities for self-expression, not to prepare them for the stage and public entertainment. Her means as well as ends were distinctly different (figures 2 and 3). In this way the two women are in a sense the inverse of one another. Duncan never really succeeded in establishing a school, or even in training more than a handful of inspired disciples. H'Doubler, on the other hand, never studied dance seriously, never performed, and only rarely demonstrated, yet her students are legion in the field of American dance education. There may be important lessons here for dance education about the kinds of learning conditions that favor the production of insightful, reflective artists. Too strong a role model can be daunting, and too iconoclastic an artist can fail miserably in the short-run training of students while doing wonders for the historical evolution of a discipline. H'Doubler seems to have been a translucent

Figure 2. A rare photograph of Margaret H'Doubler, barefooted and wearing a dance tunic, posing in a dance gesture outdoors, 1917 (Photograph by McKillop; State Historical Society of Wisconsin. WHi (X3) 29035)

presence in the classroom; she inspired but did not intimidate or over-shadow, much less demonstrate. Duncan, in contrast, was a consummate performer but erratic as a teaching presence. Deborah Jowitt reports that "Duncan couldn't, or wouldn't, spend a lot of time in any of them [her schools]. Giving systematic instruction warred with her dedication to the spontaneity of dancing."[27]

Recent scholarly research into the dance schools Duncan started in Germany and Russia has led German dance historian Isa Partsch-Bergsohn to conclude that, ironically, Duncan's real goal was, like H'Doubler's, educational rather than theatrical:

In her conversation with Lunacharsky, the Commissar of Education [in Moscow in 1921], Duncan stressed that she wanted to work, not for the theatre, but for

Figure 3. One of the few photographs of Margaret H'Doubler in dance attire, striking a dance pose, 1917 (Photograph by McKillop; State Historical Society of Wisconsin. WHi (X3) 29036)

everyday life . . . to found a school in Moscow where she could teach thousands of proletarian children, giving them joy and beauty through free and uninhibited movement.[28]

Partsch-Bergsohn contends that through the power of her theatrical name Duncan succeeded in getting Lunacharsky to give her school state support, and it officially opened in 1921.

The important link between Duncan and H'Doubler is the fact that they both radically changed the arenas in which they worked, thus rendering these areas—the concert stage and higher education—important platforms for art and social issues. The remainder of the twentieth century would be in some respects a mapping of the possibilities this redefined terrain offered. For both women, however, some things remained constant. As Koritz notes:

Duncan did not fundamentally challenge the dominant ideology that valued women for their physical qualities—beauty and childbearing—while assigning them a natural spirituality that effectively denied them a voice in the public sphere. Nevertheless, the use she made of that ideology enabled her to justify the aesthetic legitimacy of an art form created by a woman with her own body.[29]

The actions Duncan had to take to gain acceptance for dance as a serious fine art paralleled what H'Doubler would find herself doing to render dance a serious educational subject. The two major strategies here would be to dissociate the female body from sexuality and to align it with spiritual, moral, and physical worth as exemplified by Greek and Roman art in the dominant Western tradition.[30] H'Doubler's own social conservatism, as well as the institutional climate of higher education, however, would cause her to shape dance away from some of the more flamboyant and inflammatory standards Duncan embraced, which included practices such as Duncan's consorting publicly with her many lovers and not wearing the kinds of undergarments that were de rigueur for H'Doubler's dancers when performing before audiences.[31]

For both women nudity, within certain careful restrictions, could be regarded as an artful symbol of this newly freed body.[32] Several of H'Doubler's students recall her remarkable comfort with nudity. Hermine Sauthoff Davidson, a student of H'Doubler's in the early 1930s, recounted how one summer evening H'Doubler happily joined a couple of her students for a clandestine nude swim at Davidson's family's cabin on Lake Mendota.[33] The turn-of-the-century physical culture movement also saw a place for nudity. Male advocates like Bernarr Macfadden, a self-made physical culture guru, reveled in his status as a "superb male specimen" and often posed nude (in discreet profile) in photographs for the readers of his books. He also glorified the female breast as a spectacle of "superb womanhood," including photographs of bare-breasted women exercising in his book *Womanhood*.[34] Both Duncan and H'Doubler would proclaim not just the breast but the newly revealed woman's body as healthy and chaste. In 1922 Duncan wrote the following:

To expose one's body is art; concealment is vulgar. When I dance, my object is to inspire reverence, not to suggest anything vulgar. I do not appeal to the lower instincts of mankind as your half-clad chorus girls do.

I would rather dance completely nude than strut in half-clothed suggestiveness, as many women do today on the streets of America.

Nudeness is truth, it is beauty, it is art. Therefore it can never be vulgar; it can never be immoral. I would not wear my clothes if it were not for their warmth. My body is the temple of my art. I expose it as a shrine for the worship of beauty.[35]

Neither Duncan nor H'Doubler denied the sensual appeal of a dancing woman's body, but they redefined the nature of that sensuality from the base to the spiritual. Duncan is shockingly frank in acknowledging that indeed some dancing and costumes are vulgar, but that her dancing and costumes are very different; they are truth, beauty, and art. The effect is that the critics of dance are told that they are correct, there is immoral dance out there, and Duncan and H'Doubler side with them in deploring it; however, Duncan's and H'Doubler's dance and *their* dancing bodies are noble.

FRANÇOIS DELSARTE AND ÉMILE JAQUES-DALCROZE

During this developing phase of dance and physical education for women, François Delsarte and Émile Jaques-Dalcroze created very influential systems of movement training that similarly promoted the nobility of a gracefully moving woman's body clad in a Grecian gown. François Delsarte (1811–71), a French teacher and theoretician of music, acting, and aesthetics, who trained at the Conservatoire National de Musique et d'Art Dramatique in his native Paris, developed a system of movement training based on what he saw as a fixed relationship between physical and vocal behavior.[36] Delsarte also believed in a similar correspondence between physical actions and spiritual beliefs.

In the United States the major promoters and teachers of Delsartism were James Steele Mackaye, who actually studied with Delsarte, and Genevieve Stebbins, who studied with Mackaye for two years.[37] Through the work of these leaders and others, American Delsartism was widely taught in school speech and drama classes as well as privately. Delsartism's influence was substantial on the development of other expressive movement practices in America as well. American Delsartism, disseminated in part through widely popular manuals, helped to promote a union of the spiritual and the physical and supported middle- and upper-class women in a socially permissible form of expressive physical movement. Many women followed Delsarte through these manuals, whose detailed exercises linked certain actions to elevated moods, increased agility, flexibility, strength, and health.[38] The Delsarte System also supported clothing reform and the abandonment of traditional corsets because they impeded breathing.

Particularly in the 1880s and 1890s, physical training exercises emphasizing gesture and full-body actions were increasingly popular in the United States as an American adaptation of Delsartism. Elocution continued to be a primary context for America's embrace of the system, but it was rapidly expanding into the much more physical realms of pantomime, acting, and interpersonal communication.[39] The growing popularity of Delsartism among women in the United States paralleled women's increasingly frequent ventures into the public arena. Nancy Lee Chalfa Rutyer notes the American fascination for Delsarte, on the part of women in particular:

The narrower study of elocution had originally been an important part of education for men—especially for clergymen, lawyers, public readers and lecturers. As educational opportunities for women expanded, training in all aspects of expression came to be considered useful and appropriate for children, young ladies, and society matrons. . . . By the 1890s, Delsartism had spread across the United States to involve at least hundreds of teacher/performers and thousands of students. While some proponents emphasized the aesthetic principles to argue for clothing reform and artistry in everyday life, Delsartism contributed most influentially to the cause of physical culture and expression for middle-class women, constituting a context within which they could pay attention to their bodies, undergo training in physical and expressive techniques and present themselves to selected audiences in public performance.[40]

Émile Jaques-Dalcroze (1865–1950), a Swiss composer, teacher, and developer of a form of rhythmic movement known as eurythmics, studied at the Conservatoire de Musique de Genève before developing his approach to movement education based on whole-body movement. Jaques-Dalcroze's method was rich with ideas about how music and movement might be combined in exercises using pulling, skipping, and lunging while focusing on the body's place in space, timing, and awareness of form.[41]

In his own background Jaques-Dalcroze had studied gymnastics and theater as well as conducted extensively, and he correlated these practices to the system of exercises he developed. Jaques-Dalcroze, who was aware of Delsarte, extended Delsarte's principles and use of pantomime into eurythmics, a system of translating sound into physical action, as a means of helping his students achieve a better sense of rhythm.[42] One exercise, for example, involved having students walk or step in rhythmic patterns, matching their steps to the duration and sequence of musical notes their teacher was playing on the piano. Like Isadora Duncan, with whose work he was familiar, and H'Doubler, with whom he was likely not familiar, Jaques-Dalcroze was seeking movement with a new dynamic and freedom. In the experimental setting of Hellerau, Germany, where he established a training college, Jaques-Dalcroze and his faculty fashioned a vocabulary of simple gestures and movements to be used as points of departure for creative studies. Delsarte and Jaques-Dalcroze were both important influences in this era of the transformation of the body in the public sphere in America.

H'Doubler might well have been exposed to Delsarte, particularly through Genevieve Stebbins's popular manuals *The Delsarte System of Expression* and *Delsarte Pantomimes*, which were published widely between 1885 and 1902.[43] Certainly his notion of the moral function of art and the link between bodily action and the expression of emotion would have complemented her own outlook. While H'Doubler's direct experience with Delsarte's methods is speculative, she confirmed in interviews that she took classes in the Jaques-Dalcroze method while studying in New York. She reported the experience as a disappointment because, despite her excitement at finding that Jaques-Dalcroze incorporated theory, science, and a strong rationale behind his movement exercises, she saw them as a kind of movement visualization rather than movement for itself.[44] Also, department correspondence from the University of Wisconsin indicates that as far back as September 1915 Blanche Trilling, director of women's physical education, was seeking funding to hire a teacher of the Jaques-Dalcroze method, so H'Doubler may well have been aware of this movement form through Trilling's interest.[45]

WOMEN'S HEALTH AND SEXUALITY

Many of the issues H'Doubler and Duncan encountered about Victorian prudery, females, the body, and sex had been long-standing ones. These issues came to a head at the turn of the century for a number of reasons, including the fact that this was a moment of intense transition: temporally, from the nineteenth to the twentieth century; educationally, as women gained admittance to higher education; socially, as the previously discussed prohibitions on the female body began to give way; and medically, as greater understandings about health practices for women were being gained. The anthropologist Mary Douglas has noted that periods when ideological boundary crossing occurs, such as the breaking down of separate spheres for men and women and the admission of women as equals in higher education, are traditionally moments of intense social redefinition as well.[46] This was certainly true for fin-de-siècle America. As British dance historian Ramsay Burt asserts, "There is power and danger at the boundaries of the body and the idea of society . . . power to reward conformity and repulse attack but also energy in its margins and unstructured, chaotic areas."[47] It was this energy at the margins, where ideological and social relationships were being redefined, that H'Doubler, like Duncan, would use to fuel her work.

It was also within these margins that H'Doubler would affect other changes. Prior to the late 1800s, women were burdened with substantial physical liabilities because of their sex, liabilities that had historically precluded their instigating change. As medical historian Edward Shorter asserts:

One reason has now become fairly clear for the fact that women in the seventeenth century were not demanding the vote or insisting on being admitted to a university: they had an overwhelming physical disadvantage in relation to men. Before 1900, women were saddled with large numbers of unwanted children; they were less well fed than men, they were dragged down by anemia, enervated by all kinds of diseases for which there is no male counterpart, and in every way imaginable denied the platform of physical equality which is the ultimate launching pad of personal autonomy.[48]

Shorter argues that most women in the past had accepted pain as a normal part of their lives.[49] Indeed, childbirth was a leading cause of death, second only to tuberculosis, in women of childbearing age until well into the nineteenth century. So when women's intellectual release began in the late 1800s, it was inevitable that it would affect their understanding of their bodies as well. What is less well documented, however, is how intertwined attention to women's physical well-being was with their success in education. The advances made by women in American higher education cannot be separated from the advances made in society's regard for their physical health and independence. To the dictum that a child must be fed before she can learn, H'Doubler would add that her body must be strong and free to physicalize that learning experience.

2

Nineteenth-Century Responses to Women's Health and Sexuality

Art, Fashion, Dance

Educate a man and you have educated one person, educate a woman and you have educated the whole family.
Charles McIver, U.S. Commissioner of Education Report, 1907

If the college woman is a mistake, nature will eliminate her.
David Starr Jordan, president of Stanford University, 1891–1913

MARGARET H'DOUBLER HELD TWO BASIC BELIEFS FIRMLY IN place as she navigated her way ideologically through late nineteenth- and early twentieth-century prohibitions. The first was her belief that dance, especially what she initially called interpretive and aesthetic dance, has the potential to foster the emotional as well as physical well-being of its practitioners.[1] The second belief guiding H'Doubler was her determination to bring into the university a kind of dance that was oriented toward self-improvement rather than the acquisition of professional-level skills. With these as her guideposts H'Doubler steadily steered her way through the great divide between the increasingly robust and independent lived realities of women's lives and the persistent mythic representations and beliefs about their frailty and unsuitability for an active, engaged, and public life.

The American home during the period of the 1880s to the 1920s was a place where another Victorian idea—that of separate spheres of existence for men and women—was doggedly maintained. When change did happen in the 1920s, women, and especially women's bodies, became a locus in which the turbulence of rapid social shifts was enacted. Lois Banner suggests that change played out in fashion as well, where

Victorianism as a social code was based on static and kinetic visual appearances—how individuals dressed and moved. Banner notes that even slight fashion deviations, such as cutting one's hair, carried enormous social resonance. The result was that major episodes in the history of women can be seen as corresponding to clear changes in the prevailing styles of beauty. The link between feminism and fashion thus became what Banner considers a central motif of the Victorian age, and "women were designated the representatives of order, morality, and repose."[2] The result was that their challenges to these norms of dress quickly resonated in larger arenas.

It is in the details of performing daily life that small beliefs get amplified into gestural and stylistic statements, into the fashion and choreography of living. Banner says that in certain instances, trademarks of health, or the lack of it, were actually borrowed as fashion statements. "Moreover illness was a role, not necessarily a fixed condition. One could move in and out of it or, alternatively, adopt some of its features and not others. Thus a white complexion and a delicate frame did not necessarily mean a listless personality or an abdication of energy in other areas of life," she wrote of the physical fashion for young middle-class women of the 1870s.[3] Alexis de Tocqueville, writing in 1889, viewed this new American woman of the late nineteenth century as a happy product of democracy.[4] Emerging political freedoms were beginning to be played out as social freedoms, including the freedom to be energetic and yet fashionably pale. Yet he also commented on the paradox of separate spheres for men and women:

In no country has such constant care been taken as in America to trace two clearly distinct lines of action for the sexes and to make them keep pace with one another, but in two pathways that are always different. American women never manage the outward concerns of the family or conduct a business or take part in political life.[5]

GENDER BOUNDARIES

As democracy allowed freedoms, even as society might mask them with old behaviors as de Tocqueville notes, it also created new conflicts between the genders. Feminist historians Susan Groag Bell and Karen M. Offen have observed that the status of women emerged as a political issue in the late nineteenth and early twentieth centuries, when many more women experienced strains between obligations of domesticity and the beckoning new freedoms of the workplace. This tension eventually radiated out into economic and political institutions, a difficult thing for the fin-de-siècle nation in the midst of a period of social unrest and international stress. Bell and Offen cite Theodore Roszak's argument that during this turn-of-the-century period "the great sex war emerges as the foremost influence upon the cultural character and political style of the Western world."[6]

The freedoms of the body absorbed and manifested the changes in culture and style. For women especially, a conscious, as well as unconscious, strategy has always been to enact conflict on their own bodies. The more the debate raged over what women's proper roles and obligations should be, the more fierce the arguments became for what constituted pure manliness and womanliness in behavior and appearance. Interestingly, in the decades after the 1880s, these same issues were argued in America from a wide variety of perspectives, ranging from the religious to the political and artistic. The possible upset to the social order represented by a change in women's roles was substantial, and thus "popes, emperors, presidents, and prime ministers joined forces with playwrights, novelists, essayists and poets to insist upon the need to keep women in their proper place as helpmeets, mothers and sexual regenerators of men, all in the national interest."[7]

Bell and Offen adumbrate details of why sex roles polarized during this period. They point out that women were not new to the paid work force by the late nineteenth century; rather, they had been part of this expanding urban force, particularly in the newly mechanized manufacturing sector, for years. What was different, however, was that there was a significant increase in the number of women entering work in the decades around the turn of the century, and their percentage compared to men's was rising.

Immigration of non–Anglo-Saxons was also on the rise in America. In the face of consciously controlled fertility the national population was declining, such that by 1830 it had fallen to below 30 births per 1,000 women. By the late 1880s political leaders were linking the decrease in births and the increase in working women to a direct threat to national strength. This situation remained volatile for the critical fin-de-siècle decades. As Bell and Offen conclude, "Between 1880 and 1914 the problem of women's position in the family and in society troubled the public consciousness as never before."[8]

Women's suffrage advocates turned arguments about fertility and women in the work force to their own use, paralleling the renewed insistence on motherhood in this period with a corresponding call for women's citizenship. The rationale was easy: it was argued on the grounds of women's crucial role as mothers/educators and arbiters of moral behavior. If anyone needed citizenship women did, as the caregivers to the next generation of men. A similar splitting of a woman's social function would inform the argument for dance education. Increased presence of women in the public sphere was permissible if it was balanced by other traditional controls, such as rules of family responsibility in the private sphere. If the dancing body were linked to a moral spirit, then its actions were honorable. Additionally, if a strengthened moral character were linked to a strengthened body, anxieties and critics could be assuaged.

It is important to recognize how often paradoxical developments with regard to women's education occurred during this time.While women were making great strides in securing access to higher education, the late nineteenth and early twentieth centuries were also boom periods for the home economics movement. As Bell and Offen note, "Women must learn to cook, sew and care for babies even if they studied philosophy."[9] Indeed, the strategy was more to add on roles than to substitute them. In the university this often translated to separate and unequal curricula for the women students.

In 1905 Granville Stanley Hall, the first president of Clark University in Massachusetts, summed up the late nineteenth-century outlook on women's education as follows: "Now that woman has by general consent attained the right to the best that man has, she must seek a training that fits her own nature as well or better. So long as she strives to be manlike she will be inferior and a pinchbeck imitation, but she must develop a new sphere that shall be like the rich field or cloth of gold for the best instincts of her nature."[10]

Theodore Roosevelt, like Hall a man considered a friend of the women's suffrage movement, spoke pointedly in 1905 from the perspective of nationalism on the subject of "race suicide" (specifically the declining birthrate of white middle-class women): "But the Nation is in a bad way if there is no real home . . . if the woman has lost her sense of duty, if she is sunk in vapid self-indulgence or has let her nature be twisted so that she prefers a sterile pseudo-intellectuality to that great and beautiful development of character which comes only to those whose lives know the fullness of duty done, of effort made and self-sacrifice undergone."[11] Read critically, both of these debates reveal a split between the freedom that could be allowed a woman's body and the control that must be exercised over her mind. Implicit in these arguments is the awareness that there is a link between the two, but just how one might be affected by the other is unknown and potentially frightening territory. Arising in the midst of these discussions, dance education would necessarily have to define its own balance between freedom and control, by reversing this equation so that the disciplined body became the avenue to an enlightened mind.

Historian Jill Conway, in writing about women reformers of the nineteenth century, commented on the paradox of female activism unfolding in the midst of Victorian stereotypes of traditional feminine temperament:

The historians of American feminism must write a double narrative in which something more than the reversals of Looking-Glass Land must be advanced. The historian must relate the outward story of a successful agitation to some causal analysis of why this agitation, first for legal right, then for access to higher education, then for the franchise and for liberation from a traditional Christian view of marriage, had so little influence on actual behavior.[12]

The freedom and expressive pleasure Margaret H'Doubler's students found in the university dance classes were in direct contrast to the rigid rules that had governed women's personal control and understanding of their bodies in the preceding decades. In order to fully appreciate the changes the entry of dance into higher education formalized, it is important to understand the larger context of women's health and their representation in visual images at the time. Physical well-being and the freedom to move the body in the service of personal expression, outside of prescribed Delsarte exercises, were uncommon experiences for the middle- and lower-class Victorian woman. However, by the first quarter of the twentieth century they would be the physical equivalent of suffrage— emblems of a newly liberated female body functioning in tandem with a newly awakened mind.

IMAGES OF WOMEN IN THE VISUAL ARTS

The American woman's status in the second half of the nineteenth century was marked by a number of paradoxes. Scientific advances, economic developments, and cultural changes were rapidly shifting the social land- scape. They were creating a unique set of intellectual conditions that were to have a fundamental influence on twentieth-century modes of thinking about sex, race, and class.[13] Some of the forums in which many of these views were played out were those of the visual arts, fashion, medicine, physical activity, and dance. It was in these forums that the body intersected with the mind and also with nineteenth-century social paranoia about the danger of women let loose in men's public sphere.

Art-historical analyses of paintings of women of this period suggest the visual arts as an important canvas on which the moral and social missions of the time were recorded. These images are a useful starting place for an investigation of the social problems surrounding dance in higher educa- tion, because they present visually the confining norms within which the pioneering dance educator Margaret H'Doubler and her summer dance students were struggling. They also speak in visual art terms of an image of woman H'Doubler would challenge in the domains of education and the performing arts. As the feminist theorist Susan Bordo asserts, "We learn now through visual images the appropriate surface presentation of the self."[14] Historical visual images can also teach what was valued in presentation of the self in past eras.

According to many art historians, the dominant visual arts model for women from the mid-eighteenth century into the early twentieth was that of "a household nun."[15] A woman like this, who was simple, pure, and tractable, was idealized in many paintings of the time. Well into the nineteenth century, paintings loudly proclaimed that not physical activity

Figure 4. William Reynolds Stephens (1862–1943), *Summer*, 1891, a typical period image of female indolence (*Royal Academy Pictures*, London, 1897)

but physical *inactivity* was the desired goal for women (figures 4 and 5). As cultural historian Bram Dijkstra explains:

Gradually a woman's physical inaccessibility came to be seen as the primary guarantee of her moral purity. Any public or even private display of levity or physical energy on the part of women was a clear indication of the spiritual frivolity of such women and their concomitant inability to serve as efficient vessels for the care and feeding of their husband's souls.[16]

Women were idealized in this way by painters, according to Dijkstra, for the same reasons they were by poets and social critics—as a means of containing women and at the same time positioning men to exercise their (imagined) power and control: "In nineteenth-century mythology the worldly success of the male was deemed to be inextricably intertwined with the self-denial of woman." Over time the effect of this social demand of inactivity was manifested on the female body as a variety of emotional and physical ailments, "kinesthetic metaphors," they should perhaps be called. "Many late nineteenth-century women felt themselves being strangled, and felt as if they were losing their minds, caught in the patterns of a society which had come to see even expressions of insanity as representations of feminine devotion to the male."[17]

By the turn of the century a frequent image of European as well as American women in literature and the visual arts was that of a perpetual invalid. Many middle-class women—some, like Alice James and Charlotte Perkins Gilman, with literary skills to chronicle their descent into invalidism—became embittered career invalids. Tacitly, their illness was the one way they could "express covert opposition to a society

Figure 5. Albert Moore (1841–93), *Yellow Marguerites*, ca. 1880 (*Magazine of Art*, 1887)

that omitted them from the activities it valued most." Even the stalwart women's educational reformer Catharine Beecher visited over a dozen spas as a patient, taking up temporary residency in thirteen of them as she underwent repeated water cures to remedy her ill health. Biographer Kathryn Kish Sklar notes that for Beecher and the other women who visited some of the 213 female spas that burgeoned between the 1840s and 1880s, these places offered rare female communities of sympathetic peers. Their virtues were strikingly similar to those that dance education would soon offer. Spas were places where "bodily sensuality could be freely indulged, and an unwanted pregnancy might even be terminated," and where "the strong emphasis on exercise, massage, bathing and general attention to the body also provided women with an opportunity to experience sensual pleasure."[18] For the first time, the woman was treated as a whole physical and thinking person, not just as a series of symptoms, within a community of women temporarily freed from the performance of numbing daily routines and domestic isolation. As Sklar summarizes:

Under the guise of restoring their health, women could indulge their otherwise forbidden desires for physical sensuality, and some descriptions of water-cure treatments seem to express covert sexual feelings. Nudity and exhilaration were, in any case, frequent experiences during a water-cure treatment.[19]

Painfully, the fragility of women increasingly came to be held up as not just a condition but an *ideal*. More dangerously, its opposite, exercise (and its practitioners, physically active or muscular women), was labeled a pernicious evil. Lois Banner explains that "even tasks associated with housewifery and child rearing such as washing, dressing, playing in the open air, were viewed as vulgar by the fashionables. . . . This prohibition went so far that all exercise, aside from dancing, was interdicted to fashionable women."[20] While images of passivity served to contain women socially, they also presented an erotic ideal of woman. These images ranged from fainting and collapsing women, an Art Nouveau staple, to the female form metamorphosing into trees, flowers, birds, and other forms from nature, as in many of the works by Arts and Crafts artists like Arthur Mathews (figure 6).

There were many negative images of women in the late nineteenth century, ranging from the nun to the inactive woman to the simian, the primitive, and the dangerous, hysterical, or nymphomaniac woman. Images and representations of women by men blurred the boundaries between animals or landscapes and female humans in ways that paralleled scientific literature of the time, which denigrated women as the mental and evolutionary inferiors of men and closer to their primate ancestors.

Another nineteenth-century specter, that of degeneration, or reversion, as Charles Darwin labeled it, also informed social ideas about women. In his 1852 *The Origin of Species,* Darwin identified the inferiority of women as biological.[21] Herbert Spencer (1820–1903), nineteenth-century philosopher and sociologist, incorporated some of Darwin's theories into his own inclusive ideas of science, nature, and society, ideas that treated

Figure 6. Arthur F. Mathews (1860–1945), *Youth*, ca. 1917. A serpentine line of tunic-clad women dances across the California landscape and at the same time appears on the verge of disappearing into nature. (The Oakland Museum of California)

civilization as a natural, not artificial, phenomenon. Coining the phrase "survival of the fittest," Spencer reconstrued Darwin's theory of natural selection into a theory of social systems, which became known as Social Darwinism and validated social repression of women in the name of science.[22] Others, such as German philosopher Max Nordau, believed that, were norms to be challenged by such activities as women masculinizing themselves through exercise, society would sink into disarray and the human species would once again slide down to the level of the apes.[23] Even progressive turn-of-the-century thinkers like Sigmund Freud confirmed male suspicions concerning women's primitive nature and their similarity to the "savages."[24]

In paintings this drift toward masculinizing decay was depicted by images of women who were childlike or dancing women who were made to look simian, reptilian, like crossover species that were the product of interbreeding between *Homo sapiens* and a lower animal form. Fantasies about females as primitive and savage were articulated through the performing as well as the visual arts. The emblematic image of the Romantic ballets of this period, dances like *Giselle* and *La Sylphide*, is a deadly winged sylph whose beauty, grace, and frailty cloak her true murderous nature and treachery. As these art images circulated they gained social potency, becoming almost collective nightmares. Dijkstra notes that "many men began to suspect women of indulging in strange sylvan rituals, of having an insatiable urge to dance." The force leading women to enjoy dancing and to pursue it greedily was supposed to be woman's "neuro-muscular irritability," in other words, her tendency to hysteria.[25]

Dancing women thus acquired an added negative association, because rhythmic movement was supposedly one way for ill and sexually "over-heated" women to release this neuro-muscular irritability that led to hysteria. Dancing women were also supposedly sex-crazed women. They were "over-heated hysterics letting off steam," women whose emotions and "delight in physical sensations propelled them out of social control." *Nymphomania*, another label for a female condition, was coined as a way to designate women with uncontrollable sexual appetites. "Nymphomaniacs" were women described in the literature of the time as individuals who "furiously demanded coitus and died within a few days."[26] Again, the underlying fearful subject is that of a woman in sensuous physical abandon, authorizing her own appetites, her own "moves."

As Dijkstra points out, this fantasy of frantic seduction allows the man to play at being an unwilling victim, while the woman is the guilty one. The passion and strength of these women, who were so plentiful in late nineteenth-century novels, paintings, and ballets, were terrifying yet also seductively alluring. Yet while abandoned and uncontrolled motion was linked to feminine madness and insatiability, the other extreme—controlled physical strength—was also off limits to women, because it was seen as the province of men.

In an era that idealized frailty as the ultimate province of femininity, a woman's behavior that could be described as masculine was considered extremely unattractive. Toward the end of the century, as women were increasingly drawn to exercise because of its celebrated health-giving benefits, they had to be careful not to engage in activities that had "masculine-making" qualities, such as competitive team sports. Indeed, while there were strong voices favoring exercise for women, there were equally vociferous ones opposing it. Much of the dominant mythology of the time began to associate "even normal health, let alone unusual physical vigor in women, with dangerous masculinizing attitudes."[27] Correspondingly, the cultivation of moral sentiments in late nineteenth-century males was symbolized as a feminization of boys and men.[28]

The negative association of physical activity with masculinity was a major hurdle dance would have to overcome to succeed as educational material for women. The same population of middle-class American

33

women was described by nineteenth-century writer Abba Goold Woolson as "afflicted with weakness and disease" to such an extent that "feminine invalidism had become a veritable cult among the women of the leisure class."[29] Those who railed against social dance also fastened upon Woolson's myth of the evil transformative powers of exercise, particularly for women, to make their argument. Antidance author the Reverend Don Lugi Satori, in his 1910 book *Modern Dances*, crusaded vigorously to prohibit dance, saying many healthy young women who practiced it became "infected by a syphilitic young man on the dancing floor: and that far from being healthful it puts a very severe strain on the nervous system."[30]

The portrait of an inactive, frail, diseased, and morally weak nineteenth-century woman, perpetuated by the visual arts and literature, was ripe to be repudiated by dance. Yet the shift in perception that an active and energetic woman was not a social aberration but rather an ideal would have to be orchestrated gradually. More important, young girls as well as adult women would have to be identified as the victims of a life of inactivity. It would have to be recognized that this condition was not something that could be completely remedied with just a few months of college exercise; efforts would have to begin even earlier. Several decades later, H'Doubler's university dance majors would in fact study movement in the service of becoming movement teachers in secondary as well as college classrooms themselves. They would be eager to spread the gospel of the dancing body as an antidote to disease and passivity.

The need for accepted physical activity for females was acute, for there were serious problems among little girls who were socialized into inactivity. In England, where a similar situation existed, it was noted that "early strictures on movement rapidly turned healthy children into sickly young women. Less and less every year are the nerves and muscles, the restless activities of arms and legs exercised and made to purvey new vigor to the life. The body is allowed to grow stagnant."[31] The Victorian woman, living a life of forced inactivity in a cluttered and dusty home where little sunlight and fresh air penetrated, if not ill at the outset of her life as a homemaker, invariably ended up that way as a consequence of this often fatally "fashionable" lifestyle. Catharine Beecher agreed, arguing for fresh air, nourishing meals, and calisthenics as an antidote: "As wealth and luxury have increased, houses have been made tight, windows have been corked, fireplaces have been shut up, and close stoves and furnaces introduced."[32]

Not just visual art but opera and Romantic ballet echoed this condition of ailing womanhood; witness Violetta in Guiseppe Verdi's 1853 opera *La Traviata,* or Giselle in Jean Coralli and Jules Perrot's 1841 ballet *Giselle.* Art was idealizing a painful vision of distorted beauty, amplifying desirable features like unblemished white skin and a gentle manner into an extreme of sickly pallor and the listlessness of ill health.

Distortion in the quest for beauty was an aspect of classical ballet some turn-of-the-century dance revolutionaries like Isadora Duncan were to challenge. The new model of dance they would define had to make a firm stand against nineteenth-century artifice in order to present itself as a true remedy rather than just another fashion. One of the often unacknowledged virtues of dance as an art form is that, unlike the visual arts Dijkstra describes, dance has the ability not just to envision change but also to shape a subversive response, a physical image whose imitation can bring about a physical as well as a mental change in the practitioner. One means of accomplishing this would be to recast dance from a fine art into dance as an educational practice. This would be H'Doubler's strategy to establish the links among muscles, cognition, and morals. She would use dance to present a more material and less abstract physical image. First, however, there were hurdles, like the constraints of fashion, that needed to be overcome.

FASHION

Many analyses of nineteenth-century women focus on their clothing and the physical restrictions fashion imposed on them; therefore, along with social beliefs about proper activities and behaviors for women, fashion needs to be examined. Any analysis of the motions of daily life for women of this era must take into account how fashion actually made a woman physically inaccessible—an interesting metaphor for the "ideal" social state of chastity and purity. Dance historian Elizabeth Kendall interprets the fashionable dress of the time, according to a description of conventional dress from a large 1874 Boston dress-reform convention, as if its goal were to enfold a woman in layers of barriers between herself and the outside world:

American women were notorious for their mindless devotion to fashion— European fashion, since that was the only kind there was. Abroad, two traits distinguished American ladies: their ill health and their slavery to foreign ideas of style. By the 1870's this docility had got them committed to a complicated set of clothing which severely restricted the possibilities of physical motion available to them.

A woman's ordinary costume consisted of an outer dress whose waist was tightly buttoned over a corset with a tight-laced waist of its own; underneath the corset were other items, the "lower garments" one on top of another. The problem was inescapable: Every one of the lower garments has a binding fastened around the waist, and this binding is composed of a straight piece of cloth folded double. Drawers, underskirt, balmoral, dress-skirt, over-skirt, dress-waist, and belt, furnish accordingly, sixteen layers of cloth girding the stomach and the yielding muscles situated in that region.[33]

Fashion was beginning to change by the 1910s, when layers began to disappear, and dance in higher education was to become a way to vivify this newly "unpeeled" body. Fashion historian Lois Banner has observed that in the 1910s, when fashion began to change, "encased in voluminous clothing, held rigid by tight corsets, women were also encircled by a set of requirements governing their physical movements and their personal behavior."[34] Fashion was one means by which the Victorian male and female spheres were kept separate. There was also a close link between what one wore and the kinds of activity one was permitted and able to do. As would become apparent, rebellion against fashion was linked to rebellion against the behaviors fashion held in place. One kind of activity that was generally permitted for middle-class Victorian women, aside from the morally uplifting Delsarte physical culture exercises, was certain kinds of controlled social dancing, where fashion could take preeminence over health.

While a full analysis of Victorian fashion does not have a place here, certain aspects of the "dress code" are very relevant. The first is the eighteen-inch waist. From the 1820s through the end of the century, this was the stylish circumference for a woman's waist. Banner says of this that it was "a waist measurement so out of line with normal body dimensions that most women could achieve it only by tightening their corsets, a practice that caused headaches and fainting spells, and may have been a primary cause of the uterine and spinal disorders widespread among nineteenth-century women."[35]

Educational reformer Catharine Beecher also believed that tightly laced corsets were to blame for many of the serious internal disorders Victorian women suffered, including displacement of the ribs, lungs, stomach, intestines, bladder, liver, and uterus. Sklar quotes Beecher as saying, "The protracted agonies that I have seen and known to be endured as the result of such deformities and displacements [were worse than] the horrible torments inflicted by savage Indians or cruel inquisitors on their victims."[36]

While the visual art images of this era may have suggested the pale, wan, languishing woman as an ideal, adherence to fashion rules guaranteed genuine ill health. This was an issue of central concern to leading advocates for women's education. Demonstrating education's capacity to ameliorate rather than exacerbate this situation would help secure women a place in higher education and dance a place in women's education.

In the early 1850s Beecher conducted a widely cited survey among middle-class women in order to support her observation that they were always ill. In 1854 she published the results in a chapter entitled "Statistics of Female Health" in her *Letters to the People on Health and Happiness*. Sampling seventy-nine communities and over one thousand women, she found that the sick outnumbered the healthy by a ratio of three to one. In a typical community profile of Batavia, Illinois, she recorded:

Mrs. H. an invalid. Mrs. G. scrofula. Mrs. W. liver complaint. Mrs. K. pelvic disorders. Mrs. S. pelvic diseases. Mrs. B. pelvic diseases very badly. Mrs. B. not healthy. Mrs. T. very feeble. Mrs. G. cancer. Mrs. N. liver complaint. Do not know one healthy woman in the place.[37]

Surveying the health of her personal acquaintances, Beecher concluded, "I am not able to recall, in my immense circle of friends and acquaintances all over the Union, so many as *ten* married ladies born in this century and country, who are perfectly sound, healthy, and vigorous."[38]

Although Beecher and others had begun to address women's health, clearly more had to be done to improve the health of American women. It had to be done not just for their own well-being but also to position them strongly to refute the claims that education would make them even sicker.

As a precursor to the emergence of dance in the university, the final decades of the late nineteenth century reveal equivocation in many arenas about physical culture, women in the public space, women's bodies, and dance. The story has roots fifty years before that momentous summer of 1917, in the closing decades of the nineteenth century.

ANTIDANCE TREATISES

It was the appearance of "unladylike" behavior that most distressed Victorian conservatives in the last decades of the nineteenth century. This is one reason social dance, an activity that is an amplification of behavior, became the target of so many calls for prohibition in this era. For it was in social events like dances where gender relations were explored and courtship rites, feminine dependence, masculine leadership, and sexuality were expressed most freely.[39] Social dance in this context functioned as a means for physical expression for young working as well as society women, who embraced it with unprecedented enthusiasm. This is also why dance was not a subject fin-de-siècle Victorians generally thought of as a respectable part of the university curriculum, although there were pockets of gymnastic dance in women's colleges.

Dance was primarily a social and recreational leisure activity at this time, and recreation historically has been a practice where different behaviors and values can be tried on. Cultural historian Kathy Peiss says that leisure-time activities "don't reveal a unified culture[;] they may affirm the cultural patterns embedded in other institutions, *but they may also offer an arena for the articulation of different values and behaviors* [emphasis added]."⁴⁰ So at this historical moment dance took on a new social utility, becoming a cultural form in which social interactions between men and women could be reshaped. Heterosocial culture had to be redefined as America made the shift from Victorian culture to the modern era.

As part of this move into the modern age, women tested new cultural forms that explored gender in terms of social interactions with men. As Peiss explains, "Women pushed at the boundaries of constrained lives and shaped cultural forms for their own purposes."⁴¹ Peiss asserts that this full passage from Victorian culture to modernism involved a complete redefinition of gender relations. The New Woman who emerged in the early twentieth century would eventually achieve a profile of public dynamism, that of the independent, athletic, and sexual woman.

One of the first forums in which this emerging model was tested was the dance hall, a major recreational site of the time for lower-class working women. Here the sexes mingled without the chaperones who were an adjunct of middle- and upper-class mixed-couple dancing. This presented unique challenges for reformers of the time, who in the early days of the Progressive era strongly supported leisure and play. In place of the Gilded Age perspective of viewing leisure as idleness, leisure was beginning to be seen instead as a necessary period of renewal and a precious resource.⁴²

However, how to control sexual contact was an issue. As a result leisure-time activities contained recondite controls, recast as social values. According to Peiss, "Despite these changes in outlook reformers after 1900 continued to believe that the primary purpose of recreation reform for working women was to inculcate standards of respectable behavior. Like their predecessors, Progressive reformers perceived a rising tide of promiscuity and immorality in the city."⁴³ Among children recreation was also being looked to as a good means of teaching civic responsibility and moral behavior. Progressive reformers of the 1880s to 1920s were developing psychological theories about the link between physical exercise and the development of a social and moral conscience in children; young women were considered a similar population.⁴⁴

The major quest became to "ennoble relations between the sexes," especially in a situation of high-risk public contact—the dance. So while the tradition of chaperones formally ceased, informally it continued in the form of legislated and socially mandated standards. These new rules, such as having certain rows of seats in movie houses set aside for unescorted women, or mandating that theater lights be turned on during the nickelodeon sequence to prevent women from being harassed or seduced, were widely instituted.⁴⁵ However, more than any other social "amusement," dancing was perceived as having the strongest links between recreation and threats to women's morality; hence the call not just for restrictions but for its outright banishment.

Yet, at the same moment, regulated and chaperoned dances were being held in settlement houses, where, it was believed, the sedate music and careful supervision could help to improve manners and behavior and offset the bad influence of the commercialized dance hall.[46] This same impulse to make dance respectable, through a controlled atmosphere of Grecian statues in the studio and classical music as accompaniment, would also shape H'Doubler's positioning of dance in higher education.

Not surprisingly, dance as a social pastime boomed such that, according to Peiss, "by 1910 dance would have grown to be the single working woman's greatest passion, with over 500 public dance halls operating every evening in New York City alone and with over 100 dancing academies instructing some 100,000 students."[47] Thus the dance ballrooms and palaces quickly developed their own culture, one in which this formerly family amusement and neighborhood activity could be changed into a forum that legitimized working women's new public role.

Soon the dancing woman's body became the primary focus for anxious sentiments about race purity, female morality, and public decency. These sentiments were expressed in antidance treatises, books detailing the evils of social dance. In the last several decades of the nineteenth century, and into the initial decades of the twentieth, American ballroom dance became the target of an unprecedented number of these treatises. The vantage point these documents offer is provocative as well as unusual, for they were written with the goal of eliminating their subject. One reads through and into these calls for prohibition in an effort to peek past them at their target.

The mid-nineteenth-century publication of these early antidance treatises coincides with the rise of blackface minstrelsy, an art form Eric Lott has argued to be "one of the very first constitutive discourses of the body in American culture."[48] Just as minstrelsy addressed the presence of black male and female bodies in the public sphere, responses to social dance reacted in large measure to working-class women in the public sphere. Both—blackface minstrelsy and antidance treatises—are to a degree reflective of a similar impulse to control and redefine the nondominant body in a public arena.

In the mid- to late nineteenth century the performing and dancing body became a stage on which Americans argued in symbolic but intensely serious ways about conflicting gender ideals. Many antidance books and lectures were published, as well as many dance manuals, essentially prodance literature that provided middle-class men and women of the 1820s and 1830s with what Elizabeth Aldrich has noted as the keys to becoming gentlemen and ladies.[49] The majority, if not all, of the antidance authors were men, and many said they had been ballroom dancers or teachers themselves before renouncing this profession and devoting themselves to alerting others of its dangers. In fact, even those few who were not formerly dancers felt the need to address *why* they were not. J. T. Crane commences his 1849 *Essay on Dancing* by explaining that his ignorance of dance firsthand is excusable in the same way that an ignorance of what it is like to be hanged firsthand is excusable in "gentlemen who have penned learned disquisitions upon Capital Punishment. It is not needful either to dance or to be hung in order to be able to come to a conclusion touching the expediency of the performance."[50]

T. A. Faulkner begins his 1894 treatise *From the Ball-room to Hell* with a preface that includes the following autobiographical confession as a means of establishing his qualification, which for him is a shameful past:

I wish this little book to accomplish viz.: the opening of the eyes of the people, parents, who are blind to the awful dangers there are for young girls in the dancing academy and ballroom. . . . I began to dance at the age of twelve, and have spent most of my life since that time, until within a few months, in dancing parlors and academies. . . . For the past six years I have been a teacher of dancing, and for several years held the championship of the Pacific Coast in fancy and round dancing. . . . It is the greatest sorrow of my life that I have been so long connected with an evil I know to have been the ruin, both soul and body, to many a bright young life.[51]

The authority of former dancers to write antidance texts stems from an almost shamanistic force: they have traveled to the abyss of this social evil they now decry, and they have come back to warn others not to follow. This situation is rich with irony, for the descriptions many of these antidance manifestos contain are reported with such meticulous detail that the pleasure of doing is revisited in the pleasure of retelling. In essentially all of these documents actual descriptions of *the dance* itself are all but missing. Instead, what gets retold is a detailed description of what the woman dancer's body undergoes. The female body is presented as a socially charged image, a flash point for the fascination nineteenth-century women held for men. The dance is rendered translucent while the physical form it propels becomes indelible.

The following description of a young woman three months after her first dance lesson is an example of how every aspect of the physical contact of dancing was viewed as revealing personal emotions and intense physical passion. The simple abstract enjoyment of the pleasure of dancing was not even considered as a motivation:

She has entirely overcome her delicacy about being embraced in public for half an hour by strange men. In fact, she likes it now. . . . Her bare arm is almost around his neck, her partly nude swelling breast heaves tumultuously against his, face to face they whirl on, his limbs interwoven with hers, his strong right arm around her yielding form, he presses her to him until every curve in the contour of her body thrills with the amorous contact. . . . She returns to her home that night robbed of that most precious jewel of womanhood—virtue![52]

In this quote the body seems to take on a will of its own; separated from the rational judgment of the mind, it acts only on its immediate carnal appetite and the promise of sexual pleasure. Some antidance authors are titled men, "Reverends" and "Colonels," who are either reformed dancers or experienced observers (doing research for their invectives) who speak from a firsthand (horrified) position. For all of them, however, their stated objective is the same: they feel an obligation from their position of influence to warn people, particularly the parents of young women, of the dangers of balls and social dance academies. Repeatedly there is the sense that purity itself, more than just the virginity of young women who study ballroom dance, is being guarded.

A sketch accompanying the text for Faulkner's *From the Ball-room to Hell,* for example, labeled "The Dance of Death," shows a doll-like figure of an elegantly gowned woman being tipped forward by a man dressed in formal black, his limbs in an exaggerated high-stepping motion, while a black-skinned devil frames the pair from above with his outstretched arms and open bat-like wings (figure 7). In another illustration, sardonically titled "Harmless Amusement," the slight figure of a listless young woman lies in bed, her cheeks flushed with cross-hatching to suggest fever, as a man seated next to the bed buries his face in his handkerchief. "No harm in the dance?" reads the text underneath this image. "Yet the blame lieth there / For this heart-broken father / And the daughter's despair." Repeatedly the message is one of purity in danger; beyond virginity, America's future, young womanhood, is in jeopardy of defilement.

At precisely this same time, identical alarms were beginning to sound with regard to the practice of coeducation, educating boys and girls together. Coeducation had been in place since the early nineteenth century with no major objections. Now, however, these same final decades of the century that saw the proliferation of antidance documents, sermons, cartoons, and lectures also heard cries about the dangers of educating boys and girls together. As David Tyack has noted of coeducation, the anxiety demonstrated about strengthening the traditional gender order indicated that maintaining the separate spheres was becoming increasingly hard cultural work.[53] This was equally true in dance.

Femininity and masculinity, instead of being taken for granted, now required conscious buttressing. The larger social agenda seems to have been in part the struggle to keep women in their "natural" place as wives and mothers and to prevent them from challenging men in public arenas. As the historian Rosalind Rosenberg argues, this was a time when the old idea that woman's mind was limited by her body was fervently held.

Figure 7. "The Dance of Death," a popular sketch of the time depicting the evils of social dancing (T. A. Faulkner, *From the Ball-room to Hell*, 1894)

Increasing numbers of young women were entering the labor market in industry and commerce, women's reform groups were attacking urban problems, the women's movement was gaining momentum in its demand for political and economic rights, and women were demanding entry into higher education on a par with men. Thus, Rosenberg argues, "many Americans believed that the need to draw a clear line between appropriate male and female activities had become acute."[54] Ballrooms and schools were two of the most public spheres in which the sexes mixed and, therefore, these ideas might be explored.

A similar sense of the possible defilement of civilized society through dance pervades later antidance treatises as well. In 1902 Colonel Dick Maple described himself in *Palaces of Sin; or, The Devil in Society* as "a man who spent his fortune with lavish hand but awoke from his hypnotic debauch of Society's shame, to wave the red flag of warning to his fellowman." Like other antidance treatises *Palaces* calls for sanctions against balls and social dancing academies. This call, however, comes in a manner that is salaciously enhanced by the confessional and elaborately detailed accounts of these "Palaces of Sin" Colonel Maple, like Faulkner in 1894, has inhabited:

[I write] in behalf of innocent and inexperienced manhood and womanhood throughout the land. . . . I will feel that I have been repaid ten thousand times for this very embarassing task which has forced me to openly acknowledge that I was once covered with the filth of Fashionable Society.[55]

A redeemed sinner always brings out the voyeur in readers, who can sample secondhand both the allure and the shame of dance while maintaining the virtuous position of a shocked outsider. Yet audiences who read Faulkner's, Crane's, and Maple's treatises apparently took them very seriously. Since many of the authors of these books were Presbyterian, Congregational, Methodist, or Lutheran ministers, members of their congregations would likely have made up at least part of their audiences.[56] Faulkner, for example, claims in the title page of one of his books that his publications "had circulated by the million," although as Ann Wagner notes, most of his treatises were published by Faulkner himself.[57] Several of the well-worn original copies of these treatises have margin notes and underlining. In one instance a reader has written on the last page in pencil in his own hand the ten reasons why dance is a social evil.[58] Colonel Maple's preface also states that he is writing *Palaces of Sin* in response to requests from those who have heard his lectures on the same topic.

Faulkner's *From the Ball-room to Hell*, by contrast, is written in the form of a series of almost Socratic responses to what were apparently challenging questions addressed to him by *pro*dance partisans. For Faulkner, the descent from the ballroom to Hell is unequivocal. Here is a form of popular culture, he warns, whose immediate effect is to loosen the passions. Once they are aroused in both men and women there is no turning back. A social fall is tantamount to the biblical one. Indeed, one sketch in Faulkner's book shows Adam as a lustful, formally attired dancer coaxing a reluctant Eve to dance while a serpent proffering a glass of wine instead of an apple looks on from a tree. The image is, to paraphrase Sally Banes, Terpsichore in cloven hooves.[59] The connection of alcohol to dance, too, was a contributing factor in most of the efforts to prohibit dance during this time. In the Lower East Side of New York City, for example, a 1901 survey revealed that 80 percent of the 130 dance halls in 1895 were adjacent to saloons. The sale of alcohol was the foundation of dance hall business; therefore, dances were structured with three or four minutes of dancing followed by fifteen or twenty minutes of intermission to allow time for purchasing and drinking alcohol.[60]

While these antidance books and surveys represent a fear of dance, they also hint at a quest for some middle ground between popular Victorian notions of woman as either a temptress whose beauty is linked with dangerous sexuality or a pale maiden representing innocence and weakness. Played out on the dance floor, this dichotomy reveals the tension between the socially unrestrained, proactive woman and this pale, equally repugnant figure wasted away by dancing. The dance floor thus becomes an arena for negotiating a balance and defining an ideology of woman's nature and place in the public sphere. The moment was socially propitious: in 1870 less than 15 percent of American workers were women; by 1910 they made up a quarter of the work force.[61] With women entering the public sphere at such a rapid rate there was little time to observe the resultant changes; a more reflexive attitude was just to react and at least try to preserve the status quo outside of work.

For Faulkner, dance is like a drug that leads to an accelerated decline. First there are dance lessons, then attendance at a ball, sexual arousal by the physical sensation of dancing close, face-to-face and often spinning around, with a member of the opposite sex, and then loss of virginity (often by the evening's end) and life in a brothel within a few weeks. No woman, no matter how virtuous, is immune from being an easy target for seduction once she starts dancing. "I do not believe any woman can or does waltz without being improperly aroused to a greater or lesser degree," Faulkner claims. "She may not at first understand her feelings, or recognize as harmful or sinful those emotions which must come to every woman who has a particle of warmth in her nature."[62]

It is just a matter of time, then, before this woman "will one day ripen if not into open sin and shame, then into a nature more or less depraved and health more or less impaired." It is peculiar how inescapable, and yet humanly natural, the debasing effect of dance is as portrayed here. Paradoxically, Faulkner goes on to say that in fact any woman who is so cold as *not* to be aroused by the waltz is "entirely unfit to make any man happy as his wife."[63] What emerges, then, is a practice that cannot be controlled, only prohibited. To demonstrate one's humanity in the dance is also to display one's vulnerability. The result is that this type of close contact between a man and woman is seen as something that can only be sanctioned in the privacy of the Victorian home, and, of course, only between a married man and woman.

The waltz, for example, has thus become the equivalent of conjugal rites, once removed, and the ballroom a public boudoir. The physical space of the ballroom or the dance academy has also been deemed a perilous arena for the female body. Repeatedly, antidance treatises focus on the physical contact and proximity necessary for men and women to dance. The result is to render a couple's dance position an illicit embrace, and their physical contact in the swirling waltz a position for vertical, ambulatory foreplay. By locating the contact in the public space of a ballroom, the inappropriateness is increased; this is perceived as public intimacy between strangers. Faulkner elaborates:

Oh! what lady would allow any man, in any other public place, except the ballroom to take liberties with her that he takes here? Would a lady with a spark of self-respect, at any other place, place her breast against his, and allow him to encircle her waist with his arm, place his foot between hers and clasp her hands in his? This is the position assumed in waltzing.[64]

A curious phenomenon is taking place here. Just as the nineteenth-century stage was seen as a space that could compromise the virtue of a woman who ventured into it as a theatrical dancer, and the blackface minstrelsy stage was seen as a place where black bodies were appropriated and controlled, so too this other nineteenth-century public arena for dance, the ballroom, was painted as a sphere where dangerous transformations occurred. Even virtuous women could not control themselves: the only remedy was to avoid balls and ballrooms. So what was to be done? "To close the doors of the brothel, close first the doors of the dancing school," Faulkner concluded. Indeed, one of the ideals of the Victorian distinction between private and public space, women's and men's separate spheres, was the notion of how controlled spaces could impart a sense of order to social interactions through carefully planned, controlled, and deliberate patterns of movement.[65]

In contradiction to these claims by antidance treatises implying an increasing licentiousness in dance styles, social dance historian Richard Powers says that dance positions did not change significantly during the entire nineteenth century. Generally the manuals specified that partners should stand "not too far [from] and not too close" to each other. This meant that certainly no more than their hands were touching. Some dance manuals even suggested women look slightly to the left, which would have directed their faces away from their partners and reduced the intimacy of face-to-face exposure.[66] Social changes were far more dramatic during the century, bringing medical discoveries about disease and the functioning of the body and increased anxiety about foreign immigrants and influences. These social changes contain their own ambiguities that in some ways parallel the curious dichotomy of fearing dance as a site of the breakdown of control while at the same time seeing it as a means of establishing and maintaining control.

As frightening epidemics of cholera, typhus, typhoid, and influenza raged, the nineteenth-century body was being conceptualized as a newly knowable entity, one that could reveal a moral significance in the laws of life through its own workings.[67] That this same body should have been regarded with anxiety by Victorian religious men is not surprising.

As Elaine Showalter, Bruce Haley, and Patricia Vertinsky have documented, the body, women, doctors, exercise, and religious men have a strange and intertwined history in the late nineteenth century.[68] Haley, like minstrelsy historian Eric Lott, places the Victorian body at the center of broadening nineteenth-century social discourse. Citing the emergence of physiological psychology and the notion of a healthy body and mind being interdependent, along with the belief that education should develop the whole man through physical as well as mental training, Haley outlines a world in which a quest for personal control, social order, and moral significance coincided.[69]

This discourse of health and disease also included xenophobia, in one instance directed at Parisian dance teachers. J. Townley Crane's 1849 antidance *Essay on Dancing* hints at the threat of foreign influence in America in the form of French-trained Parisian dance teachers: "From this elegant city, renowned for vice and moral pollution of every description, do troops of dancing-masters issue forth every year, and come upon the surrounding nations as did the locusts of the Egyptian plague. . . . [In France] a virtuous woman is not the rule, but the exception, and one-third of the children are of uncertain parentage."[70] Similar fears about the mixing of immigrant and lower-class adolescent children with those of Anglo-Saxon descent and the middle class are reflected in cries against coeducation for high school girls at this time.[71]

Apart from claiming that two-thirds of all prostitutes once attended social dances and that "the most accomplished dancers are to be found among abandoned women," the antidance authors fail to establish dance as the sole cause of these social evils. The strongest rebuttal Faulkner offers to the rhetorical question of why more dancing women are not mothers is that "the dance floor exercise will relieve all fear of maternity." Paradoxically, the implication is that if a woman dances she is at risk for getting pregnant, but if she does happen to conceive the dancing will "force the termination of the pregnancy."[72] The authors do not succeed in establishing a cause-and-effect relationship between dance and social problems, but their anxiety was undoubtedly real. To them the sight of any man taking a woman in his arms at a dance, unless they were a married couple, was a distressing display of improper intimacy.[73]

46

The most tangible effect couple dancing produced was likely an elevated mood, the very thing these antidance treatises were in a sense attacking and the focal point of both the protest against and the pleasure in the dance. One could not have done better in the service of the new Victorian ideal of seeking a mind-and-body union than to enjoy how the physical motion of waltzing radiated into a stimulated mental and emotional state. Yet one of the repeated complaints about dancing from its detractors was that it did nothing for the mind.

No social dance form seems to have been immune from antidance rhetoric. Round dances, square dances, the waltz—all are named and implicated in the perils to civilized life posed by social dance. The venue, too, seems unimportant: *all* social dance is the target. From dances in private parlors to huge public balls, the complaint is the same: the female body in America is imperiled, particularly for middle-class women at unchaperoned and public dances.

Antidance treatises are only part of the story of antidance sentiment in America in the late nineteenth century. Cartoons, sketches, sermons, and lectures echoed the sentiments of these writings, presumably thrilling the audience with tales from the sordid front. The cartoons in particular are curious, not so much illustrating the texts as supplying their own narrative with the blunt directness and didacticism of engravings made for a child's book. Interestingly, when one compares these antidance tracts to the prodance guidebooks, it becomes apparent that point by point both addressed many of the same issues. The difference is that the prodance authors came to precisely the opposite conclusions, claiming that dance was a socially valuable and healthful practice. The numbers on both sides were voluminous. Elizabeth Aldrich based her compilation of dance etiquette on "scores of [pro]dance and etiquette manuals from the 1800s," and Ann Wagner counted more than 350 primary antidance books and tracts in researching her *Adversaries of Dance*.[74]

One of the most persuasive antidance treatises was written by William C. Wilkinson, who faults dance for being a late-night, stuffy indoor activity, a complaint that curiously echoes Beecher's earlier concerns about the health dangers the Victorian home posed for nineteenth-century women. To make his point, Wilkinson posits a gymnasium run like a ballroom in an effort to undermine the argument that dance offers good physical exercise. "What would be thought of a gymnasium that should carpet its floors, and close its windows and announce its hours of exercise commence at 10 P.M. and end at 3 A.M., interrupted by a sumptuous midnight feast . . . and in dress that represses respiration. This is the dance as it is!"[75]

Antidance treatises reveal a certain ambiguity as to just what constituted a healthy body for the Victorian American woman. The implication was that physical health reflected a kind of certainty about one's body, which offered a starting point for other certainties. This was potentially subversive social knowledge for a culture that wanted women to maintain the social and gender status quo. Haley posits that "in sport the healthy body was an instrument not for understanding the ineffable, but for ritualizing an obedience to the reasonable."[76] It was precisely in this regard that the dancing body broke from Victorian convention. It refuted expectations that only specific kinds of physical activity could, and should, be agents of moral and spiritual fitness. Implicit within the concern that dancing could lead to moral degradation was a belief in the link between the physical and the spiritual, the mind and the body. Within a few years the playground reform movement would be arguing for physical activity as a means toward mental fitness, building on the implicit bonds the Victorian fears revealed.

Similar fears about the health dangers that education imposed on women were echoed by Dr. Edward H. Clarke of Harvard Medical School in his influential 1887 book *Sex in Education*. In this book Clarke claims, "If girls had to compete intellectually with boys, with no allowances made for their menstrual periods or special needs, the result would be 'monstrous brains and puny bodies, . . . flowing thought and constipated bowels'— in other words, mastery of algebra at the expense of the ovaries. . . . [B]y emulating boys academically, girls would lose their health and might become sterile. Why should we spoil a good mother by making her an ordinary grammarian?"[77] Dr. Clarke's argument may be yet another implicit call for suppression of women in which concern for their childbearing function is couched as concern for their personal health.

G. Stanley Hall, the late nineteenth-century psychologist and educator, shared some of the views of the antidance authors, yet he was a proponent of dance as part of physical education for women. Hall believed that the body took primacy over the mind and that women should be assisted in improving their health and vigor through physical training. Like the antidance authors, Hall was arguing for a controlled female body as the only safe form of woman to have in the public arena. "First to know, then to control female development" was his motto. In particular, physical culture was important for Hall because it represented service to the state rather than intellectual training, which he felt would have merely been for personal development.[78] Indeed, even a leading prodance book of the time, William Blaikie's 1899 *How to Get Strong and How to Stay So*, stated flatly that it was better for a woman to be physically fit than to know history.[79] The implication was that educating the mind and training the body were mutually incompatible activities for women. If the mind was taxed by learning, then the body would suffer, and healthy female bodies were more important to the nation than amateur historians.

As Vertinsky notes, Hall's model supports Michel Foucault's analysis that as scientific discourse about the physical requirements of the body expands, the human body is brought increasingly within the orbit of state, institutional, or professional power.[80] Hall had a concept of the body that argued for the formation of moral character along with physical development as part of motor education. The era of these antidance treatises was a time of broadening discourse about women's social and biological bodies and increasing anxiety about how society could control them.[81] The models of women's education that Hall put forth elevated the female physically while deprecating her intellectually.

In antidance treatises the mind, too, is seen as unable to control the powerful physical response that the dancing woman's body will have. The body leads and the mind follows. So there is no talk of persuading or educating women to resist men's advances in the ballroom; once the body is awakened to sensual urges, the logic seems to be, the intellect and reason are powerless to intervene.

Curiously, men, too, are depicted as victims of their passions, but this is dismissed as simply the way it is. In contrast, women are seen as more socially malleable: on the dance floor they are led by the man, a microcosm of the world outside in which society must "lead" them. The evangelist M. B. Williams, while decrying the dance as "unspiritual and immoral," says, "It remains a physical necessity for men to attend brothels," and hence they surely will not be able to rein themselves in at dances. "Are there, then, no circumstances under which the modern dance is justifiable?" Williams asks in his treatise (actually a collection of three sermons against theater, dance, and drink). "A young man might dance with his grandmother," he answers sarcastically, "if she was not rheumatic."[82] So it is the woman who has to be rendered sexually impotent for the exchange to be safe. It is accepted that men will go to brothels and have carnal appetites, but it is women's passions that society decides to control.

Feminist art historian Martha Banta has argued that, as of the 1893 Columbia Exposition, the idealized nineteenth-century woman's body, young, Protestant, and northern European, was seen as a metaphor for America. With this metaphor it is possible to posit the attempted controls on the nineteenth-century female social dancer as emblematic of the perceived threat to the nation posed by spiritual degradation, immigrant dilution of its Anglo-Saxon stock (what Theodore Roosevelt was calling "race suicide"), and diminution of its moral strength.[83] Once the physical sphere women occupied was no longer as controlled socially as it once had been and they began to trickle into the work force, efforts at restriction shifted to more interior space, women's bodies. In the decades to come, the process of justifying dance as a legitimate public activity for women would shift to higher education, where a new ideal of womanhood would be articulated. Women themselves were discovering through dance that they could use their bodies to express such things as sexual desire and individual pleasure in movement, emotions forbidden up until now in any respected public realm. This capacity for emotional expression would be the centerpiece of the dance education program Margaret H'Doubler would craft at the University of Wisconsin.

3

Women, Physical Activity, Education

A Nineteenth-Century Perspective

Not one girl in ten had the air and look of good health. . . . If we neglect the body, the body will have its revenge. And are we not doing this? Are we not throwing our whole educational force upon the brain? Is not a healthy city-born and bred woman getting to be as rare as a black swan? And is it not time to reform this altogether? Is it not time to think something of the casket as well as the jewel? Something of the lantern as well as the light?

Editor of the *Boston Courier*, 1858.

THE BEGINNINGS OF DANCE IN AMERICAN HIGHER EDUCATION ARE nested in a larger period of health reform and in the larger question of why dance education emerged as a part of the physical education curriculum. The late nineteenth and early twentieth centuries saw several booming movements of reform, including the Progressivism of the 1900s and 1910s, when general reformist ferment connected with social optimism. All of these general reform movements saw proper personal hygiene as a precondition for social and human progress. This was not a spurious connection. One was an essential foundation for the other, and the belief ran deep that a "pure" individual would lead to a "purer" society. The result was that good hygiene came to be regarded as a moral obligation, and women's bodies were swept up in this growing discourse about the model "fit" American. There were more ominous extensions of this philosophy in the 1920s, however, and some reformers saw hygiene and eugenics linked. "They are really both hygiene—one individual hygiene and the other race hygiene," observed Irving Fisher, a professor of political economy at Yale who also revealed a dabbling in the subject of "healthy minds" in his 1921 presidential address to the Eugenics Research Association.[1]

Not all of the Progressive health reforms were as clear-minded as the notion of dress reform and the institution of physical activity for women, particularly college women. Among the other health reforms proffered that did *not* endure were diets emphasizing uric acid, Graham flour, skipping breakfast, "thorough mastication," avoiding excessive amounts of protein, "muscular vegetarianism," and sexual restraint.[2] These other reforms, more fads than revolutions in thinking, were short-lived and had limited success in comparison to the fitness crusade. The dance program at the University of Wisconsin might be considered one of its most outstanding and enduring examples.

Actually, a change in women's attitudes toward their bodies preceded this larger change in the social status, behavior, and fitness of women. For a long period women agreed with society's belief that their disadvantaged status was justified and that they were "inferior, diseased and poisonous."[3] Middle-class nineteenth-century women in America found the medical profession and the clergy the most outspoken dictators of "proper" bodily behavior. American and English doctors established strict sexual codes, maintaining that sex for women was an unenjoyable duty and that those who enjoyed and indulged in it were threatened with cancer and early deaths.[4] The result was that women were induced to become passive breeders. The middle-class Victorian male frequented prostitutes for physical pleasure, at the same time lobbying for rigid standards of decency and respectability. As Ronald Pearsall details in his study of Victorian sexuality, the duplicity resulted in convoluted attempts at propriety and invented language to hide anxiety about bodies:

The whole subject of sex became forbidden, confused and diffused into the most unlikely areas. The more pressed could see sex in everything: the shape of a grand piano became indecent and its legs were draped to avoid giving offense to tender-minded young ladies. The English language became a minefield; not only, predictably, did breasts become bosom, but legs became limbs or, to point the argument even more powerfully, "unmentionables."[5]

These verbal prohibitions on even mentioning female body parts hint at what must have been the Victorian woman's daily lived experience of the dangerousness of her body. Although it may have been "the body" that was chastised as sinful, the body has been "notoriously and ubiquitously associated with *the female*," and intuitively the Victorian woman must have recognized this coding.[6] Philosophers from the modern positivists to Descartes and stretching back to Plato have long depicted the body as an enemy of objectivity, as existing in opposition to the mind and as more allied with the natural than the rational world. These are all descriptors of the female as well.

EDUCATION BECOMES PHYSICAL

Given this history, it is possible that, were it not for the medical urgency of making women's bodies stronger, the revolution of dance education would not have happened. For just at the moment that she was gaining the right to develop her intellectual capacities in higher education, the American woman might have preferred to leave behind her gender's ties with the physical. But in this instance she had no choice. The welcoming of the American woman into higher education would be swiftly followed by the awakening of her body in the same environment. Both had become social necessities. Earlier, women's bodies and minds had been restricted, and illness had loomed as a painterly ideal, but now the awakening of these same bodies was coming to be seen as a social imperative for robust and responsible motherhood.

What H'Doubler did almost intuitively in the first quarter of the twentieth century was to offer an alternative to the mind-centered approach of traditional higher education. For women waking from the physical slumber of the Victorian age, H'Doubler's classes offered a new vision of the body's role in intellectual insight. The body became central in the conscious reproduction and transformation of culture in H'Doubler's studio. The rationalist bias that saw reason as the major tool for gaining knowledge of reality was now challenged by a new model that saw the empiricism of the senses as equally important in influencing perceptions of reality. The implications for education would be enormous.

Similar battles were fought on both sides of the Atlantic. Scandinavian gymnastics, Swiss ideas about child development and the importance of natural play to it, and the British love of sport influenced the development of physical education in the United States. In describing the development of British physical education, historian Paul Atkinson delineates three basic systems of physical education that arose in the nineteenth century and played themselves out along the lines of class and gender. This model is useful, for it suggests a trial-and-error approach to finding the right fit for students of a particular age and gender:

In the boy's public schools there emerged a distinctive concern with sports and games which verged at times on an obsession. In the elementary schools, on the other hand, such physical training that was provided was meted out in the form of military drill. In the girls' high schools and public schools, toward the end of the century, therapeutic exercises imported from Scandinavia were preeminent. By the end of the century the girls' schools had also adopted games similar to those of the boys' schools, and it was in the girls' schools alone that the various strands of physical education were welded into a comprehensive scheme of physical education.[7]

This trial-and-error approach never appealed to H'Doubler, whose starting point for dance education was a broad theoretical view of what good educational goals were and how dance might address these. Her most immediate task was to find a place for dance in what William James in his 1901–2 lectures on "The Varieties of Religious Experience" was calling "the religion of healthy-mindedness."[8] She did not have to look far. Between 1860 and 1920 the graceful side of physical activity was increasingly lauded as being particularly valuable for hygienic reform. In contrast to the more competitive, aggressive, and straining types of physicality, activities like riding, swimming, fencing, skating, and walking could be recommended to adults of a wide variety of ages as well as children.[9] Good hygiene was seen as a moral obligation because physical well-being was equated with spiritual propriety. Graceful physical activity was a safe, expeditious, and lifelong avenue to a healthy body and mind.

Manliness, too, was undergoing a redefinition during the early 1900s. Since the late 1850s German immigrants had brought an influx of *Turn-vereine* (gymnastic societies and gymnasiums) to the United States, and this generated an interest in physical fitness throughout the larger society, first for men and then for women. By the end of the decade there were more than seventy gymnastic societies around the country.[10]

Relatively inexpensive, available in all seasons and all weather conditions, the gymnasium was one solution to the new, less physically active lives city dwellers experienced compared to their country ancestors. The eager young men who took up this fitness regime in America, while maintaining its gracefulness, pushed it toward an ideology of perfection, believing "the muscles are the only organs of the will."[11] Exercises that had been designed to test the muscles and encourage a complete range of motion of the joints and limbs became feats of balance and stamina in "manly competitions." Eventually transformed into something more genteel, these activities would in later decades become the roots of dance education, but for now gymnastics was a pragmatic masculine enterprise, albeit one with latent aesthetic elements.

The parallel and horizontal bars, horse, weights, and climbing equipment were all used in varieties of vigorous competitions for men. In addition, in a discovery that would prove useful for dance as well, this rhythmic, indoor movement activity was also found to be invigorating play for the mind that complemented the muscle building.[12] Here was a physical way to ameliorate the widespread American disorder of nervous exhaustion. Health was being redefined as "perpetual youth—that is, a state of positive health. . . . Health is to feel the body a luxury as every vigorous child does."[13]

Exercise was also beneficial for sublimating the less laudatory aspects of human behavior: "Physical exercises give to energy and daring a legitimate channel, supply the place of war, gambling, licentiousness, high-way robbery, and office-seeking. . . . It gives an innocent answer to that first demand for evening excitement which perils the soul of the homeless boy in the seductive city," wrote Thomas Wentworth Higginson in an 1861 *Atlantic Monthly* article on gymnastics.[14] This capacity for rhythmic physical movement to offer release from negative social behaviors was one element of this early gymnastic activity that H'Doubler and the women at the University of Wisconsin would also discover and promote.

One of the leading figures in formulating a system of gymnastics at this time was Diocesan (Dio) Lewis. A former physician who practiced medicine in the 1840s and who shifted from treating disease to trying to prevent it, Dio Lewis wrote books on sexual hygiene and nutrition as he developed his philosophy of education. According to fitness historian James Whorton, Lewis insisted that "physical education was the indispensable foundation of all other education and that the American school system could never succeed at its task until it gave physical education as central a place as intellectual pursuits and character training."[15]

Beginning in 1854, Lewis started to formulate his system of gymnastics. As Whorton elaborates, "His goal was to find exercises that would have the excitement of free play but could be combined to develop whole body flexibility, coordination, agility, and grace of movement." Interestingly, his first "student" was his wife, whom he reported to have cured of tuberculosis with a regimen of exercises including walking, wood-sawing, and other functional tasks. Lewis was ambitious with his physical exercises; he was interested not only in great muscular strength but also in the mental and moral improvement of practitioners. The first question that should be asked of a young lady when she enters a school, he suggested, was not " 'how have you progressed in Latin?' but 'Miss Mary, how is your spine?' "[16] This is a telling anecdote and one that moves the old complaint about society needing better mothers, not grammarians, to a new plane. Here the female body is being assessed for its well-being as a precursor to tuning the mind. The body is no longer fit at the *expense* of the mind; rather, Lewis's view is that each *complements* the other.

By the spring of 1864 Lewis had incorporated his gymnasium as a normal institute for physical education, and within six months it produced America's first class of trained physical education teachers. Four years earlier Lewis's method had received the approbation of a respected body of educators when the American Institute of Instructors, meeting in Boston, had endorsed his system as "eminently worthy of general introduction into all our schools, and into general use." It was this group that endorsed his plan for creating his institute and thus paved the way for its popularity among future physical education teachers. Lewis's students found they were in demand, and as soon as they graduated they were hired in schools around America, according to an 1885 circular authored by John Philbrick on "City School Systems in the United States."

Lewis went to significant lengths to see that women had more than equal access to his school. Half of his first class of fourteen pupils was female, and to encourage more women to enroll he set their admission fees 25 percent lower than men's. Whorton reports that Lewis officially justified this as offsetting the disparity between men's and women's earnings, but, more important, he seemed to want to address pointedly the rampant ill health of women at the time. He was well versed in the issue, and in fact he had borrowed many of his exercises from Catharine Beecher's own program of physical reform for women.

What Lewis did so well, however, was to institutionalize, and to a certain degree standardize, physical education instruction. Pupils came through his door as those listless, languid, "vanishing" women of Romantic painters' canvases, and they left as Duncanesque Samothraces, women grandly revivified and forcefully healthier. After addressing the training of instructors, Lewis next opened the Family School for Young Ladies, where he took in "delicate" teenage girls and dosed them with a regimen of heavy exercise and study. Each day started with ninety minutes of his special brand of gymnastics. Unfortunately, the school was destroyed by fire in 1867 and was never rebuilt. However, in just three years it trained nearly three hundred girls and achieved remarkable improvements in the girls' vitality.

It mattered little at the time that his vision for his successful students extended no further than healthy motherhood; Lewis had initiated a breakthrough in the kinds of physical activity females could not only tolerate but master. Lewis's endorsing physical activity for females while supporting the status quo for their sex, thus fitting women for motherhood, was typical of most women's physical-activity advocates of the time, including Catharine Beecher. The rationale seems to have been to push hard at one frontier of social change at a time. Also, Lewis and others firmly believed that, for women, biological destiny took precedence over all else.

Biological destiny governed men also; however, for them physical health was a religious, civic, and racial duty. The following statement reflects one of these views of the male obligation.

He who neglects his body, . . . who allows it to grow up puny, frail, sickly, misshapen, homely, commits a sin against the Giver of the body. . . . Round shoulders and narrow chests are states of criminality. The dyspepsia is heresy. The headache is infidelity.[17]

No "quality of life" or "enhanced well-being" sentiments cloud the issues here; for men as well as women the body is social property, and letting it run down is like being a negligent tenant or unfaithful spouse. The idea of the body as social property is a double-edged concept, for it allows society to mandate that individuals keep themselves in good health, and it also allows for social control in areas like education, fashion, and public use of the body that might not be welcomed.

By the 1870s a number of systems of physical exercise were being advocated. In addition to military drill, which modeled itself after Civil War training, free Swedish gymnastics and several systems of weight training and sports and games were increasingly practiced.[18] More telling, by the 1870s many members of the medical profession had become major advocates of this new "muscular Christianity," or "muscular morality," as it was also called. Although the term *physical education* had actually been invented in the 1820s by William Andrus Alcott, a doctor turned physical health reformer, a group of 1870s physicians, including Lewis, is credited with initiating the modern physical education movement.

Were there any doubt about the physically remedial orientation of early physical education, the fact that its founders included these physicians, actively interested in preventive health measures, resolves it. The physician's outlook is prescriptive; she identifies a problem and assigns exercises to address it, and the student ceases the physical activity once the problem is corrected. It was this legacy that would inform the focus and orientation of the women's physical education program in which H'Doubler would found her dance curriculum. In 1861, on the cusp of this boom in physical education, Edward Hitchcock, Jr., son of an 1830s health reformer, was appointed professor of hygiene and physical education at Amherst, thus introducing physical education at the college level. Hitchcock maintained his post at Amherst for the next fifty years, cementing the field's presence in academia.

The real academic breakthrough for physical education in higher education, however, came in 1879, when Dudley Allen Sargent, a devotee of preventive medicine and holder of a medical degree from Yale, was given a professorship at Harvard. Sargent was zealous, pragmatic, organized, and a fervent believer in the health benefits of exercise. His system was one of the most widespread physical training programs in higher education into the first few decades of the twentieth century, and many women's college gymnasiums today still have the pulleys and rings Sargent invented. As Whorton describes the system:

The Sargent System that he instituted at Harvard's soon to be famous Hemenway Gymnasium was structured around exercises on pulley-weight machines (many of Sargent's invention) that could be adjusted to the strength of the individual and focussed on the cultivation of specific muscles. The system also involved "mimetic exercises," more than fifty activities designed to imitate the movement of various forms of labor and sport.[19]

With this second university appointment in physical education, the standing of the field improved significantly in American colleges. Sargent's own background as a former gymnast, circus acrobat, and private gymnasium operator gave him a broad repertoire of movement forms from which to draw. By 1885 Sargent's weight machines and codified exercises were in use by nearly fifty colleges and clubs around the nation. Three years later Sargent initiated his Harvard Summer School of Physical Education, a major training ground for established teachers who wanted to go into teaching diverse aspects of physical education. By 1912 Sargent boasted that 270 colleges had programs in physical education, three hundred city school systems required it, and there were five hundred YMCA gymnasiums with eighty thousand members, as well as more than a hundred gymnasiums connected with athletic clubs, hospitals, military bases, and miscellaneous institutions.[20]

Soon Sargent's graduates were fanning out to other universities: Edward Hartwell, M.D., took the Sargent System to Johns Hopkins; William Anderson, M.D., was director of the Yale Gymnasium and was instrumental in establishing a national physical education association; Luther Gulick, M.D., was a graduate of Sargent's program who studied the growth of physical training within the YMCA; and R. Tait McKenzie, M.D., directed the physical education program at the University of Pennsylvania.[21]

A consciousness of Hellenic idealism permeated all these men's outlooks on the value of physical training. The goal was to attain for American society the Greek ideal of a sound mind in a sound body, the very ambition Isadora Duncan paraphrased in her vision of a new American dance:

not the tottering, ape-like convulsions of the Charleston, but a striking upward tremendous mounting, powerful mounting above the pyramids of Egypt, beyond the Parthenon of Greece, an expression of Beauty and Strength such as no civilization has ever known. That will be America dancing.[22]

As educational models shifted, so too did the rhetoric, but not the goal, of this physical education movement. For example, as Progressive models emerged as an educational ideal, the notion of efficiency became absorbed into physical education ideas of well-being and the conservation of energy. The result was that the fit body was talked about as a vehicle of "efficient service," a means for attacking with discipline the great moral, financial, social, and political problems of the nation. "Endurance and its parent efficiency were vital to the life of the country," Whorton summarizes. "Economic productivity and military strength required hardy bodies and agile minds, so physical education was a patriotic duty."[23]

Over time the more faddish aspects of the physical education movement and its fanatics dropped away, and the steadiest concern remained improving the physical and moral health of Americans through exercise. Physical and moral health was seen as a road toward Christian as well as human perfection and, most important, a way to build a better world in an era of the city as an industrialized jungle. It helped that there was also a growing awareness that muscular exercise improved mental functioning, that, in Whorton's words, "muscle power generated brain power."[24]

This growing awareness of the possible links between mind and body enhanced dance's attractiveness to educators. The fascination with more rigid exercise forms of movement like gymnastics was beginning to fade by the end of the nineteenth century. Spontaneity and unpredictability, attributes central to interpretive dance, were two qualities most of these earlier fitness regimes had ignored. Now, however, the concept of fitness itself was about to evolve outlooks more compatible with subtler aspects of physical well-being, namely, the aesthetic and the graceful. This development had major resonance for dance. Bicycling, too, had some of these subtler qualities and, by the century's end, was on its way to becoming a new and enormously popular physical activity—especially for women, who could perform it while seated and garbed in modest attire.

One of the most salutary effects of this shifting late nineteenth-century interest in physical education was its effect of destabilizing the long-standing mind-centered approach to knowledge and understanding. The body was coming to be seen as having a much more central role in intellectual insight and in the reproduction and transformation of culture. Instead of perceiving the body in opposition to the mind, the crusaders of fitness were actually pushing toward union, or at least a friendship between the two. It would remain for later twentieth-century feminism to extend these nascent notions into a regard for the body as a cultural text and a social construction. Already, however, the groundwork had been laid for dance as an exemplification of a mind-body union. Indeed, dance is a medium through which cultural understanding is represented and in which change can be envisioned and sampled.[25]

WOMEN, SPORT, AND EDUCATION

One of the earliest forums in which the nineteenth-century woman envisioned and sampled change was that of female sports and physical education. Here was an arena not just of aspirations but where actual changes could be implemented. Women's entrance into the world of sport and physical education represented a critical breach in a long-standing barrier between women and physical activity.[26] It was a necessary first step toward the eventual founding of dance as a discipline in higher education. With this new access a variety of physical freedoms and a loosening of prohibitions on the body would eventually follow, but it would be a long battle and a hard-won victory.

By the last decade of the nineteenth century most "girl's" colleges had taken the lead from physical education for men and adopted physical education programs of their own, also equipping themselves with gymnasiums. Activities would come to be defined as appropriate along very strict gender divides. Athletics and intense competition were important for manhood and wartime readiness, while sports for girls were used to develop leadership qualities, sociability, and "health"—defined differently than for the males. By the mid-nineteenth century, for example, Vassar required physiology and hygiene courses during the freshman year for all women in an effort to keep them healthy enough to learn. In contrast, physical education for men was often instituted for very different reasons. It was supposed to foster enjoyment of fierce competition as well as grace in losing. Along with this came the lessons that strength was a moral as well as physical attribute and that some are destined to lead and some to follow. Harvard and Yale, which had gymnasiums at this time, had no required physical education for men; rather, it provided the gymnasium to give young men the opportunity to work off excess energy. The hope was that this would reduce the number of student pranks rather than serve as a health measure.[27]

Women's colleges did not have the same tradition of including physical education, nor the same reasons for it. Organized physical education for American women had actually begun in the 1830s and 1840s, when Catharine Beecher, Emma Willard, Almira Phelps, and Zilpah Grant insisted that calisthenics and other physical activities be incorporated into the curriculum of the female seminaries. In the early 1900s, gymnastics, in fact, served as a synonym for physical education. Two men—Matthew Vassar, who established Vassar College in 1865, and Henry Fowle Durant, who founded Wellesley College in 1875—were also strong supporters of developing women's ability to handle noncompetitive exercise and higher education. Vassar and Wellesley both included exercise in the curriculum from the start; Vassar also had bowling alleys and a riding school in the gym, or "calisthenium," and offered flower gardening, swimming, boating, and winter ice-skating. It was these reformers, concerned about women's ill health and the need to make women stronger, who began to develop appropriate physical exercises for girls and women.[28]

As feminist sports historian Patricia Vertinsky explains, Emma Willard prescribed exercises fashioned to improve the posture and gracefulness of her pupils at Troy Female Seminary. Her assistant, Almira Phelps, elaborated upon exercises for health and beauty in her *Lectures to Young Ladies*, and Zilpah Grant instituted a systematic course of calisthenics at Ipswich Seminary. Catharine Beecher, however, considered herself the inventor of the system of calisthenics increasingly employed in the 1830s and 1840s by other reformers such as Dio Lewis.[29] In academia this was a welcome addition to the curricula. As Thomas Woody noted, "Physical training came into the women's colleges, in the later part of the Nineteenth Century, on a great tidal wave of popularity."[30] By the early 1900s, in fact, many institutions had established separate departments of physical education for women.

The physical education programs for women, however, were established with difficulty. The kinds of arguments made to situate physical education (or physical training or physical culture, as it was sometimes still called) as a part of the curriculum of female education would also have an important impact on how dance would position itself in the university, within women's physical education.

Ironically, although there was increasing awareness of the benefits of physical exercise for men during the middle decades of the nineteenth century, it was at this time, as women began to be admitted to seminaries, normal schools, and high schools, that the curriculum for women (rather punitively it seems) "emphasized book-learning to the almost total exclusion of provisions for health." Cries of alarm to change this came from a number of fronts, including the medical and health establishments. As early as December 1837 a long article appeared in Boston's *Medical and Surgical Journal* stating, "There is something radically wrong in the present system of education among young ladies. Their physical condition does not receive from parents or teachers that consideration which it deserves." Woody summarizes the rest of the article: "Briefly, the faults are these: girls go to school early and are confined there long hours; they have not enough exercise in the open air; they have too many studies; they finish their education too young and are hastily prepared by anxious mothers for society."[31] The larger view of what women were being educated for was not being addressed; instead, the curriculum in practice became almost punitive in its narrowness and negation of the physical toll of mental work.

Similar observations were made in *Education of Girls* by Nathan Allen:

From six to sixteen years of age, girls are confined closely to school, except about twelve weeks vacation each year. No systematic provision for physical culture is made at the school, neither is there sufficient exercise taken outside for a proper and healthy development of the body. . . . In no part of female education is there so much need of reform as in physical culture. If the standard of scholarship is to be raised higher and higher in all our schools for girls, and no greater attention is to be paid to the laws of health and life, grave consequences may well be apprehended. With rare exceptions, there is no system of gymnastics, or calisthenics, provided in schools for girls, and, generally speaking, no regular and systematic exercise that is adapted to promote their highest physical development.[32]

With such restrictions on young women's physical activity in school, illness seems almost programmed into the curriculum, as if to confirm fears that study would indeed make females sick. Julia Brown, a historian of women's physical education, has observed that schools became *in loco parentis* and tried to protect students as a way of meeting society's expectations. Repeatedly, the portrait that was being painted is that of girls forbidden to run, slide, or race as the boys did, restricted exclusively to school duties and the indoors. Partly this was a matter of decorum, but it was also a consequence of women's attire and social roles. Vertinsky says:

A general feeling of the time was that the constitution of women could only bear a certain amount of moderate exercise. Walking was fine if pursued sedately; gardening was.acceptable so long as both the sun and stooping were avoided. All children could play shuttlecock and skip with ropes, but girls were advised against such active sports as tag and follow the leader.[33]

Here again a curious cause-and-effect *il*logic occurs in the placing of blame. Women, admitted to education, are given the added pressure of academic achievement and yet restricted from the kinds of stress-releasing physical activity permitted men. Strangely, too, women teachers are targeted as being partially to blame for tight corsets as a fashion. Woody reports that "some critics gave teachers the chief credit for the prevailing tight-lacing habit and declared that 'lady-teachers' waists' were smaller than those of any other class of women who earn their daily bread."[34] One senses resentments of a different sort creeping in here, almost a "blame the victim" mentality.

The introduction of physical education into women's curricula finally came about in large measure as a response to outside pressures and models for change created by influential women leaders such as Beecher, Willard, and Phelps. The success of the public playgrounds and gymnasiums effectively led to an educational model for how to strengthen girls and women physically. Granville Stanley Hall, writing in 1902, claimed that since the first gymnasium was opened in New York in 1869, "over 475 gymnasia, training more than 86,000 young men, have been established in 610 city or large town associations of the country."[35] Boston, for example, opened a public gymnasium for women two years after opening one for men. The response to the women's gym was extraordinary: within three months ninety-seven thousand girls and women had reportedly used the gym's facilities under the direction of Elizabeth C. McMartin, a student in Sargent's Normal School.[36]

This public enthusiasm, coupled with the efforts of a number of leaders of women's education, began to effect significant changes in higher education. Both Emma Willard and Catharine Beecher, in founding their female seminaries, included from the start vigorous programs in health education, calisthenics, fresh-air activity, and bathing, all reconstituted as health regimens. Beecher was aware that public enthusiasm was not enough, as she outlined a larger goal of trying to instill order in what she saw as the troubling disorder of American society in the 1820s and 1830s. Beecher believed restoring clarity to gender roles, with the female's role redefined as that of being a healthy mother, was the way to "instill morality and social probity in generations to come."[37] For the next several decades the larger goal for Willard, Beecher, and other leaders of women's education would continue to be that of defining this new portrait of the American woman as ethically and intellectually vital and physically vigorous.

"PROPER" PHYSICAL ACTIVITY

The process of searching for what constituted effective, yet also socially proper, physical activity was from the start a major concern for reformers. Up until 1891 domestic work, in schools where the women students did unpaid housework for their dormitories, was counted as physical exercise. It is an interesting parallel that in women's mental institutions of the time, particularly in England, floor scrubbing, laundry, and ironing were also introduced as physically therapeutic activities for the female inmates.[38] In both instances there is a patronizing inference as to the kind of physical activity for which women are best suited, and a suggestion of what will and should be their physical roles after they leave their respective institutions— college and asylum. Even Beecher's system of calisthenics, rather than looking to help women enjoy restful recreation or tone muscles, was instead created to correct the female form and to provide appropriate physical discipline to fit women better for "women's work"—that is, motherhood and domestic matters.[39]

From the 1890s forward, housework began to diminish as a part of the college exercise curriculum; one imagines this was because it offered little mental recreation and was not very popular with the female students. Corrective gymnastics, work on apparatus, and eventually dancing began to dominate the exercise curriculum.[40]

Gradually, the reasons for continuing physical education changed, and with this change came a more dramatic shift from activity that was drill-like to activity that, while still potentially boring in its repetitiveness, also provided mental stimulation and had aesthetic qualities. In higher education, women's colleges were the first places to register this shift. At Mount Holyoke in 1862, for example, the calisthenics teacher, Miss Evans, was asked to travel to Boston to learn Dio Lewis's system of gymnastics. Reportedly, some educators had raised objections to calisthenics because they were too "dance-like," but one also imagines the women were beginning to feel the tedium of the repetitious monotone. By the following year students were lobbying for facilities improvements as well, and at the commencement ceremony Ellen Parsons read her graduation essay—a plea for a women's gymnasium.[41]

In quick succession other leading women's colleges placed physical education strongly in the curriculum. When Smith College opened in 1875, it had a teacher of gymnastics, and physical education was accorded a level of importance equal to the academic departments. Wellesley College opened the same year with a motto that announced, "Good health is essential to good scholarship."[42] By the end of the nineteenth century most women's colleges had adopted some form of physical education and had built a gymnasium.

More important, by the century's end, physical education for women would be regarded increasingly as a preventive as well as a curative practice. An important event marking this transition was the formation in 1885 of the American Association for the Advancement of Physical Education.[43] Here was a respected organization that believed women were not inherently weak creatures but rather the victims of ill health, and not from study but from inactivity. The association represented an organized effort to develop programs for all based on medical advice and education. As a result, the ideas underpinning a physical education curriculum were formulated. The final transition for women's physical education would be the reconceptualization of physical education as having important social as well as physical benefits.

The placement of dance in the curriculum would bridge these last two notions of physical education for women as a preventive and also a socially valuable act. Indeed, by the 1911 meeting of the Directors of Physical Training of Women's Colleges in New England, there was a strong consensus that present departments were too narrowly concerned with just "the problems of exercise." Sports, games, dancing, stunts, and tumbling were advocated as substitutes for gymnastics, particularly since these activities could be continued after college.[44] Men's sports, by contrast, emphasized competitiveness and winning—echoing the ethics that drove American business. In this way sports served, and would continue to serve, as a major vehicle for defining and reinforcing gender differences, particularly among those who could afford higher education, the middle and upper classes.[45]

In general these shifts can be linked to new educational theories that emphasized the student as a whole person, where mind and body were unified. The implications of this were profound for physical activity in higher education, for now moral and social behavior as well as the proper use of the body were seen as the province of education.

This made dance, specifically the "aesthetic dancing" style current in the late nineteenth century, an especially attractive choice for educators seeking proper use of the body that also benefited moral and social behavior. Vassar College began offering "aesthetic dancing" in 1898 in an informal arrangement, with the teacher not being regular, full-time faculty. By the first decade of the twentieth century, some form of this loosely defined "aesthetic" or "interpretive" dancing could be found in most women's college catalogues.[46] However, it was a recreational pastime, not a part of the academic curriculum. In 1910 Dr. Thomas Wood of Teachers College at Columbia stated his belief that games and sports and dancing should replace the various systems of gymnastics in this country. Barnard College introduced what it called a "natural" dance class in 1913, an outgrowth of Swiss natural movement, and clog dancing in 1920.[47]

However, the growth of physical education as a college subject was considerably slower than these dates suggest, for it would be several years before the instructors would be full-time, regular faculty. The majority of these early women's physical education teachers also taught one or two other academic subjects or carried unrelated administrative duties. For example, at Mills College in Oakland, which opened in 1871, the instructor of physical culture also taught Latin until 1899, when the first full-time teacher of physical education was hired. At Smith College the gymnastics teacher also taught elocution until 1887, when a full-timer was hired. At Emir, history and elocution were among the duties of the physical culture instructor until 1914, when the first full-time women's physical education instructor was at last hired at this college—which had been founded in 1855. At Vassar, which taught students calisthenics from the time it opened in 1865, the gymnastics teacher also served as president's assistant until 1883, when the first full-time teacher of physical education was employed there. Similarly at Wells Seminary, the physical culture teacher also taught history or physiology and at times also served as the librarian.[48]

The solidification of physical and movement training for women in higher education unfolded in a manner parallel to the professionalization of the faculty. Underlying these changes was a fundamental shift in the perception of women from their being weak because of nature to their being weak because of social environment.[49] One way to hasten the legitimacy of women's physical education for many institutions was to give prominence to medical measurement and inspection of the women's bodies. In this way the progress toward well-being could be quantified.

Statistics about how much weight women gained over a semester, the increase or decrease in inches of their muscles, changes in their eyesight, degrees of joint rotation in ankles, and straightness of backbones were collected and published in great detail in tables of "anthropometric records."[50] This kind of record keeping continued to be crucial for the survival of women's physical education programs for many years. The feminist advocates of this change remained vigilant for decades, renewing their argument and defense periodically as repeated challenges arose.

As the first generation of women graduated from institutions of higher education in Britain and the United States, medical inspection was followed up by surveys of the reported health of graduates and alumnae. Continued concern and watchfulness were necessary on the feminists' part: despite the evident success of women's schools and colleges, medically informed opposition to their work remained current for several decades. It was therefore imperative that the benefits of mental and physical exertion be demonstrated.[51]

Additionally, for years women with medical degrees were counted as a key part of the faculty of many women's physical education programs. In programs without a physician, the gymnastics teachers played a key role in the monitoring and promotion of physical vigor and in the detection and treatment of weaknesses or disorders. This served both the physical education classes directly and the cause of women in higher education indirectly. It was a way to answer the lingering concern about women damaging their reproductive capacity by too much intellectual work or their feminine demeanor by too "masculine" forms of exercise. As Paul Atkinson notes:

The development of physical education in parallel with medical inspection was therefore firmly grounded in debates over women's capacity to withstand the rigors of intellectual effort. The feminist pioneers of educational reform took medical opposition to heart, and their collective response to it became thoroughly characteristic of the ethos and organization of school life.[52]

Framing physical education for women as scrupulously scientific and medically supervised helped to cushion it from criticism. However, some residual, medically informed opposition to women in schools and colleges continued for several decades.[53]

Victorian ideals about proper gender behavior constrained the progress of physical education and sports for women in higher education much longer than it did for men. Until well into the twentieth century women were generally forced to be as "ladylike" as possible, both on and off the playing fields, or else risk being ridiculed and scorned.[54] Clearly the vision of a physically active woman challenged long-standing definitions of male and female and prompted a call for returning to conservative behavior norms. Physical activity was seen by many as desexing for women.

Therefore, the heads of women's physical education programs in higher education had to be careful to create programs that differed significantly from the men's programs—and kept up conservative appearances. Manners were thought to be a key sign of morality, so how one "performed" sports assumed a moral intonation.[55] As sports historian Kathleen McCrone notes, "Behaving like a lady meant adopting the bourgeois values associated with being female and it appears to have been a prerequisite for nineteenth-century sportswomen."[56]

One way to do this would be to offer classes (gymnastics and, later, dancing, for instance) that did not duplicate the men's classes. Passivity, the desire to nurture, intuitive morality, and affection were all assumed to be innately female characteristics.[57] Since these affects were supposedly rooted in the biology of women, it was believed that physical education should reinforce these behaviors. It was believed, for example, that women were physically frailer, their skulls were smaller than men's, their muscles were more delicate, and their nervous systems were finer. Dance could be an ideal means for maintaining ladylike appearances while respectfully skirting these imagined biological differences. It simply was not mentioned that dance could address the mind, nervous system, and muscles; these would be virtues generations in the future could explore.

The larger tension governing many debates about sex roles in the nineteenth century concerned the ways in which sexual boundaries might become blurred. While the focus of this examination is primarily women, middle-class ideals of manhood also underwent a significant shift during the nineteenth century. They moved from a standard based more in the community and the qualities of a man's soul to one based on individual achievement, "muscular vigor," "fair play," and the (fit and powerful) male body. In men's physical education these new values were manifested as a rapid rise of competitive college athletics and outdoor activities.[58]

For men who lacked the physical, moral, and intellectual vigor to be leaders, sports and games were also arenas in which individuals could learn how to be graceful losers in life if necessary. One of the lessons competitive athletics was supposed to teach was that "what a man achieves is a result of industry and self control."[59] If someone failed, it was his own fault due to lack of diligence. For women the situation was more complicated, because while they seemed governed by a similar outlook about failure, their opportunities were much more circumscribed. It was decidedly "unfeminine" to be competitive. Concepts of gender therefore became even more polarized into metaphors of a controlled female (body) and a freer, vigorously competitive male (body).

The athlete in many ways represents the brave, competent, and idealized hope of the man, or woman, perfected. It is a starting place for a scenario of the future. Dance has always acknowledged this in its framing of the performing body onstage. So the way that dance would be conceptualized in higher education would directly respond to this legacy of assembling the perfect human specimen through disciplined physical activity. Eugenic thought continued to be very strong during this period, and many who advocated vigorous athletics were also involved with eugenics. It was in fact still widely believed that individuals inherited *acquired* characteristics, such as fitness. Fit mothers were thus really a means toward breeding fit children. Vertinsky confirms how pragmatically women's health was regarded: "The physician's concern for the physical betterment of the late nineteenth-century female then was not for her sake alone but for the sake of her unborn child."[60]

The "well tuned" male athlete, therefore, was the image of the "ideal sire." The 1890 Convention of the American Association for the Advancement of Physical Education, for example, featured an address by L. H. Gulick, a medical doctor and physical educator, who insisted that physical education offered a fundamental means for building the nation "as it worked to develop a superior race."[61] Athletics stood at the juncture of the transformative process that so preoccupied Americans of this era. It stood between gender definitions and between images of women of the past and dreams of women of the future.

One of the tasks for educators would be to demonstrate that conventional perceptions of femininity and more active participation in physical activity were not incompatible. Dance is arguably the oldest arena in which women were permitted to be physically active in public, so there is a certain logic in its eventual choice as a "new" discipline for this newly active college woman. Other social constraints at the time, however, and particularly the long-standing associations of dancing women with loose morals, presented different problems the early advocates of women's dance education would have to overcome. The larger issue linking both was that of bodily and spatial mobility. The freer the activity in those terms the greater the public hostility and resistance.[62]

There was reason to be hostile toward free activity, because some physically active women did become socially activist women. For example, in England the Gymnastics Teachers Suffrage Society established itself in 1909. In the great suffrage procession in London in the summer of 1911 this society proudly marched behind its own banner.[63] Generally, however, it was not easy to establish a clear causal relationship between physical freedom and social activism, although detractors of dance for women did repeatedly try to link physical activity directly to undesirable activist behavior.

Women were caught between two extremes of physical activity—excessive control and excessive physical freedom—and neither was socially acceptable. While excessive freedom carried connotations of loose morals and social agitation, moving too far to the extreme of controlled strength conjured up another prohibition for the physically active woman—that of manliness. McCrone notes that the cult of athleticism was in essence "a cult of manliness," so if women joined in on an equal footing they could not be simultaneously projected as sexual objects by men, a situation that was disconcerting to some men. The following quotation from an editorial in a badminton magazine of 1900 reveals the anxiety produced by just the imagined image of a woman engaged in aggressive physical sports.

Beauty of face and form is one of the chief essentials [for women], but unlimited indulgence in violent, outdoor sports, cricket, bicycling, beagling, otter-hunting, paper-chasing, and—most odious of all games for woman—hockey, cannot but have an unwomanly effect on a young girl's mind no less on her appearance. . . . Let young girls ride, skate, dance and play lawn tennis and other games in modera-tion, but let them leave field sports to those for whom they were intended—men.[64]

It is clear that the forces behind the introduction of physical educa-tion for women into higher education were as complex as the responses this gesture generated. More broadly, they reflected "the anxieties of middle-class Americans discovering their bodies."[65] Contemporary femi-nist scholars have argued that the notions that emerged out of the debate about the ideal female form and function were essentially conservative and that they fed into increasingly harsher efforts to control and regu-late women's bodies. They suggest this was part of a redefinition of the separate-spheres outlook and part of an increased control of women and their bodies as industrialized society grew more stressful.[66]

Within nineteenth-century debates of the individual versus society and nature versus culture in the development of humans, however, lay a larger notion of what David Armstrong has labeled the political anatomy of the body.[67] It was the tensions between ignoring and acknowledging this body that informed the issue of women in American higher education—just at the point that dance entered the university.

MAKING A PLACE FOR DANCE

The continuing concern women's education reformers had with women's health and concepts of femininity confirms how intertwined these is-sues were and, correspondingly, how interconnected their solution would become. Particularly for dance education pioneers, the introduction of creative movement into the college curriculum would entail addressing a host of other related issues. One of these was femininity.

Feminist historian Mary Beth Norton has observed what she calls the paradox of nineteenth-century femininity. On the one hand, woman's ideal role was so sharply defined as to be oppressive, yet on the other hand, this was the same era that saw the founding of the women's rights movement, the burgeoning of higher education for women, and the entry of women into professional occupations like teaching and librarianship.[68]

69

It should be added that this was also the era that saw the first formal acknowledgment of the expressive (female) body in higher education, through the introduction of creative dance into the curriculum.

This paradox of strict constraints coexisting with unprecedented new opportunities for women is relevant to a number of issues central to dance in higher education. It reveals how many of the Victorian positions could be argued to their opposite if one were crafty enough in reasoning. It also illuminates the bonds between educational validation of the arts and social acceptance. Contradictions were prevalent in this era—and useful, for those who knew how to manipulate them.[69]

REDEFINING WOMEN'S SPHERE

American society in the late nineteenth and early twentieth centuries was rapidly industrializing, social orders were skewed, and gender roles were starting to be challenged. Once universities began to welcome American women in this era, they did so in part out of financial necessity. Increasing numbers of men were opting for business rather than college and its implied path to the ministry and teaching, and the universities needed students.[70] At the same time, however, the curricula were being revamped with new courses in political science, economics, sociology, medicine, law, engineering, and business administration in the hope of winning back men.

While this professionalization of the curriculum has been acknowledged by some historians as a way of ensuring middle-class status through exclusionary rules, Norton suggests it was as much about gender separation as class.[71] At the outset it was assumed men would be the population to benefit from professional training, while women would stay in *their* sphere in the university, that of the liberal arts.

Norton sees within this accommodation a more pervasive strategy of educational reformers to "work out a new modus vivendi between middle-class men and women." The larger divide of sex differences would remain, now played out in different curricular emphases: "Social reform and teaching became women's domains and the new professions were for men."[72] Here, too, we find important background for dance in higher education, for these tensions of the moment clinched the framing of dance in the university as an enterprise of *teaching*, not professional dancing. Obviously Progressive reformers were using the term *professionalization* in a different sense than this, but its use supports the fact that dance became an academic subject in a climate where the only accepted public spheres in which a woman might practice it would be teaching and social reform. Pragmatically, then, dance would be conceptualized in both spheres. Gender distinctions in higher education were about to change, yet with the changes some traditional divisions about the genders remained the same.

The woman who deviated from the basic domestic ideal of the time was constantly in danger of being labeled a dangerous, unsexed, monstrous creature capable of frighteningly risky behavior. Reformers quickly learned, then, that the way to render educational subjects safe was to purify them, restructure them, and *then* permit women to study them. (It was like a grown-up version of childproofing an environment before letting a child loose in it.)

As historians Sara Delamont and Lorna Duffin comment, "Any deviation from the male-dominated classification of behaviour could lead to labels of witchcraft, prostitution, hermaphroditism and subhumanity and leave the woman polluted."[73] Delamont and Duffin conclude that the most successful feminist campaigners were those who managed to minimize hostile reactions by manipulating rather than violating the classification system. While Delamont and Duffin are speaking of someone like Catharine Beecher, Blanche Trilling and Margaret H'Doubler also neatly fit this model. Trilling and H'Doubler were pioneers who also knew how to be peacemakers.

While working within established classifications, Trilling and H'Doubler reshaped dance to be educationally valid by offering it as a distinctly female form of physical exercise. It is one thing to allow women into the university on a separate and unequal basis, but to structure a discipline, particularly a physical discipline, so that its virtues echo precisely those qualities society wants cultivated in one sex is a recipe for sure acceptance. It is almost as if the education reformers were responding firmly and finally to a document like the Englishman John Morley's 1874 "Sex in Mind and Education," one of many such nineteenth-century articles warning of the dangers of the same education for different sexes:

There is sex in mind as distinctly as there is sex in body; and if the mind is to receive the best culture of which its nature is capable, regard must be had to the mental qualities which correlate differences of sex. To aim, by means of education and pursuits in life, to assimilate the female to the male mind, might well be pronounced as unwise and fruitless a labour as it would be to strive to assimilate the female to the male body by means of the same kind of physical training and by the adoption of the same pursuits.

Morley concludes: "There is sex in mind and there should be sex in education."[74]

Ironically, he was right to a degree, for in order to get sex out of education it would first have to be dramatically put in. The uniqueness of the two genders would have to be articulated, the myths exploded, and the fears confronted before males and females could be addressed equally by academic institutions. The differences between what men and women could do would have to be articulated in some areas, including physical education, as a means of circumventing the illogical argument that cognition is as gendered as the body.

4

Blanche Trilling

Leader and Visionary in Women's Physical Education

[The difference between dance and acrobatics is] a difference
of total effect. . . . The acrobat, however bad or good, appeals
to the mind rather than to the senses. We admire his skill. . . .
In dancing, the physical skill is ancillary to another effect.

T. S. Eliot, 1925

IN THE SUMMER OF 1951, BLANCHE M. TRILLING, THE FORMER DIREC-
tor of physical education for women at the University of Wisconsin, was called back from retirement to write a detailed account of
the development of the women's physical education program for the
university. The project was the idea of the dean of education, and he
assigned Frances Cumbee, a graduate student just finishing her doctorate
in physical education, to work with Trilling, researching the data and
typing up Trilling's recollections.[1]

The resulting unpublished 136-page history, found among Trilling's
uncatalogued administrative files in the University of Wisconsin–Madison
Archives, is a remarkable document. It is important as much for what it
chronicles about the early history of women's physical education in higher
education as for what it coincidentally reveals about this little-known
woman who, it might be said, made the university safe for dance.

Although Margaret H'Doubler is customarily credited with beginning the nation's first program of dance in higher education, Trilling,
who directed the Department of Physical Education for Women from its
inception in 1914 to her retirement in 1946, created the context that
made it possible for a dance program to flourish. Trilling oversaw all

of H'Doubler's work. She gave H'Doubler the "assignment" to bring back some dance content fit to be taught at the university. Then, with H'Doubler, she steadily pushed and prodded that content into curriculum units, and finally into the nation's first college dance major. Trilling also persistently ran interference with university administrators, often deans and presidents, arguing for a larger legitimacy for the physically sentient woman's body in higher education.

THE UNIVERSITY OF WISCONSIN

As one of the nation's premier land grant institutions, the University of Wisconsin was funded through the Morrill Federal Land Grant Act of 1862, which offered federal aid to states in order to support colleges whose curricula included agricultural and mechanical instruction.[2] As a result of the influx of this federal money, these public colleges were reshaped into institutions emblematic of a newly democratized educational system looking to foster American research and American scholarship. These colleges were also charged with reexamining the training and preparation of the American farmer and the American mechanic in the new industrial age.[3]

The University of Wisconsin existed with this particular mandate toward public service and toward making higher education accessible for whole new populations of Americans. With the Morrill Act came the legislative and financial incentive to reshape this state university even further to "promote the liberal and practical education of the industrial classes in the several pursuits and professions of life."[4]

Geographical forces acted upon the university as well. Madison was one of the more western outposts among American universities, which at this time were still heavily concentrated in the East. Particularly with regard to the arts, westward expansion has always brought with it an opening of new possibilities and a lessening of the restraints of formal traditions. The lake-studded farmland of Madison would become a rich field for academic and artistic mingling and reinvention.

WOMEN IN WISCONSIN

Despite its expansive academic potential, the state of Wisconsin exhibited conflicting attitudes toward women, their place in society, and their rights. On the one hand, here was a place where women's news and opinions often appeared anonymously in abolitionist journals, "temperance sheets," and other reform newspapers, even before Wisconsin became a state in 1848. Yet it was in Wisconsin that Mathilde Fransziska Annke published her newspaper, the first in any state published under a woman's name. Women's organizations abounded in the state—temperance unions, women's alliances, ladies' clubs, Progressive reform groups, and, of course, suffrage groups.[5] Most symbolic of Wisconsin's support of women as equal citizens was that in 1919 Wisconsin became the first state in the nation to ratify the Nineteenth Amendment, giving women the vote.

The state's conflicting attitudes toward women extended to the university. The regents of the university had originally endorsed coeducation in 1851, making the University of Wisconsin a pioneer in courses for women in higher education, but this was in direct conflict with the university charter.[6] The result was that for the next fifteen years, during which time the Morrill Act added additional imperatives encouraging gender and racial equality to the university's mission, women students continued to be restricted to the Female College on campus. The state legislature, pressured by taxpayers, had specified in 1866 that all departments of the university should be open to women.[7] Dr. Laura Ross, a pioneering physician in Milwaukee and a founder and the first president of the Wisconsin Woman Suffrage Association, said tartly of the exclusion of women from certain departments in the university: "Girls can be defrauded of their rights to a thorough education by narrow, bigoted men entrusted with a little brief authority."[8] When at last the first six women completed the regular college curriculum in 1869, President Paul Ansel Chadbourne, who had made a condition of his accepting the presidency the strict separation of male and female students, threatened for weeks to withhold the women's degrees, until the regents forced him to consent.[9]

In theory, the new land grant colleges offered both male and female students what was then an unprecedented educational opportunity. Yet, as Catherine Clinton documents, "despite the equal-admissions policy, women were often at a disadvantage" because of continuing subversive tactics to maintain "gender differentiated curricula." Clinton elaborates:

For example, in 1865 at the University of Wisconsin, forty-one male students were enrolled in traditional college courses, with no women registered in them. At the same time, sixty-six women were students of the "normal school," with no men enrolled in this program.[10]

Clinton explains that Clara Colby, one of the first women to challenge these restrictions at the University of Wisconsin, asked to be admitted to classes in Latin and philosophy, which were all-male. University of Wisconsin president Chadbourne objected, but she managed to enroll and went on to Phi Beta Kappa membership and to serve as class valedictorian. Colby then became founder, publisher, and editor of the national *Women's Tribune*. Years later, in 1901, in a consciously ironic tribute to former President Chadbourne and his politics, President Birge christened the building that housed women's activities, including the first women's physical education classes, Chadbourne Hall.[11]

Despite Colby's successes, the college continued to discourage women from enrolling in men's classes. Until 1871–72, when women were at last granted full access to the college's curriculum, female students continued to be barred from registering for a course if men had already filled it. Women were also required to use the library on different days than the men, thus effectively continuing their second-class status, albeit in less direct ways.[12]

It was not until 1876, twenty-nine years after the university was chartered and thirteen years after women were first admitted, that the first program in what was then called "physical culture for ladies" began at the university, run out of an impromptu gymnasium.[13] And it was not until the fall of 1889 that the program was formally expanded and situated in a very small room in the front of the third floor of the dormitory then known as Ladies Hall. The 1889–90 Wisconsin catalogue indicates that physical education began as a voluntary program: "A ladies class in gymnastics was voluntarily maintained in Ladies Hall during the winter with gratifying results."[14]

The teacher of the program, Miss Clara E. S. Ballard of Boston, had graduated from the Allen School of Gymnastics, one of the more respected training centers for gymnastics teachers at the time. Ballard had been what Trilling calls "induced to come, to equip a gymnasium, and to run it at her own expense," charging students a small fee, which she used to support herself. Not only Ballard's status but also the conditions and terms of her employment indicated the generally low regard the university held for her work. Ballard, however, reportedly came to Madison with a strong determination to introduce physical education into the university, and she was aggressive in securing space and equipment for her classes. Interestingly, however, the 1890–91 catalogue states that these gymnastics classes, in addition to being taught by a trained instructor (Ballard), "are under the general supervision of a thoroughly educated lady physician."[15]

That year, 1890, Ballard was hired by the university at a fee of $750 for eight months' service, but the conditions still remained that she must provide all her own music for exercises and that she had to clear "her" classroom, the music room, of chairs daily before the brief two-hour period she was permitted to use it.[16] Ballard was diligent about formalizing the work she was doing. She systematically measured and examined her female students. As a result, she introduced methods of data collection at the University of Wisconsin as a way of scientifically documenting her students' physical improvement, a measurement practice that persisted for many years (figure 8).

Beginning with the 1894–95 catalogue, measuring women students became a requirement: "The students will be examined as to their physical condition at the beginning and close of each year."[17] By the 1900–1901

76

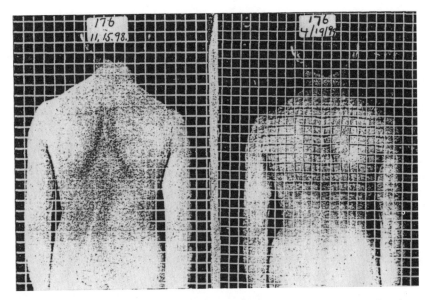

Figure 8. An example of photography used in the anthropometric examination of students to determine the extent of physical deficiencies and inequalities (Courtesy University of Wisconsin–Madison Archives)

academic year this requirement had attached to it the notion of a quick remedy for posture and alignment problems as well:

Every [woman] student will have a physical examination on entering the department, in order that the physical condition may be known, and suitable exercise prescribed for individual cases. A second examination is given during the second semester in order that the improvements and benefits of the course of exercise may be shown.[18]

Trilling, in her historical account, notes with an edge of alarm that the 1915–16 catalogue reveals a growing medicalization, or what she calls a "take over by the Infirmary," of this aspect of monitoring women's involvement in physical activities. It also can be read as a tacit means for controlling, and in the process demeaning, women students. Trilling quotes from the catalogue's description:

The organic condition, stage of physical development, and degree of motor efficiency attained by each entering freshman and sophomore are determined at the opening of the college year by a series of examinations and tests made by the Department of Clinical Medicine and the Department of Physical Education.[19]

Trilling objected to this locating of women's progress in physical education in the infirmary and medical wings of the university. To her, physical

77

education should be a path to the discovery and acquisition of new skills, community bonds with other women, moral and spiritual values, and, as part of this, the cultivation of practices of lifelong well-being. She resented the university's framing of it as short-term physical therapy, something to do—like bed rest and drinking fluids for a fever—and then abandon once the situation improved. With her directorship firmly in place she succeeded in shifting the focus in women's physical education from a short-term remedy to the acquisition of lifetime habits of physical exercise. After this 1915–16 catalogue entry, there was a gradual decrease in the number of "anthropometric measurements" made of women students. From a high of fifty-five in 1895 it dropped to five in 1920 and zero in 1935.[20] If anything was measured now it was the skills developed in each activity. Aims and objectives changed from developing specific muscles and ranges of motion to addressing the mind within the body—attitudes, standards of conduct. The full person.

GROWTH OF THE WOMEN'S PHYSICAL EDUCATION CURRICULUM

The women students' passion for physical culture was considerable from the very outset and overrode administrative resistance, spurring the dramatic growth of the women's physical education curriculum. At the time Ballard taught, attendance was not compulsory, fees were charged, and there were the inconveniences mentioned above. Still, a great many female students took the classes regularly and considered the exercises beneficial and interesting.[21] Ballard had clearly tapped into an appetite for physical activity among the women that was only just beginning to be addressed.

In the fall of 1894 physical education became a requirement for women at the University of Wisconsin. The catalogue of that year reads: "Gymnasium work is required of young women of the Freshman and Sophomore classes, on two days of the week, one hour each day."[22] This requirement would continue until 1910–11, when it was increased to four periods each week for all freshman and sophomore women. Trilling notes with some irony that this requirement of activity for women preceded the requirement for men, who continued to practice military drills, which were considered adequate exercise for them. Which students did what activities changed, as well as when in the school day the physical education classes were offered. With the beginning of Trilling's tenure in 1912, individual differences would begin to figure into the requirement, and efforts would be made to match students with those classes that promised to be most beneficial to their individual needs.

This was an important development, for it was not just about individualizing physical education activities but also about recognizing the emotional and intellectual individual within each exercising body. For dance to become an academic subject, linking the mind and the body was essential. In an aesthetic form of education both the mind and body, the psyche and soma, are addressed, and both respond to the conditioning, training, and insight education affords.[23] While no one theorized it at the time, this emergent awareness that a distinctive sensibility is nestled within each body brought with it the additional understanding that not just raw will but private proclivities also determine physical success. The world of American higher education would turn when dance entered the curriculum, in ways profound and lasting for many dimensions of education.

Ballard's classes grew in popularity, and soon faculty wives were lobbying for their children to have special classes so they, too, could participate in the rhythmic drills and swinging exercises with Indian clubs, dumbbells, and wands. It helped the status of women's physical culture at the university considerably that the resultant children's classes included several faculty children, among them the daughter of Charles Van Hise, then a professor of geology and soon to be president of the university, and the son and daughter of Dr. E. G. Birge, a recent University of Wisconsin president.

The university wives were not alone in their recognition of the educational virtues of dance. Wisconsin had been settled by many German and Scandinavian immigrants, who themselves boasted a tradition of recognizing the health benefits of gymnastic exercises. They clung tenaciously to customs they brought with them from their home lands, for example, beer drinking. In 1884 a city-wide battle erupted over university president John Bascom's efforts to ban liquor sales in Madison. The German immigrants enlisted the brewing industry's Wisconsin Association for the Protection of Personal Liberty, won press support, and pressured Bascom to back down. This defeat contributed to his eventual departure from Madison.[24]

A love of gymnastic movements and dance was another old-country passion the Germans brought with them to Madison. The town had a thriving Turner Society, where gymnastics classes were offered, German was spoken, and German foods were served—all intended to support immigrants in maintaining their Germanness. It was home to the Kehl Academy of Dancing and Deportment, Wisconsin's oldest dance school.[25] Founded in 1880 by a German immigrant, "Professor" F. W. Kehl, the school framed its dance services with the following statement printed on the 1895–96 season brochure, a mission statement that reflects the larger sentiments the Madison, and by extension the university, community must have held for dance: "The manifold advantages to be derived from dancing, as an exercise, the great delight it affords as a recreation, its refining influence on manners, are becoming each year more fully recognized."[26]

In 1898 Kehl moved his school to a large brick-and-stone studio he had built, and that site served for many years as the location of balls attended by Madison's best-known families, including university faculty and their spouses. Kehl married Barbara Hoeveler, daughter of a family of talented Madison musicians and dramatic artists, and together they ran this dancing school, renamed Professor Kehl's Palace of Pleasure and Education in 1899. This title, as well as Kehl's own labeling of himself as "Professor," offers an interesting glimpse of the kind of legitimation academic endorsement and training were thought to confer. It also suggests, prophetically, that the blending of the title "Professor" with dance was at least a commercial possibility in turn-of-the-century Madison.[27] So was the linking of "pleasure" and "education."

SMALL BUT TELLING CHANGES

Throughout these years of steady progress toward establishing a real place for women in the University of Wisconsin, the college catalogue registered small but telling changes in its verbal descriptions of its offerings in physical education for women. The 1894–95 catalogue lists what is the first reference to physical education of any sort for women in the university, framing it under the following goal: "To secure a good physique, strength, better health, self-control and grace."[28] Writing in her unpublished history of the program, Trilling notes that in the following year "self-reliance" was added to the objectives. Up until this point the objectives of the University of Wisconsin and that of other college and university women's physical education programs were very similar. The 1898–99 University of Wisconsin catalogue, however, registers the beginning of a shift in goals.

The object of training for women is for the purpose of maintaining and conserving the *health first* [italics added], and incidentally there are derived benefits of a very valuable character such as the acquisition of grace, muscular control, self-reliance and strength.

Trilling notes that it was not until 1903 that mental health through physical well-being was mentioned in the catalogue. The catalogue statement reads:

The main objects of training for women are the acquiring and maintaining of good health and the producing of a good physical foundation for mental health. Other results are poise, control, grace, and development.

Two years later, in the 1905–6 catalogue, the words *games and sports* and *interest* make their first appearance:

The aim is to give students such exercises, games and sports as will best create and maintain a vigorous health. The department endeavors to reach a large number of students, especially the weak and undeveloped; to give to all exercises that will be not only beneficial but interesting.

The cumulative effect of these small, telling changes was that the whole thrust of the women's physical education program gradually changed from a corrective to a proactive emphasis. Instead of addressing physical problems and malformations in women, the focus of the program became physical activity as a means for insuring physical well-being. With this last statement from the 1905–6 catalogue the mind suddenly enters the picture as well, and being "interesting" becomes a goal and a virtue of the curriculum.

With the 1910–11 catalogue the tone shifts noticeably to much more wide-ranging objectives and deeper personal goals. This shift seems concomitant with the arrival of Clarke W. Hetherington, from the University of Missouri, as director of physical education. For the first time the aims and objectives are presented in a numbered list with much more specific details of what is expected from the students and what they in turn can expect from the course work. The Physical Education Department goals are beginning to be framed in the style of "legitimate" academic pursuits. As one reads through this list of six goals, each one can easily and neatly be addressed by the soon-to-be-developed dance program. The six objectives for 1910–11 were as follows:

1. The development of organic power, the basis of vitality, the prerequisite of physical and mental efficiency.

2. To assure and maintain good posture, a harmonious muscular development and a reasonable degree of body skill and grace.

3. To provide incentive and opportunity for every student to secure at least one hour of physical recreation daily as a balance to the sedentary demands of University life.

4. To conserve the social and moral values of games and sports and to secure to every student the fullest opportunity for their practice.

5. To develop the "habit of exercise."

6. To train teachers of physical education and directors of play for service in educational institutions, clubs, playgrounds, municipal recreation systems, etc.

Physical activity and organized team sports were coming to be seen as strong vehicles of political socialization as well during the first two decades of the twentieth century. The child-saving reform movement, which had begun in 1880 and continued strongly until 1920, prompted new insights into how physical activity could be tied to social training and how the rules and regulations of sports and games might be used to shape young people for an increasingly corporate and organization-focused society. Trilling must have rightly sensed that these arguments of child development reformers could be applied with equal validity to her work with physical activity in higher education. The new psychological theories of child development were assuming that "a link existed between carefully organized physical exercise and moral vitality and cognitive alertness," and Trilling's program eagerly embraced this new outlook.[29]

Trilling must have studied the University of Wisconsin catalogues with extraordinary care, for in her history of the program she cites the most minute changes in wording and accords them great significance. For her the 1912–13 catalogue's slight rewording and combining of the first two objectives into one to read "Prescribed courses are designed to secure a high degree of organic power, harmonious physical development and a reasonable degree of skill and grace" indicates significantly that "individual differences were being considered." Trilling has two final entries in regard to changes in the catalogue aims. The first is to note that in 1915–16 the aims were reorganized and placed under three headings: "Student Growth and Development," "Training of Teachers," and "Extension," and the second was to add the objective of making "worthwhile social contacts" as a desired outcome of physical education activities. What Trilling does not say is that these program objectives were now being authored by her. For the next twenty years, until the 1934–35 University of Wisconsin catalogue, they would remain the same. These new aims would be seen as the academic context and rationale for Trilling's dance program.

THE EVOLUTION OF FACILITIES AND INSTRUCTION

The women's physical education program aspirations grew more rapidly than their facilities. It was not until June 1897, three years after the construction of a gymnasium for men, that the University of Wisconsin completed the remodeling of Ladies Hall (soon to be Chadbourne Hall) to include a sizable room for women students' gymnastic training to replace the small temporary space that had been used before. This was the first specific space for women's physical activities in the university, and it signaled an important step toward legitimacy and permanence. Earlier Pauline Bower, a graduate of Anderson's Gymnasium of New Haven, and then Sara Boudren, of the Boston Normal School of Gymnastics, had taught the women's gymnastics program. With the completion of Ladies Hall's remodeling, Abby Shaw Mayhew from Wellesley College was engaged for the next academic year as instructor of physical culture and mistress of Ladies Hall (figure 9).[30]

In another unpublished internal history of the women's physical education program at the university, this one handwritten in 1916 by a

Figure 9. Margaret H'Doubler with faculty colleagues, 1910 (*left to right*: unknown, Mary McKee, Abby Shaw Mayhew, H'Doubler, unknown) (Courtesy University of Wisconsin–Madison Archives; in the collection of Julia M. Brown)

collective of five members of the "play committee," Mayhew is celebrated as "a trained woman whose life was consecrated to the healthful development of girl's bodies." The authors report that in 1897 "she began immediately to organize the work at Wisconsin so that no woman should pass out as a graduate without at least two years of regular gymnasium training."[31] Mayhew apparently taught her own combination of apparatus work, club swinging, drills, and Delsarte. This inclusion of Delsarte is the first direct precursor to dance being taught at the University of Wisconsin.

Mayhew also initiated a series of "open lessons," shrewdly conceived public events where her women students could demonstrate in annual spring showings their expertise with the Indian clubs, dumbbells, and Delsarte exercises. The 1916 department report notes:

It has been declared recently by an alumnus, a Professor of French at the University, that the drills of these days were remarkably well finished and perfect in their rhythm. Music always accompanied their movements and it is indeed pleasant to imagine a group of animated girls swinging clubs in perfect unison while a circle of enthusiastic parents and friends watched attentively from the balcony.[32]

This description is almost painterly in its evocation of the pre-Raphaelite and neo-Grecian images of bacchantes decorously gamboling on the grass.

Institutionally these open showings provided important groundwork for promoting dance, for they suggest almost a reinvention of the innocence of women's bodies moving rhythmically in public. What might never have been possible in a big city of the time like New York, Chicago, or San Francisco, where dancing girls still evoked strongly negative moral associations, had slipped by in Madison.[33] Here, in an essentially rural outpost, where the only other image of dancing girls came from the Kehls' Palace of Pleasure and Education, dance could forge a fresh association with purity, artistry, and education in the public mind.

There is an interesting model here, for later in the twentieth century, during the late 1980s "Culture Wars," when the performing arts came under serious attack by the religious right and were accused of presenting images of indecency and immorality, the arts redefined themselves in relationship to education and society. The social utility of the arts once again began to be discussed and emphasized in much the same way that dance was redefined as an avenue toward personal expression when it entered the university in 1917. So the arts would once again look to forge fresh bonds with education. Then, as now, this seems a consciously pragmatic act as well as a means of starting over, back at a point where one can clarify the goals, objectives, meanings, and values the arts convey in a climate freer of social tensions than the "outside" world.

THE MAY FÊTE

Several years before it formally offered any dance classes, the University of Wisconsin was home to a popular college dance phenomenon of the early twentieth century, the May Fête (figure 10). More spectacle than art form, more sensual release than disciplined expression, the May Fête was an exhibition of amateur dancing performed by would-be bacchantes in a variety of homemade tunics and elf costumes. Old photographs of the University of Wisconsin May Fête of 1907, the first year it was staged, do not suggest dancing so much as playful yet graceful posing. The impression one gets looking at this scene is that of the kind of "cutting-loose" activity one might have done at a big family gathering, much as one might have engaged in a game of charades. So what is showcased here in 1907 is more the women's *yearning* for activity than a full realization of it.

Even at this early date, the university apparently did its best to support this activity. All women's regular gymnastic and physical education work was directed toward the preparation of the May Fête, from the resumption of classes after Easter break until the performance the last week in May.[34] The fact that the May Fêtes were deemed significant enough to disrupt regular classwork suggests the importance this display must have held for the women's physical education instructors as well as the university administrators.

Figure 10. The maypole dance at the University of Wisconsin May Fête, 1913 (Photograph by McKillop; courtesy University of Wisconsin–Madison Archives)

One can imagine that these fêtes provided a persuasive public demonstration of how women in the university were managing to maintain their health and grace while engaging in intellectual work. Instead of rote physical activity like the men's military drills, these May Fêtes were framed as genteel dances of antiquity, interpretive, dignified, and chaste; they might have looked like finishing school demonstrations showcasing the college woman who had not lost her feminine charms just because she was studying biology. Those concerned about the potential masculinizing effects of learning needed only to gaze at these lilting women in gauzy white gowns to be assured that all was right with the world. Women could study biology and still cavort on spacious lawns under maypoles in "beautiful exhibitions of dancing and music which turn the campus hill [Bascom Hill] on one May afternoon of each spring into a fairyland of color and movement" (figure 11).[35]

Trilling's description of the May Fêtes suggests they really functioned as university-wide talent shows:

Figure 11. A group of women students posing in their flowing gowns, slippers, and flower garlands as part of the May Fête, 1913 (Photograph by McKillop; courtesy University of Wisconsin–Madison Archives)

They had piano solos as part of the program then, Delsarte was still in vogue, the Girl's Glee Club sang, there were readings, club-swinging, and several dances, a Norwegian dance and the May Pole dance itself. In 1908 an evening of quite elaborate dances was presented. German, French, Negro, Danish, Norwegian, Swedish, Russian, Irish, Spanish and American dances, each representative of its particular nation, were undertaken by freshmen, sophomores and advanced classes. In 1909 a small, but certainly a real, May Fête was given on the upper campus in which dances and marches were performed just as the sun was setting over Main Hall.[36]

These original May Fêtes reveal a pervasive primitivist yearning of the time, a yearning whose fulfillment would also help significantly to shape dance in academia. Writing about modern dance photography in a statement that also illuminates the emergence of creative dance in the university, dance scholar Joan Acocella has noted:

When modern dance was born at the end of the nineteenth century, it arose from the primitivist impulse so widespread at that time: the urge to heal the split that the modern world was thought to have created between nature and the human soul. Consequently, a primary article of faith for the creators of modern dance—and a principle reinforced by the example by the ancient societies that, as primitivists, these dancers took as their models—was contact with nature. They imagined themselves outdoors.[37]

Photographs of the early University of Wisconsin May Fêtes show groups of young women, clad in loose, ankle-length layers of white,

Figure 12. University of Wisconsin women students performing outdoors in the annual May Fête, 1914 (Courtesy University of Wisconsin–Madison Archives)

moving around a huge maypole densely hung with ribbons and situated on a grassy glade on campus (figure 12). Closeups, however, reveal an uneasy self-consciousness to these young women despite the naturalness the setting evokes. A detail of a 1913 May Fête performer, for example, shows a young woman in a shapeless dark dress with an animal pelt draped across the front, poised on one foot with her head held stiffly, one arm reached outward and the other up holding a flute (figure 13). The pose looks designed, as if arranged to mimic a statue of Pan rather than arrived at from some inner understanding of movement impulses. The problem is not just the nature of photography of the period; it did require the subject to remain still for a lengthy exposure time, but there are also many stunningly vital naturalistic images of women, taken with the same technology, that have none of the artificiality of the early May Fête photographs.[38] Rather, the University of Wisconsin women here have the stiffness of figures in family snapshots caught in the midst of a silly good time they are not quite sure they want documented.

The not-quite-naturalness these photographs convey is not so much about the women's unease at not being real dancers—as similar photographs of amateur student productions might reveal; rather, it suggests a discomfort in the fact that they were dancing *at all*. The impulse to

Figure 13. May Fête, 1914. Detail of a woman student posing as the Greek god Pan, wearing an animal pelt across her chest. (Photograph by McKillop; courtesy University of Wisconsin–Madison Archives)

reenter nature as a dimension of modern life is there, but the means for doing so are yet to be defined. There was a testing of sorts to see if dance would be, could be, or should be a means for doing this.

These May Fêtes, along with the Delsarte classes, and even aspects of the music hall dance entertainments in the big cities, were stylistically part of a climate of late nineteenth-century symbolism in art. These dancing women in the May Fêtes were, like the Symbolist poets, enacting art as vision more than as literal representation. The Symbolist poets' academic cousins—the women of the university dance program—would help inaugurate a new notion of dance as serious art with the capacity for representation in addition to vision. Movement in nature, in unfettered garb, was simply the start. In the right hands, *could* it become a shortcut to idealized personal insight? That was also a goal desired by Symbolist poets of the time.[39] By 1917 the new dance program would absorb the May Fête, rendering it, in Trilling's words, "better organized, larger, more attractive and more popular."[40] Public bodies were on their way to becoming disciplined, trained, orderly bodies.

The quest for personal insight would be a key link between theatrical dance outside the university and the practice of modern dance within it. The more one uncovers the evolution of dance in higher education, the clearer it becomes that the arrival of creative modern dance in the university in 1917 was an evolutionary event distinct from the emergence of modern theatrical dance and in response to educational changes. While dance in the academy definitely paralleled a similar emergence of modernism and the articulation of the individual female voice in American theatrical dance in these initial years, one did not simply piggyback on the other.

Modern dance arose in the university for some of the same reasons it arose in outside society: the social moment was right; the evolutionary forces for women, for the body, for female sexuality, and for physical independence were all reconfigured in such a way that what had been unthinkable for so long suddenly became possible in both realms. This suggests that in universities, art forms may evolve and progress, propelled by scholarship, administrative leadership, and academic mandates. Within academia these forces are at least as potent as societal pressures outside. The dance program that Trilling and H'Doubler would create would be part of a larger stylistic development of dance, from the lighter symbolic references of nature in the May Fêtes into a newly rich form of nonnarrative dance, dance on the cusp of abstraction, dance that could have the prestige of intellectual achievement, dance with the capacity to represent the nuances of real life.

Interestingly, Trilling's account of the first decade of dance at the University of Wisconsin is almost completely devoid of any mention of the larger rationale governing decisions regarding curriculum changes. However, her statements and criticisms of women's physical education rules prior to her arrival reveal a great deal. For Trilling, women's physical education seems to have been her passion, her profession, and her life. Her intense focus on effecting change in it suggests that she saw it for precisely what it was: the linchpin for women's professional advancement in society.

Trilling apparently made considerable use of her forceful personality to effect this advancement. Frances Cumbee recalled two favorite stories about Trilling. One dates from World War II, when most of the telephones were removed from the academic buildings to conserve resources. Reportedly, when the crew arrived in Trilling's office to ask her which phones she wanted removed, she said, "None! I don't want to have to go into every faculty member's office when I want to talk to them." So Lathrop Hall remained the only building on campus with every one of its telephones intact. On another occasion, a gathering of male administrators in the office of the president of the university was handing out cigars in celebration of the birth of a child for one of the deans. Looking out a window, the president saw Trilling approaching the building, and he shouted to the men, "Hurry and pass them out. Miss Trilling is coming and she'll take them all!"[41]

Trilling never married, which was the rule for many professional as well as college-educated women at the time. In the 1880s schools began to dismiss women teachers who married, a policy that originated in Washington, D.C., and moved westward.[42] Married women bore children, and the notion of a pregnant woman teaching children was abhorrent to Victorian sensibility. As feminist historian Catherine Clinton argues: "Within the ideology of the culture, childbearing and a career simply did not mix."[43]

Within the universities through the 1890s, other forces were at work. Marriage, even among progressive couples of the time, still meant frequent childbearing, and the responsibilities of the household and raising the children fell on the woman. So it became an either-or choice between domestic duties and childbearing, and a single life outside for educated women of the time, and many of these beliefs persisted into the early years of the twentieth century. As Clinton notes:

More commonly, women with careers, especially educators, resolved the conflict between marriage and career by remaining single. Only 40 percent of women with careers in education were married, and only 25 percent of them had children. In fact, many women educators openly scorned marriage, applying the radical feminist critique that marriage was "legalized prostitution" whereby a woman abandoned her rights, her individualism, and any chance for spiritual fulfillment. Most of these women lived independent lives—yet few were alone. . . . Ostensibly, these women led lives of dedication and self-sacrifice, but they also needed recognition and some reward, despite their rejection of traditional female roles. Professional careers (in academe, law, medicine, and eventually reform and social work) afforded this feminist vanguard avenues for major contributions to late nineteenth-century American society.[44]

The lifestyle choices that social realities pressed on Trilling became choices her students and faculty also made. Margaret H'Doubler, Trilling's young faculty protégé, married at the age of forty-five, very late in life for the time, and she remained childless. Several of the living graduates interviewed from these inaugural years of the dance program at Wisconsin never married.[45] This was not atypical for educated women generally: "A 1908 study of the women graduates of the University of Wisconsin, for example, indicated that 100 percent of the 1869 alumnae were married, while only 54 percent of the women who graduated in 1900 and only 41 percent of the class of 1906 were."[46] The situation for women in British universities was even more severe. Between 79 and 85 percent of women academics teaching between 1884 and 1904 never married. This fell to 67 percent by 1924, yet into the 1930s there were still British universities where women were expected to resign upon getting married.[47]

Trilling's standards for what women's physical education should be—a centerpiece of the modern woman's life—and her aspirations for how to achieve this and at the same time confer academic legitimacy upon these activities clearly informed all of her curricular decisions. Short-term goals seem never to have deflected her from her larger objective of making activity a centerpiece of modern women's lives, unstated but implicit in each change of catalogue wording, each institution of a new course. Trilling's own voice echoes through the following concluding statement from the 1916 handwritten department history, a history she apparently commissioned because it was undertaken while she was director.

So this movement [of women's physical education], which had such small and inauspicious beginnings, has grown at Wisconsin until now it constituted one of the most important of all the University's activities. Because of its never ceasing struggle to generate the very fittest physically, physical education had become so vital an element in the lives of many of the girls that, at the present time, its influence and the greatness of the results which it has achieved are almost immeasurable. And because, throughout the twenty-seven years of its growth, the ideal of American womanhood has been most consistently maintained, the movement at Wisconsin is becoming every day more energetic, more intense, and more powerful not only in building up sound bodies, but also in bringing the girls to a realization of true dignity in manners. A sound constitution, a good understanding, a benevolent heart, an honest and upright personality, these are the characteristics which physical education, if wisely administered, may develop in an individual, and these are also the ideals of Wisconsin. . . . May we go on upbuilding [*sic*] the physical and moral fiber of a great people![48]

According to Trilling's documentation of burgeoning enrollments in gymnastics classes, the women's increasing use of their gymnasium facilities finally led to a request by Wisconsin alumni in 1908 for the construction of "a new women's building."[49] Trilling recounts these developments as the tale of an inevitable rush of progress, shrewdly managed and wisely steered.

Figure 14. A 1910 postcard of an artist's rendition of the newly completed Lathrop Hall, labeled "Woman's Building." The dance studio would be created on the top floor of the right-hand wing behind the three small windows. (Courtesy University of Wisconsin–Madison Archives)

LATHROP HALL

The new building the alumni asked for was to be Lathrop Hall (figure 14), named after John H. Lathrop, the first chancellor of the university. Architecturally and stylistically the building is an intensely feminine space, a Victorian home expanded to enormously public dimensions.[50] From its dedication ceremony to the interior details of its design, Lathrop Hall embodied the tensions and aspirations of women's physical education in the university. Strong yet decorative, public yet very private and discreet about the functions that went on inside it, Lathrop Hall, like the Department of Physical Education, was a good setting for the essentially clandestine innovation of H'Doubler's dance curriculum.

The building debuted at an April 1, 1910, dedication ceremony presided over by two women, Miss Florence Buckstaff, class of 1886 and a member of the Board of Regents, and Mrs. Anna Spencer, a member of the university summer session faculty, who spoke respectively on "Eternal Values in a University" and "The Personal Development and the Social Responsibility of Women."[51] The triad of concerns these titles suggest is telling, for it was precisely within the matrix of academic values, personal development, and social responsibility that women's physical education, and soon dance, would exist.

This new five-story building, which decades later would come to house dance in many studios, classrooms, and faculty offices, was at the time of its opening conceived of as a women's center, and dance had no place in it (figure 15). Trilling quotes a contemporary description from *Wisconsin* magazine that makes Lathrop Hall sound like a self-contained city exclusively for women:

[It is] a large and handsome building, thoroughly equipped to serve as a center for the social life of the women, containing among other conveniences a spacious drawing-room, a gymnasium, a swimming pool, and a cafeteria-restaurant serving 3,000 meals a day which have the distinction of being the best for the money in Madison![52]

Indeed, the feeling that emerges from Lathrop Hall, even to the early twenty-first-century visitor, is that it is a haven for women within the university. Although architecturally massive and featuring private club–like details of dark wood paneling, wainscoting, and hardwood or tile floors in the corridors, offices, classrooms, and studios, the interior spaces of Lathrop Hall feel private and protected. The building, which was popularly referred to as the Woman's Building in its early years, is accessed by relatively steep and narrow stairways on its front and back façades.[53] Once inside the central hallway one finds no exterior windows, just a dark, interior space.

With its huge basement cafeteria, faculty kitchen on the first floor, bowling alleys, swimming pool, laundry for swimming suits, apartment in which the janitor and his wife lived, indoor track and huge gymnasium, locker rooms, showers, classrooms, offices, library, posture rooms, and formal wood-paneled parlor with a massive fireplace, Lathrop Hall suggests the marriage of a Victorian home with a turn-of-the-century parlor and recreation center (figure 16). The central ground-floor interior of Lathrop Hall is like the main thoroughfare of an old European city, where all that one needs is contained in a few hundred yards of individual "vendors."

Architecturally, Lathrop Hall is not an environment that invites looking out; rather, its whole ambience focuses on interiors on many levels: personally, here is where women are asked to explore their emotional resources through dance; physically, here is where women increase their aerobic and cardiovascular endurance; and psychologically, this is a place where the linkage of the mind, the body, and the emotions is explored. Its windows are small and placed high and deep within the cement façade. Inside, in nearly windowless settings, one finds customarily outdoor facilities—a swimming pool that did have some windows and the

Figure 15. Women students in Lathrop Hall Gymnasium, 1914 (Courtesy University of Wisconsin–Madison Archives)

Figure 16. Reception room, Lathrop Hall (Courtesy University of Wisconsin–Madison Archives)

indoor track that circles the three-stories-high gymnasium at the third-story level. It feels like a safe, private, and indeed almost invisible site from which women could challenge conventions and discover the physical pleasures of activity.

For all the metaphor of its design, however, the building was functionally impractical in some respects. Trilling minced no words when she summed up Lathrop Hall's functionality by calling it "an architect's dream come true and a Physical Education Director's nightmare." For her it was a painful example of "the aesthetic dominating the practical." Trilling decried the vast wasted space between the two wings of the building, saying this valuable central area had been left undeveloped and filled with beams and props such that it was suitable only as storage space.[54] It interfered with her penchant for efficiency and her expansionist notions as director of women's physical education.

BLANCHE TRILLING IN MADISON

The opening of Lathrop Hall and the beginning of Trilling's tenure as director seem synonymous, yet it was not until two years after Lathrop Hall opened, and immediately after Mayhew departed to take a new post with the YWCA in China, that Blanche M. Trilling formally arrived in Madison. Trilling had been aggressively recruited by Clarke W. Hetherington, who had been impressed with her when she taught under him at the University of Missouri. Trilling regarded Hetherington as an inspirational mentor, "an idealist, a statesman and a prophet in the field of Physical Education."[55] Hetherington had created the physical education major at the University of Wisconsin in 1911, making it one of the first colleges in the Midwest to establish a professional course for the training of teachers of physical education.

Trilling had precisely the qualifications that were needed for director. She was a graduate of the esteemed Boston Normal School of Gymnastics, one of only four teacher-training schools of physical education in the United States at the time and the prototype for American women's college physical education and sport programs. In 1909, just after Trilling graduated at the age of thirty-three, the school became the Department of Hygiene and Physical Education at Wellesley College. The Boston Normal School had been founded in 1889 with funding from the Boston philanthropist Mary Hemenway and the steady efforts of Amy Norris Homans, who had directed Hemenway's various projects since 1877.[56] The program in Boston was modeled on Stockholm's Royal Central Institute of Gymnastics, and for Homans its tacit mission was to place its graduates in leadership positions as directors of college and university programs around the country.

Homans saw to it that the curriculum included the most up-to-the-moment medical information, and she frequently brought in professors from Harvard and physicians from Harvard Medical School to teach. Initially, Swedish gymnastics were the main focus, but by the 1890s, the period during which Trilling was there, the curriculum had broadened to include swimming, games, dancing, basketball, boating, tennis, and athletics. Homans believed firmly that a good woman was a quiet woman, and she reportedly had a large sign in the gymnasium with the following quotation from *King Lear*, which served as her motto: "Her voice was ever soft, gentle and low; an Excellent thing in woman."[57]

Trilling came to Wisconsin from the University of Chicago Teachers College, where she had served as acting and then associate director of physical education since 1910. Trilling's own biographical entries in her department history indicate that it was the opportunity to work with Hetherington again, as well as the lure of heading up "one of the most modern and best equipped women's buildings in the country," that drew her to Wisconsin.[58] Here was the ideal setting and persuasive administrative backing for a woman who wanted to change the nature of female physical education in America's universities. Of Trilling's appointment Hetherington wrote:

She came to the profession with a background of social graces and education in music, and the professional discipline and spirit inspired by Miss Homans. To that she added intelligent courage, devotion, tactful manipulation of social problems, energy, and administrative ability. She has carried through a rare piece of work and made the Wisconsin organization a power.[59]

When Hetherington left Wisconsin in 1918 for California, where he became state supervisor of physical education, Trilling was already deep into developing her program at Madison. She would not leave the university until her retirement in 1946, after thirty-four years of leadership.

Once she arrived in Madison in the summer of 1912, Trilling was immediately appointed assistant professor of physical education and director of the women's gymnasium. Her timing could not have been better. The professional course leading to a degree as a teacher of physical education was one year old, and at the conclusion of Trilling's first year, in June 1913, the Department of Physical Education graduated its first three majors.

University files contain a brief reference to the hiring of Trilling that first year. However, that her previous post was associate director of physical education at the University of Chicago Teachers College reveals that she was recommended by Clarke Hetherington specifically because of her ability to head up the new major in women's physical education teaching. Indeed, her job description reads: "She will have direct charge of the prescribed activities for all first and second year women and of the normal practice and practice teaching of the women students in the professional course. She will lecture on the Special Technique of Children's Play and Games, and of Dancing."[60]

Correspondence from Trilling's early years at Wisconsin reveals a woman who was steadily searching for and sampling creative movement activities for the future growth of her program. She seemed to honor the past as well. Trilling's files contain several original books of sports and games for children from the early 1800s, as well as a reproduction of a seventeenth-century English book of sports and a reproduction of a Parliamentary order from 1643 demanding all copies of this sports book be burned because they endorsed the enjoyment and toleration of sports on Sunday. At the time Trilling took command of the women's physical education program at the University of Wisconsin, this kind of thinking was not all that remote, yet her preservation of these materials suggests an amused disdain for such an unenlightened outlook. This was the past that she, and the program she was creating, was rejecting.

One revealing document in Trilling's personal file is a copy of a 1900 summary of the standards of physical fitness for a teacher of women's physical education, which reads as follows:

She is expected to be positively well, organically sound, free from defects, functionally normal. *She is responsible for making her body her trained servant or her efficient machine* [emphasis added] and then giving it the respect we of the Twentieth Century bestow on both of these. Soundness, vitality, endurance are her first business assets and absolutely necessary advertisements of her work. Her condition carries conviction of the value of physical education or goes a long way toward effectually disproving it. She is expected to be able to do hard work and keep fit, and illness is or should be considered inexcusable if not actual disgrace.[61]

This statement reads more like a manifesto, or a call to arms, than a passive description of what an effective physical education instructor should do. Almost militaristic in its demands, it suggests an angry and adversarial relationship between the Victorian woman and her body. The image of a woman's flesh here is that it is something to be conquered, subdued, and made to serve her will and her mind. This document sounds as if it might have stood as an oath of allegiance of sorts for the new profession of women physical educators. Its tone seems deliberately inspirational but also intimidating. It suggests the moment as being a rare opportunity to make profound changes, and yet it also reveals a mindfulness of the enormous pressures on women to make sure the physical education instruction they devise for other women is a success on all fronts.

The care and energy with which Trilling fashioned her program at Wisconsin reveal just how seriously she took this mission and her responsibility to women, their bodies, and the status of the physical education of both the minds and bodies of female students in the university. Beginning in the fall of 1915, at the start of her fourth year in the university, Trilling began lobbying aggressively for a separation of the men's and women's physical education programs. There are copies of her letters to women academics in women's physical education programs at the Universities of Minnesota, Illinois, California, Texas, and Iowa and at Stanford soliciting arguments for her own battle to free herself from the supervision of a men's physical education director in Wisconsin. In fact this separatist struggle would take Trilling fifteen years to win, for the men's and the women's physical education departments did not separate until 1930. Trilling continued to shape women's physical education into the kind of program she wanted while she waited for the official separation.

Trilling's steady insistence on having the women's physical education program separate from that of the men was something of which Homans would have heartily approved. Within this demand was an important rationale: namely, only women, who shared the same physiology, and the same gender ideals, can design and oversee women's physical education programs. Trilling was also well aware of the evils rocking the world of college men's athletics at a time when violence in football and gambling were commonplace. In a well-known incident in intercollegiate football, a college team was faulted for using alumni as players and even slipping the janitor onto the team. Julia Brown, professor emeritus of women's physical education at the University of Wisconsin, remarked, "Trilling wanted women's physical education and athletics to be appropriate to their gender. She was a major influence on why women's athletic associations did not advance to intercollegiate competition. Instead she promoted 'sport for all' in an atmosphere where games might be followed by a friendly social activity such as sipping tea and singing songs together."[62]

Trilling had also learned strategy from Homans, and she had arrived mentally prepared to be one of the few women in the university faculty. Homans had coached her graduates in how to deal with often hostile male colleagues who had not yet accepted the idea of higher education for women, let alone a female colleague.[63] Trilling learned to balance her style between a Victorian feminine ideal and the image of a New Woman, depending on the situation, the circumstances, and her patience. She always required that her students acknowledge her entrance into the classroom by standing up when she stepped in.[64] This is a gesture that suggests the importance she assigned her role as a professor of women's physical education and correspondingly the importance she attached to the act of education for women.

Indeed, Edith Boys Enos, now in her nineties and a University of Wisconsin alumna from the initial years of the dance program, recalled

Trilling vividly more than seventy years later. In a letter about her strongest memories of her college years she writes:

Blanche M. Trilling was a visionary. She wanted to have the finest Physical Education Department for Women in any public university—and she did. Patrician, Miss Trilling, short and sturdily built, was a firm (no nonsense) administrator and respected by students and faculty.[65]

TRILLING AND DANCE

Just what prompted Trilling to want to introduce creative or modern dance into her curriculum is not certain. What is clear is that dance of some sort, whether it be country dances, national folk dance forms, Delsarte's system, or Jaques-Dalcroze eurythmics,[66] was familiar to her from her own training at Boston Normal School of Gymnastics as well as from the curriculum she inherited and reshaped in Wisconsin. Born in Syracuse,

Figure 17. Blanche Trilling as a young woman, during the period of her life when she was a music student (Courtesy University of Wisconsin–Madison Archives; in the collection of Julia M. Brown)

New York, in 1876, Trilling attended finishing schools in Virginia and Tennessee, as well as the Cincinnati College of Music to study piano and harmony (figure 17). "I imagine that's where her interest in dance may have come from," Brown said. "She often taught music and even folk dance as part of the rhythm classes in physical education."[67]

Trilling was also a director who was adventuresome in trying out new subjects for her program. In her lectures to physical education students she repeatedly stressed the importance of an eclectic curriculum. "Tempting girls," she called it, "by offering a wide range of activities—giving large opportunities for selection—giving students an opportunity to become proficient in some form of vigorous activity which she will preserve after leaving college."[68]

Trilling herself taught a number of courses, both theoretical and studio ones, because it was often neither feasible nor practical to engage specialists in all the subjects she wanted to offer. In the summer of 1916, for example, she ended up teaching country dance herself on what was probably a last-minute basis. She wrote a hasty note in mid-July to a sheet music company in New York to request twenty copies each, promptly, of three different country dance tunes "for use in my summer classes, and the session is already half over."[69]

Trilling's forte, however, was as an administrator, what the visionary women's physical education director Homans had trained her to be. Indeed, Trilling's own writings resonate with a larger portrait of physical education and its values, virtues, and battles for academic legitimacy. A series of lecture notes and class handouts from the courses Trilling taught during the 1922–23 and 1923–24 academic years offers a rare glimpse of her own thoughts on these points.

Lecture II for her Seminar I,[70] for example, begins with a series of revealing, if fragmentary, phrases about women's physical education: "Break down prejudice against profession (Very name against it, and arouses antipathy)," she writes, as if dissecting the problem prior to formulating a battle plan for how to gain legitimacy for the entire field of physical education in the university. Next, she notes: "Difficult to find place in curriculum—studies with mental content given the preference—always asked to take last place in schedule." Here, too, Trilling identifies another major problem for the field: as long as physical activity is regarded as not having mental content, its status in the university will remain low. Conceptually the indivisibility of mind and body needs to be demonstrated. Trilling apparently intended these as notes to herself, but one can imagine her amplifying them in lecture. Indeed, this same lecture continues with a surprisingly modern assessment of the 1920s outlook on the body: "Our entire mental life is influenced by our bodily condition and has a vital connection with it. Why then, if we have accepted this new idea of relation between mind and body, do we have such difficulty in establishing a place for physical education?"

While Trilling argued adamantly for an increased academic status for physical education, she suggested that physical education brought with it a different set of standards and criteria. "Physical educators have made the mistake of demanding the same amount of credits for physical education as for any other subject," she headlined in Lecture II. "Cannot measure it by counts or credits. Must show itself in physical fitness, personal conduct, character, good habits, lofty ideals, obedience to nature's laws." At other points Trilling's lecture notes echo strong Progressive sentiments, as in the following capsule summary she offers students of how "society is slow to adopt new ideas and new practices":

We are largely governed by traditions. Old idea of school was an immovable, unfiltered desk—which tortured the body while it trained the mind. Technical schools came in and we added the bench—the laboratory—the work shop—where a child put into practice ideas learned at the desk, and gradually the gymnasium and playground.

Trilling then forcefully anchors the current need for physical education in another evolutionary model—that of the diminution of physical activity in twentieth-century lives: "If our system of education is to meet our national need, it must be continually modified to meet our changing conditions, and one of our most important needs at this time, is the introduction into the school program of at least a portion of the physical exercise which was in the past supplied from other sources." For Trilling the mission of women's physical education was first to offer physical education opportunities for all. Always it was the lay learner rather than the specialist whom she saw as the ideal consumer and beneficiary of her program.

Indeed, in the fall of 1929 Trilling was the outspoken opponent of women's participation in the 1932 Olympic Games. Speaking at the northeastern Wisconsin teachers' convention that fall, Trilling said she opposed women's participation in the Olympics because "it means specialized athletic training for a few instead of opportunity for a great many taking part." Trilling believed firmly in the democratizing influence of team sports, and this remained for her one of its most vital functions. Muscular reactions could constitute a private moral realm, particularly for an efficient team player, and for Trilling this was a loftier goal than competition. She noted, "Until there are ample playgrounds and gymnasiums in all schools and until every girl has the fullest opportunity to engage in athletics, let the schools conserve their energy and money instead of spending both on a form of sport that is, at best, of doubtful value. Let them choose rather to build up a kind of athletics that it will realize the ideal of the women's division—'A team for every girl and every girl on a team.' "⁷¹

This drive to present such a range of physical activity that every woman might find something that suited her eventually led Trilling to begin searching for a way to bring interpretive dance into her program. When in 1915 she had asked for an instructor in Jaques-Dalcroze's method and was turned down for lack of funds, she did not abandon her goal; she merely shifted her sights closer to home. Her summer sessions, with their special training programs for physical education teachers, were booming, particularly in the "Singing Games and Folk Dance" classes. What Trilling wanted next was someone who could teach what she was then calling "Esthetic Dancing."

At the close of the 1916 summer session, Margaret H'Doubler, the young basketball and baseball coach who had been hired from the 1910 graduating class, asked for a year's leave to study at Teachers College at Columbia. Trilling consented, and she offered a condition: H'Doubler was to return with some form of dance "worthy of a college woman's time" in the university. This was to become a prophetic directive for dance education, a phrase tantamount to Serge Diaghilev's often quoted order to Jean Cocteau, to create dance works of surprising creativity, "Etonné-moi, Jean!" Astonish me! Diaghilev told Cocteau. Find dance worthy of the university woman's time, Trilling told H'Doubler.

5

Margaret H'Doubler and the Liberty of Thought

To preserve individuality and save it from herd-like conformity
is one of education's most important challenges.
Margaret H'Doubler, no source, undated

Those who deal with institutions are situated very differently
from those who deal with ideas. The latter should insist on the
liberty of thought and keep the horizon clear; the former must
accept the material most immediately applicable to purposes
of support and construction.
John Bascom, president of the University of Wisconsin, 1874–87

WHEN BLANCHE TRILLING MADE TWENTY-SEVEN-YEAR-OLD MAR-
garet H'Doubler her emissary to the world of New York dance
studios in the autumn of 1916, neither she nor H'Doubler
could have foreseen how fortuitous this selection would prove to be.
Initially, their roles were simple: Trilling was an administrator, desirous of
expanding her curriculum, and H'Doubler was a young instructor, eager
to please but with a firm sense of standards concerning what she thought
was educationally meritorious (figure 18).

Trilling knew H'Doubler as an enthusiastic and inspirational physical educator. The students adored H'Doubler and worked hard for her,
almost regardless, it seemed, of the sport she was teaching. Under her
instruction hundreds of University of Wisconsin women each year took
active part in basketball classes, intramurals, and tournaments that she
organized.[1] According to H'Doubler, Trilling's reason for connecting her
with dance probably stemmed from a silly skit in the year-end faculty show
in May 1915, when Trilling had chosen the tall and stately H'Doubler as
her partner.

In the early days, when Miss Trilling came, it was the policy of the department
every year to give some kind of entertainment for the students. This one year Miss

103

Figure 18. An official faculty portrait of Blanche Trilling (State Historical Society of Wisconsin. WHi (X3) 28939)

Trilling and I did a dance—she taught the dancing when she came. Our stunt was we did some kind of a skit, and I don't know why she thought I might be able to do some dancing. That's how she happened to ask me. I had forgotten that, that's very important.²

A dated and labeled torn photograph of what was likely this event is preserved in a Women's Physical Education Department scrapbook (figure 19) in the University of Wisconsin–Madison Archives. Above the caption "Miss Trilling and Miss H'Doubler" is a photo of Trilling, *en travesti*, as a Dutch boy in pants and a short straight wig, gazing admiringly at H'Doubler, who wears a flowing full-length gown. H'Doubler curtsies deeply and demurely, her face all but hidden by a coiled blond wig and a large fan. From this photograph it is difficult to assess what it might have been about H'Doubler's dancing ability that impressed Trilling. What does show through readily, however, is how comfortably H'Doubler acts the subservient role. Her bow reveals homage as much as greeting.

MARGARET H'DOUBLER'S EARLY YEARS

Much more than obedience, however, made H'Doubler the right person to be Trilling's emissary (figure 20). H'Doubler was as fiercely loyal to principles of education, and to what she saw as situations that fostered the spiritual growth of the mind, as she was to physical activity for all women. It helped considerably that she had been raised in a family climate of methodical and orderly invention. Born April 26, 1889, in Beloit, Kansas, to Charles and Sarah H'Doubler (the H-apostrophe-Doubler is an Americanized version of the original Swiss family name Hougen-Doubler), Margaret Newell H'Doubler was the second daughter and the third and last child of this prominent Swiss immigrant family, which also included her older sister, Pearl, born in 1885 and her brother, Frances Todd, born in 1887.³ The Hougen-Doublers' relatives had arrived in the United States in the early 1700s and had resided primarily in Illinois and Pennsylvania.⁴

H'Doubler's father, Charles, was born in 1859 in Warren, Illinois, where he was known as "a man of many and pronounced talents," including artistic photography, often of his daughters.⁵ H'Doubler's early experience with having her image recorded and then publicly displayed, at a time when having one's photograph taken was a rare and infrequent occurrence for most Americans, may have contributed to her ease with working in a field where public moving images of the body were the products. In the 1920s and 1930s H'Doubler's dancers in fact posed nude for a series of dance studies photographed outdoors in Madison near Lake Mendota.⁶ Although these photographs are now lost, their very existence suggests again that for a woman at the end of the Victorian era,

Figure 19. Blanche Trilling and Margaret H'Doubler in costume for a spoof scene at a faculty party. This photo was artfully torn and folded prior to being glued in a department album. (Courtesy University of Wisconsin–Madison Archives)

Figure 20. A faculty portrait of Margaret H'Doubler with bobbed hair (State Historical Society of Wisconsin. WHi (X3) 28938)

H'Doubler had extraordinarily open views about photography, public images, and women's bodies. She was a modern woman.

H'Doubler's presentation of herself reveals a similar sensibility. Many of H'Doubler's pupils have remarked on her flair for tasteful yet very fashionable attire. She dressed as if she would be looked at, and at the same time her choice of understated attire put her in control of herself to an unusual degree in a situation of public display (figure 21). Her comfort with being regarded as an image, and her skill at shaping the public presentation of herself, were useful qualities that would eventually help position H'Doubler as the author of a new public image for dancing women. This openness also extended to her comfort with her own body. Several of H'Doubler's students recall how relaxed she was about nudity. Hermine Davidson, one of H'Doubler's students in the early 1930s, recalled her stripping off her clothes on a hot summer evening and going skinny-dipping with Davidson in a quiet corner of Lake Mendota. Another student, Ellen Moore, remembered another sweltering midwestern summer day several years later when H'Doubler, in a social chat with a couple of women students at home, simply peeled off her shirt and continued chatting in her bra and slip.[7]

H'Doubler's father set a fine model of one who is creative, inventive, and yet supremely practical, qualities that would serve Margaret H'Doubler as well in the invention of dance as an academic discipline. H'Doubler has recalled her father as a man whose inventions, particularly of electrical machinery, resulted in a number of successful patents. She remembers him as "a man of many abilities and inexhaustible energy who encouraged his family to venture into new and exciting opportunities."[8]

H'Doubler's mother complemented Charles's creativity with practical design skills of her own: she costumed the young H'Doubler and her sister in intricately hand-finished and detailed, lace-covered dresses. Here, too, was a valuable model: when H'Doubler introduced a new form of aesthetic movement for women in higher education, she also had to create the appropriate fashions. The result would be a much copied H'Doubler-designed Greek tunic, in the style of Isadora Duncan and her ilk, which students were to sew for themselves for use in daily class as well as the eventual lecture demonstrations of Orchesis.

The young H'Doubler was precocious. Raised in an environment of privilege with carriages, vacations, private tutoring, and piano lessons, H'Doubler read extensively from an early age, particularly Greek mythology, Aesop's fables, poetry, and operas. H'Doubler graduated from a one-room schoolhouse in Warren, Illinois, and began high school in 1902, at the age of thirteen. In 1905, during H'Doubler's senior year, the entire family moved to Madison, where H'Doubler's brother, two years her senior, had been accepted to finish his undergraduate degree in math.[9]

Figure 21. Margaret H'Doubler, in fashionable period attire, standing on the steps of Lathrop Hall (Courtesy University of Wisconsin–Madison Archives)

At high school in Madison, H'Doubler participated eagerly in basketball, field hockey, and eurythmics, the major movement forms open to females at the time.

H'Doubler entered the University of Wisconsin in 1906, intending to study either biology or medicine. As an entering freshman she also took her obligatory physical education class. "I loved it!" she recalled many years later of that initial experience. "I said I know *now* what I'm going to do."[10] H'Doubler returned home that evening and announced to her parents that she was going to be a gym teacher. Her parents wisely, and prophetically in regard to the dance major she would one day design, suggested that because there was no such major yet she should put together her own comprehensive course of study. Four years later H'Doubler graduated with a major in biology and minors in chemistry and philosophy.

Although she rarely mentioned it in her later life, H'Doubler did sample what passed for early dance in the university at the time. She was among the hundred or more coeds in the 1908 and 1909 May Fêtes. For the 1909 program H'Doubler's family watched her in the grand maypole dance waltzing with 109 other young women, and also in the massive final pageant, which boasted up to four hundred female students dancing in various groupings designed around a central theme.[11]

The other early exposure to dance H'Doubler had at the University of Wisconsin was through the folk dance classes taught by Dr. Dennison, a medical doctor and instructor in the women's physical education program. Dennison taught the Louis Chalif method of mail-order dances; Chalif mailed descriptions or scripts of his dances to teachers, who would decipher them as best they could as they instructed the students in follow-along sessions. H'Doubler reportedly mastered several Chalif dances, learning the steps to waltzes, schottisches, mazurkas, and polkas.[12] This was, however, a dry and eviscerated way to learn dance, and predictably H'Doubler enjoyed the accompanying piano music more than the routinized dancing. She was beginning to form a sense of things she did *not* want to do, and regimented social dancing was one of them.

Knowing what one does not want can be an important skill for discovery in the arts and education; the luck of good timing also helps. H'Doubler graduated from the University of Wisconsin in May of 1910 and was promptly hired as an assistant instructor, along with three other new graduates, to teach in the just-formed Department of Women's Physical Education that fall (figure 22). Two years later Blanche Trilling arrived as the new director of women's physical education.

With her own classes in basketball, baseball, and swimming booming in the university, H'Doubler spent the summers of 1911, 1913, and 1914 participating in physical education workshops, including one held at the

Figure 22. Margaret H'Doubler (left, in white) coaching women students in baseball, ca. 1914 (Courtesy University of Wisconsin–Madison Archives; in the collection of Julia M. Brown)

Sargent School for Physical Education in Boston. Sargent had developed his highly successful system of weight machines and mimetic exercises in the 1870s, shortly before he was named a professor of physical education at Harvard. The Sargent Summer School H'Doubler attended had begun in 1887, and it quickly became a popular continuing education session for teachers like H'Doubler looking to expand their knowledge and repertoire of physical education activities.[13] While the Sargent method was essentially all exercises, Melvin Ballou Gilbert was engaged by the school to teach "aesthetic dance," as it was called for the women, and "gymnastic dancing," as it was renamed when taught to the men.[14]

H'Doubler reported that her initial enthusiasm at learning the Gilbert and Sargent methods quickly turned to disappointment. "It was just a dreadful course. There weren't any values—you learned a bone name in anatomy—there was nothing significant about the skeletal structure for movement or anything like that, nothing. Something would have to happen to hold me in this field," she said, reflecting back on that time years later.[15] Repeatedly for H'Doubler, the pivotal experiences as she was building her nascent model for dance education seemed to be what did not work, what was incomplete, what left her expectations for movement education unfulfilled.

In 1916, at the conclusion of her sixth year of teaching, H'Doubler asked Trilling if she might have a year's leave of absence to study philosophy and aesthetics in the graduate program at Columbia University. The fall of 1916 was an amazing time to be in New York, particularly for a young woman alone. John Dewey was lecturing frequently at Teachers College at Columbia, having just published his *Democracy and Education* that same year. The pivotal Armory Show of avant-garde art had happened in New York a mere three years earlier. The term Dada was coined in Zurich and flowering in New York. Internationally, psychologist Carl Jung's *Psychology of the Unconscious* was published, and Albert Einstein had just articulated his theory of relativity. H'Doubler said the following of this time:

[It] was a very interesting time to be in New York . . . because there was a revolt in all the arts. In music . . . new forms were appearing . . . the same kind of thing in painting, and it was also happening in dance, but that was not very well known. There were a few who were dissenting, not teaching ballet, but the more I saw, the more I disliked it. It was merely miming; it was different movement but imitating and being told what to do. The people who were dissenting and trying something different were as limited in their thinking as the ballet in theirs.[16]

H'Doubler was part of the first generation of professional American women, women who substantially rejected traditional female roles to accomplish what they did. Judging from their choices—H'Doubler did not marry until she was forty-five and remained childless—they seem to have had firm social ethics and high social respectability. They led lives of selfless dedication to a profession rather than domesticity.[17] Having chosen to forgo the customary path, these women made academia, medicine, or social work the source of the satisfaction others might have found in a traditional family life. It was a serious choice for these early twentieth-century women, one that would have to offer rich rewards of a different sort to justify the sacrifices.

Therefore, when Trilling uttered her famous request to H'Doubler as she left for her year in New York, "Try to find some dance worthy of a college woman's time," both women knew this was a serious demand.[18] For some time Trilling had sensed that dance could be more than the rigidly artificial five positions of poorly taught classical ballet and Chalif dance-by-number. Years later H'Doubler delighted in recounting this exchange: " 'I was horrified,' I said and I asked Miss Trilling, 'I? Teach dance and give up BASKETBALL?' Tears came into my eyes, and I said,

'I just couldn't think of that. I don't know anything about dance' "
(figure 23).[19]

H'DOUBLER IN NEW YORK

With Dewey's educational admonitions framing her search, H'Doubler's
hunt in New York would be for methods as well as content. Culturally
and educationally, as well as artistically, ideas and ventures were in an
extraordinary state of experimentation and flux throughout the nation,
and particularly in higher education, during this period. American colleges were trying to balance the challenges of general culture and what
Thorstein Veblen would see in 1918 as the dangers of having business values central to American education. It was, he wrote in a widely publicized
article of the time, like "riding two horses at the same time—vocation and
general culture." Unless the pursuit of knowledge were separated from
training for professional work, he warned, higher education in America
was in danger.[20]

Figure 23. Margaret H'Doubler and her 1912 championship University of Wisconsin
women's basketball team. This photograph was deliberately and artfully torn and folded, as
was the style in early twentieth-century photo albums. (State Historical Society of Wisconsin.
WHi (X3) 28937)

Matthew Arnold had earlier complained that the land grant colleges were calculated to produce miners, engineers, and architects rather than "sweetness and light." When H'Doubler departed for philosophical and aesthetic study in New York, she was determined to bring back some of those missing dimensions of the curriculum to Wisconsin. "Sweetness and light," she reasoned, could be made as scientific, rigorous, and socially useful as engineering or architecture.

There was also a larger climate of what Merle Curti has called "cultural nationalism" brewing. Cultural nationalism was essentially a quest to foster indigenous American scholarship that would free Americans from imitating the scholarship of Europe. The way to create an authentic American culture, it was believed, was to have scholars trained at home "in an environment and by methods that shall subject the form and relate the content of their knowledge to the high tradition of their own language, literature and inherited culture." There were shortcomings in the life of the mind in America, intellectuals worried, and this agenda of cultural nationalism, of which H'Doubler's quest for a worthy dance form might be considered a prime example, had as its goal to stimulate Americans to greater literary and scientific achievements. These achievements would carry a distinctive American identity and give voice to distinctly American understandings of the world and democratic America.[21]

Throughout her subsequent life as an educator, writer, and dance education theoretician, H'Doubler seems to have been most steadily and profoundly influenced by her exposure to Dewey's philosophy stretching back to her year at Columbia. While at Columbia, H'Doubler was asked to be the graduate student member of the Educational Philosophical Club, where she gained admission to regular discussions about education theory attended by Dewey and William H. Kilpatrick, among others. "I got terribly excited about what this human mind, what this human being, really is, the values and all, and it got me very stimulated," she recalled later. In particular, H'Doubler says she read extensively on the role dance had historically played in older civilizations and different cultures. "From there I commenced to build up and tried to see what could be done in our civilization," she said in a statement that echoes the cultural-nationalistic sentiments of the time.[22]

Initially, H'Doubler hoped to fulfill quickly Trilling's request to find some interesting dance. She arranged to arrive in New York a week or two before the fall semester began at Columbia, so that she could visit several studios free from the pressures of what she knew would be substantial academic demands. She was promptly disappointed. The majority of the studios H'Doubler visited before Columbia began all offered poorly taught classical ballet, or weak imitations of it. (This was, after all, twenty-eight years before George Balanchine arrived in America to begin to build a world-class American identity in classical ballet.) "I am just not getting anywhere and I am so disappointed and I am sure you will be disappointed," she recalls writing to Trilling of this initial search. Thirty years later, the memory of the second-rate ballet classes she had seen would still remain sharp: "It's mostly anti-human structure and anti-human function from a biologist's point of view," she sniffed in a 1952 interview with her former student Diane Gray.[23]

Interestingly, the most consistent thing H'Doubler found was a desire to break free from the constraints of classical ballet.

Whenever I would hear of somebody that was teaching, I would go and try to get in the class to see. And there were some who had broken from ballet. I would talk with them and they would say, "I don't know where I am going, I don't know what this is all about. I just know that I don't want ballet."[24]

H'Doubler soon found, however, that while the dance teachers she was visiting had indeed abandoned ballet, they were teaching their new movement vocabularies in the same rigid and doctrinaire manner. "It was a question of imitating their movement, but they were different movements from the ballet. That still wasn't what I wanted."[25]

In a 1963 interview, H'Doubler was even more outspoken and specific about what was missing in the studios she visited:

The so-called dances that came out of such training always seem to be nothing but a stringing together (in an artistic manner) of the technical movements studied. They were without significance. In the few studios where there was a breaking away from this formal technique there was no sound theory or philosophy or reason for what was being done. It was either cultist or a blind imitation of personalities.[26]

What H'Doubler was looking for most pointedly was a form of dance that was as unencumbered as possible by personal style and fixed vocabularies. This dance form also had to be logical enough physically to survive scientific scrutiny and a kinesiology-based analysis of its uses of the body. In essence what H'Doubler was looking for, although probably neither she nor Trilling fully realized it at the time, was a form of dance that could be made to fit into the institutional frames they already knew would surround it. It was not a matter of finding the right ready-to-go dance but rather the right fixer-upper dance, a dance that, like a first-time buyer's house, had a good foundation and great potential.

This may well be why, for all of her interest in ferreting out interesting dance while she was in New York, H'Doubler never once referred to having seen any concert dance. Between the fall of 1916 and the spring of 1917, Ruth St. Denis performed extensively in New York and toured frequently across the country. In the fall of 1916 Isadora Duncan had just returned to New York from a South American tour, and her lover, Paris

Singer, underwrote an invitational performance by Duncan and six of her graduates at the Metropolitan Opera House. Yet H'Doubler never mentions any of this even happening, much less her having attended Duncan's or others' concerts.

It was not then, nor was it ever, dance as a performing art that really engaged H'Doubler. The New York dance world, as she recounted it from that 1916–17 visit, was a world of dance studios, dance teachers, and dance pupils. As H'Doubler framed dance for higher education, it was not a world that needed to include a sense of dance as a theater form, or even of dance as an art form with a history. It would be many years before these dimensions of dance were gradually added to the Wisconsin curriculum, in a choice that was just as pragmatic as the initial decision to exclude them.

GERTRUDE KLINE COLBY AND BIRD LARSON

At about the same time that H'Doubler was searching out dance in New York, two other important early pioneers, Gertrude Colby and Bird Larson, were also beginning to develop their versions of educational dance. Mary O'Donnell, who later directed the dance program in women's physical education at Teachers College at Columbia, suggests in a 1936 article that H'Doubler was in contact with Colby and Larson during this period of exploration. "There was the opportunity of knowing Gertrude Colby and the late Bird Larson and in Miss H'Doubler's many discussions with them surely dance history was made by that remarkable triumvirate," she wrote in the leading dance publication of the time, *Dance Observer*.[27] In later years, however, when H'Doubler spoke of her influences during this period, she rarely mentioned Colby's and Larson's names, as if she had never even met them.

Gertrude Kline Colby was the only dance educator at Columbia at the time H'Doubler was there, so one must assume H'Doubler had contact with her. Colby's own history in some respects parallels H'Doubler's early years. She first studied at the University of Minnesota, her home state, and was initially interested in physical education. She, like H'Doubler, at first planned to study medicine. However, by the time Colby had moved on to graduate work at Teachers College at Columbia, her field of study was corrective gymnastics. In New York her interest rapidly changed to dance as she, like H'Doubler, made the rounds of various dance studios, including those of Gilbert, Chalif, and a Russian named Kurylo. She also spent three years studying Dalcroze eurythmics. Upon graduation Colby was appointed to teach at the Speyer School, the Progressive demonstration school for Columbia.[28]

From 1913 to 1916 Colby worked on her program of movement education for children in the Speyer School. The program Colby designed used natural movement to foster self-expression in children in a curriculum that was intended to be integrated with the full school program. What she developed was her own system of natural dance, creative movement that started from the interests of the children and their native movement proclivities. The Speyer School closed in 1916, but Colby continued on the faculty of Columbia, training many teachers in her method of "natural dance" children's dance instruction.[29] Colby was also apparently influenced by attending performances by Isadora Duncan and Ruth St. Denis, whose own quests to find an individual voice in movement as performers offered a professional parallel to her search as an educator.

In 1930 Colby oversaw the revival of the 1913 Teachers College dance/drama production *The Conflict*, a heavily allegorical "health" pantomime about the conflict between "the forces of Ignorance and Enlightenment for the possession of Humanity."[30] In her foreword to the script of this revival Colby lauds pantomime as "the essence of all dancing," a statement that suggests a radical contrast to H'Doubler's quest, which was to unlock through education the freely expressive, nonnarrative body within each individual, the antithesis of pantomimic gestures. Colby once recounted the four greatest influences on her teaching of dance: her association with Madame Alberti, a teacher of dramatic expression, her own great love of music, the educational attitude of the Speyer School, and Isadora Duncan.[31] With the exception of the Speyer School experience and a general interest in Duncanesque dance, these influences were far removed from the kinds of educationally reflective influences like Dewey's philosophy that shaped H'Doubler's conception of dance education.

Bird Larson was the other prominent pioneering dance educator in New York with whom H'Doubler must certainly have come into contact during her year there. The daughter of Swedish immigrants, Larson, like Colby, was born in Minnesota. A fine pianist, she taught school for five years in a small Minnesota mining community before leaving for New York to take her master's degree at Columbia. She had initially planned to major in home economics or mathematics, but she learned en route to New York that physical education was the emerging field for women. Upon arrival she switched her major, and she completed her graduate work in 1914, studying Delsarte movement at the same time. From 1916 to 1923 she was assistant professor of physical education at Barnard College, where, with limited actual experience in dance, she began to tilt the women's curriculum from athletic skills to dance pageantry.[32]

Larson, who, like Colby, was of the same generation as H'Doubler—Larson was just two years older—came into her movement interest through volunteer work with wounded war veterans. It has been speculated that in rehabilitative work with the veterans, Larson may have begun developing her own theories of body movement. During the years of World War I, Larson was very influential in New York dance education circles; however, she left academia in 1923, because she felt it did not allow for the kind of experiments in natural movement she was interested in pursuing. Highly opinionated, she rejected Isadora Duncan's style as too romantic and Ruth St. Denis's as too eclectic and too much influenced by foreign styles. Her search was for a basic movement vocabulary that would extend beyond popular performing techniques.[33] Larson eventually developed a system of movement training based on the laws of kinesiology, anatomy, and physics. Her emphasis was on developing oneself fully through dance, and to do this she stressed movement that originated in the torso.[34] After leaving Barnard, she spent the rest of her professional career in her own New York studio, experimenting with her students and performing for general and invited audiences. Larson died in 1925 at the age of thirty-eight, following the birth of her only child, well before she could satisfactorily develop her ideas about dance education.

ALYS BENTLEY

While Colby and Larson may not have influenced H'Doubler specifically beyond Colby's use of improvisation and Larson's emphasis on a scientific basis for movement, their very presence as independently searching dance teachers must have, at the very least, given H'Doubler tacit encouragement. Their presence likely spurred her own search for a more educational form of dance, for again, in reflecting on this period later in her life, H'Doubler summed up the other efforts in dance teaching as "nothing but endless imitation and endless petty rivalries. It [was] anti-educational in all the ways we [were] talking about at Columbia."[35] While H'Doubler pronounced dance teaching practices antieducational, the field of women's physical education was thriving, and the profession of theatrical American dance was coming into being at the same time. The two disciplines seemed destined to meet.

Most of the pioneering women in dance and physical education were attempting to bridge the two domains of dance art and education, at least temporarily, and to bring back to higher education fresh hybrids of educational theory and new movement forms. It is not surprising that Teachers College at Columbia, and the current ideas of John Dewey, offered a fertile basis from which Colby, Larson, and H'Doubler began their investigations. Only H'Doubler, however, relentlessly kept her education theory values at the forefront of whatever dance she was sampling. Perhaps because the determined Trilling always seemed to be looking over her shoulder during these formative years, H'Doubler persistently worked to reshape dance to fit high pedagogical and educational standards. Her first allegiance was always to academia, to serving the broad student body, which made her choices much clearer. It was the dance that would be changed, not what she demanded of it.

Toward the end of her second semester of graduate study, H'Doubler began to get anxious about her failure to find any worthwhile dance to bring back to Wisconsin. For a while H'Doubler thought her search had ended after she took her first class in the method of Émile Jaques-Dalcroze from a man named Porter Beegle.[36] Her intuitive sense of what she did not want, however, soon alerted her that although this movement form had the contours of a systematic investigation, it was in fact not one:

I thought this is it. It has some theory, some science back of it, some reason for it. But then it, pretty soon, was a dead end for me because it was really movement for music—That was his main purpose. They were true to what they were doing but it didn't mean dance to me. How did I know what dance was at this time? Myself, I didn't. I just didn't.[37]

H'Doubler began writing Trilling repeatedly, saying, "I shall never teach dance," although she was well aware that Trilling had already announced a new dance class taught by H'Doubler for the summer session of 1917. Finally, in April, Trilling wrote H'Doubler with one last suggestion: "I wish you would look up a woman who does not teach dance but is a music teacher and has her students move in relation to music. Her name is Alys Bentley."[38]

H'Doubler found Bentley directing a music studio for children in Carnegie Hall. Bentley's approach was highly idiosyncratic. Her teaching of creative music to children, for example, involved having each child sing his or her own made-up song rather than learning any set melodies or lyrics.[39] At first Bentley was reluctant to allow H'Doubler to study with her, because she primarily taught children.[40] H'Doubler, by now fairly desperate, was persistent in explaining what she called "her problem" (i.e., finding dance worthy of taking back to Madison). Eventually, Bentley relented. She expressed great interest in H'Doubler's problem, and after cautioning her that she took only students she wanted to, she put H'Doubler in a class with seven girls who had been studying with her for years.[41]

The class began with all the students lying flat on the floor. Instantly H'Doubler knew she was at last seeing the kind of dance for which she had been searching:

I said of course! Get on the floor where we are relieved from the pull of gravity, no balance—I had anatomy and all these things before I went to her. Where you could work out and see what the structure response was to [a] change of position in movement. Why it was like a quick flash. I got so excited.[42]

What excited H'Doubler was that in simply following Bentley's directions to work with flexion, extensions, and rotations of various joints, without any further explanation, it all became clear. H'Doubler suddenly realized that lying on the floor, removed from the pull of gravity, it was at last possible to get the body to move with true freedom and to explore the structural changes of position that resulted from relieving the joints from weight bearing.⁴³ This would be ground zero, the clean slate from which she would begin her new discipline of dance education and from which she would commence most dance lessons she taught over the next forty years.

H'Doubler's actual contact with Bentley was very limited. Speaking in 1972, she estimated that she visited Bentley's studio "once or maybe twice a week for perhaps a month." Yet the effect was instant and electrifying:

She freed us by this business of getting down [on the floor]. I could see it right away. And I thought, yes, get a technique worked out that is based on the body structure, the structural responses first, and know body technique, and then you can have the knowledge of how to develop your own style.⁴⁴

Equally profoundly, Bentley avoided all the slavish imitation of other movement teaching methods of the time. The emphasis was, just as Dewey would have advocated, on utilizing each child's natural impulses for expression and individual inventive use of movement in the learning process.⁴⁵

Bentley's response to H'Doubler's enthusiasm was to invite her to stay and continue to work with her in New York. "Stay here in New York and develop this because you never can do it in a university. Whoever heard of anything artistic coming out of a college?" she asked H'Doubler.⁴⁶ For the time Bentley was right; in 1917 the performing arts, especially dance, were not disciplines one studied at a university.

Here again H'Doubler's devotion to academia was tested. Even without such an invitation, Bird Larson had left her job at Barnard and set up her dance headquarters in her own private studio. H'Doubler, however, never wavered from her goal. "I don't want studio work, I want to teach," she told Bentley.⁴⁷ H'Doubler's response and Bentley's dismissal of the possibility of doing anything artistic in a university reflected similarly fixed views of teaching and artistic endeavors. These two women were simply reflecting the common assumptions of the time: that art happened outside the university, and meaningful educational teaching only happened within. H'Doubler's efforts would soon begin to suggest new possibilities within the university with regard to teaching *and* artistic endeavors.

H'Doubler seems to have been very impressed with Bentley's air of personal as well as artistic independence. Years later she recalled Bentley as having beautiful curly, short hair, a daring style for any respectable woman of the time and particularly for Bentley, who was in her early sixties when H'Doubler met her.⁴⁸ A curious little book Bentley wrote and published in a limited edition in 1933, *The Dance of the Mind*, reveals her as having distinctly strong social views as well. Subtitled "A Phantasy," it is a parable written in the form of a nonrhyming epic poem about how hunger for money and power saps men and women of their humanity and health. As much anticapitalist as pro a variety of health regimens, *The Dance of the Mind* has about it the simplistic ambiguity of a private fitness regimen touted as a cure for a global malaise.[49] Yet within this idea of the interrelatedness of personal well-being and social order lies what would soon become H'Doubler's own philosophy about the social and educational value of dance.

BRINGING DANCE BACK TO MADISON

Just before she had to return to Madison, H'Doubler made one last pilgrimage to gather more material as she pondered how to reshape this dance for the university woman. H'Doubler went to Boston for a few days to visit her brother, who, having just graduated from Harvard Medical School, was doing his internship at Peter Bent Brigham Hospital.[50] She decided to couple this with a stop to visit Drs. Dudley A. Sargent and Carl Schrader, two early pioneers of physical education teaching at the Sargent School in Boston. H'Doubler had a continuing need to verify her own emerging ideas about dance education with "the experts" and to secure their approval and encouragement. Unfortunately it would take years for her to get it. "I used to talk to people around and I kept running across people like myself who were starting to find dance or studying dance," H'Doubler said. "I would talk to them about this point of view and they just thought that I was crazy, really. [So] I thought well, I'll just talk to Dr. Schrader and Sargent while I'm in Boston." Evidently, Drs. Schrader and Sargent were not particularly interested in H'Doubler and her discoveries in dance education. She relates nothing more of their conversation than to say, "They didn't have the slightest idea of what I was talking about."[51]

H'Doubler made one more professional visit while in Boston. Just before she left, she called on Amy Norris Homans, who was on the women's physical education faculty at Wellesley College. Homans was a former head of the Boston Normal School of Gymnastics, where she had been Trilling's respected mentor. "She was such a cultured person herself," H'Doubler recalled. "She was very much interested in finding the kind of dance of which she would approve. I thought Well, I'm going to see Miss Homans, she'll know what I am talking about. The way I had heard of her, I just thought she must be tops. I went to see her and I was excused and in the hall in about five minutes. I don't believe she listened to me for ten minutes, it was the smoothest dismissal. I was just out in the hall."[52] While H'Doubler often downplayed in interviews how it was she found the ideal recipe for dance in the university, she took pride in recounting her perseverance in the face of initial discouragement from Homans. Throughout her development as an educator she was always very respectful of older women professionals, and when their acknowledgment of her accomplishments finally came, she was delighted. H'Doubler concluded her visit in New York, according to her own account, by "working as hard as I could until I had to go back."[53] She did, however, make one final dramatic gesture. It was the style of the time for women to wear long hair twisted up into a bun or braid, but for some time during her stay in New York, H'Doubler had been experiencing hair loss. When she sought help, she was told that the only remedy was to discard the switch of false hair she wore atop her own and get her remaining hair cut short. For H'Doubler this was both terrifying and an enormous relief. For years she had been dreaming of having short hair. Having seen Alys Bentley with her curly short hair only intensified H'Doubler's desire to strip herself of her own long tresses. Yet she was also aware how socially unacceptable it was at the time for a woman to bob her hair.

Shortly after returning to New York from Boston, a few days before heading home to Wisconsin, H'Doubler acted on impulse to realize her wish. Dashing into a barber shop, the only place where one could get hair cut, H'Doubler sat down quickly and asked for her hair to be trimmed short. For the next several weeks she carefully tucked up her new short hair in such a way that no one would know what she had done. Sometime after her return to Madison, she would confess her short hair to Trilling. For the time being, however, her comments suggest she felt reckless and wonderfully free, while still sharply aware of how she would be censored socially if anyone found out her secret. "Here I was in New York, studying dance, short hair, New York, and what would they think back there? Ruined woman. So I didn't know what to do about it."[54]

H'Doubler often retold this anecdote, which seems to contain several truths about her willingness to try a number of daring things and then shyly recoil. Beneath her surface identity of modest, obedient midwestern daughter, H'Doubler had a spirit of steel. She seemed to have a strong natural instinct for what was right for her, and once decided she rarely veered from the path she set for herself, even if it meant countering convention. Yet H'Doubler was also the perfect first-generation feminist in her ability to cloak a radical and rebellious agenda with a veneer of docility and conservative respectability.

Even within the feminine enclave of women's physical education, higher education was an environment that seemed to demand intellectual daring and aggressiveness to get ahead and at the same time to require ladylike reserve from the few women on the faculty. After nearly a year on her own in New York, H'Doubler was learning how to balance both roles. She was returning to Madison with the kernel of a new course in dance education. She had fulfilled Trilling's request, and in the process she had found her way into a domain that would occupy her for the remainder of her life.

6

Margaret H'Doubler and the Philosophy of John Dewey

[Art] is something more than the mere technical skill required by the organs of expression: it involves an idea, a thought, a spiritual rendering of things, and yet it is other than any number of ideas by themselves, it is a living union of thought and the instrument of expression.

John Dewey, director of the Dewey School, 1896–1904

JOHN DEWEY IS IN MANY REGARDS THE FATHER OF DANCE IN AMERican higher education. While he probably would not have disputed it, he was, in all likelihood, unaware of his paternity. It is therefore useful to explore John Dewey's philosophies of experience, nature, democracy, and art in relationship to the theoretical base for the beginnings of dance in American higher education. It can be argued that Dewey's philosophy of experience offered the ideal rationale, and at an extremely propitious moment, for dance in American education. The link between Dewey's ideas and their enactment in the dance classroom was H'Doubler, who was a student in one of Dewey's 1916–17 seminars at Teachers College at Columbia. H'Doubler, who would teach the nation's first college dance class a few months after she met Dewey, was profoundly affected by Dewey's new concepts as she formulated her ideas of dance education. Moreover, the existence of Dewey's theories was essential as a rationale for H'Doubler's shaping of the transformation of dance from a questionable social practice outside the university into a valued educational one within it. H'Doubler was on assignment, seraching for a model of practice, and her contact with Dewey offered her a theoretical base at the same time.

By examining H'Doubler's teaching and writing, this chapter will explore how Dewey's ideas were manifested in both H'Doubler's dance classes at the University of Wisconsin, beginning in 1917, and her subsequent influential writings on the place of dance in education. The connections among Dewey's own limited experience in the arts, his exposure to the movement training of Alexander Technique, and the applicability of his ideas for dance will also be examined. In particular the unique affinities that Dewey's theories held for dance will be investigated. Dewey's own experiences with movement will be considered as having contributed to his formulating notions of education that offered ready utility for dance education theory. Last, this chapter investigates the consequences of this Deweyan approach for dance education.

DEWEY AT COLUMBIA

H'Doubler met Dewey during the 1916–17 academic year while studying philosophy and aesthetics in the graduate program at Columbia University as a twenty-seven-year-old basketball coach on leave from her job at the University of Wisconsin. Her encounter with Dewey's ideas would be transformative for her in much the way contact with them would be for the chemist turned art collector Dr. Albert Barnes the following year.[1]

Two requests extended to H'Doubler during that sabbatical year would put her in the position of being the catalyst between Dewey's ideas and the dance. The first request was Trilling's, to "try to find some dance worthy of a college woman's time." The second request came soon after H'Doubler's arrival at Columbia, when she was asked to be the graduate student member of the Educational Philosophical Club at Teachers College.[2] There she became part of regular discussions about educational theory led by William Heard Kirkpatrick and John Dewey.[3]

In the fall of 1916 Dewey was just beginning his second decade teaching in the Departments of Philosophy and Psychology at Columbia and leading seminars with Kirkpatrick at Teachers College. The courses Dewey taught stemmed from his prevailing interests at the time, particularly his interest in developing a philosophy of experience. Consequently, he taught "Theories of Experience" and "The Analysis of Experience," courses in which he sought to establish that reality is to be identified with experience instead of eternal phenomena. At about this same time Dewey was also clarifying and defending his theory of knowledge and his position that thinking, or reflection, is inquiry and that factors involved in thinking or knowing must be viewed within the context of inquiry. As George Dykhuizen noted, this was in sharp contrast to the prevailing view of reality as a ready-made, fixed world waiting to be known.[4]

The implications for dance, and in fact all art, of a new view of cognition based on experience are substantial, for art deals with a bringing-into-being of the *un*known. Instead of a departure from life, this process, viewed through Dewey's new explanation, suggests the disorder of creation in the arts as a vivid model of how understanding in the world proceeds. It was during these first ten years at Columbia that Dewey wrote *How We Think*, a book that revealed to American education this "problem-based approach" as a vital teaching device.[5]

Dewey posited that when any act of inquiry or reflection was examined, it would generally have the same pattern of steps toward understanding as any other. It would begin with a problem and proceed, through testing of possible solutions, to a resolution.[6] This had long been true for science; now Dewey was about to posit that it was also true for the rest of life, including art.

DANCE AND *IN*EXPERIENCE

Ironically, the fact that H'Doubler knew nothing about dance when she set out for New York would, in this situation, prove to be a virtue. For it would take an outsider, someone who could evaluate with skepticism the popular private dance teachers of the time and see objectively what was missing educationally, to find the kind of dance Trilling wanted in the university. This was the practical side of H'Doubler's quest. Equally important for this outsider, however, was a strong sense of what values drove American higher education. Certainly Dewey's ideas on "Experience and Thinking" and "Thinking and Education"—chapter titles in his *Democracy and Education*, just published that year—must have suggested to H'Doubler a larger pedagogical context for what she was seeing as she toured New York dance studios looking for a model of rich content and effective teaching to bring back to Wisconsin. One can imagine H'Doubler embarking on her search through a host of private New York dance studios, each with a dance teacher's own "true" method of dance instruction. Meanwhile John Dewey's admonitions about the evils of mind-and-body dichotomies in education were ringing in her ears:

It would be impossible to state adequately the evil results which have flowed from this dualism of mind and body, much less to exaggerate them. Some of the more striking effects may, however, be enumerated. In part bodily activity becomes an intruder. Having nothing, so it is thought, to do with mental activity, it becomes a distraction, an evil to be contended with. For the pupil has a body and brings it to school along with his mind. And the body is, of necessity, a wellspring of energy; it has to do something. But its activities, not being utilized in occupation with things which yield significant results, have to be frowned upon. They lead the pupil away from the lesson with which his "mind" ought to be occupied; they are sources of mischief.[7]

This sounds like a blueprint for a rationale for dance in the university and a road map for introducing the affective domain into physical education. Part of H'Doubler's task would be to articulate the links between mental activity and physical activity, to delineate the ties between an engaged mind and a knowing body. H'Doubler's own writings also attempt to address the misleading dichotomy of mind and body. Her approach is to highlight what she defines as the "kinesthetic sense," which according to H'Doubler "reports to the mind the exact state of muscular contraction, the range of joint movement and the tensions of the tendons in any movement."[8] She stresses the unifying function of the kinesthetic sense as providing a means for integrating inner and outer experience. For H'Doubler this fusion of inner and outer experience produces the fullest meaning in an art form: "If inner and outer rhythm are one, communication is rich and complete, if not the dance is likely to be too physical, too much of the body rather than the mind through the body."[9]

The dancing body had to be shown to yield "significant results," products beyond the quantitative gain in individual muscle strength or range of joint motion that women's physical education had traditionally charted up until now. The products also had to be more profound than mere amateur dance shows like the ubiquitous May Fêtes of college campuses.

Here, too, Dewey's insights must have led H'Doubler, for "Thinking in Education" concludes with the following summary, which sounds tailor-made for H'Doubler's conceptual task:

Thinking is the method of an educative experience. The essentials of method are therefore identical with the essentials of reflection. They are first that the pupil have a genuine situation of experience—that there be a continuous activity in which he is interested for its own sake; secondly, that a genuine problem develop within this situation as a stimulus to thought; third, that he possess the information and make the observations needed to deal with it; fourth, that suggested solutions occur to him which he shall be responsible for developing in an orderly way; fifth, that he have opportunity and occasion to test his ideas by application, to make their meaning clear and to discover for himself their validity.[10]

This inductive method of knowledge acquisition is precisely how understanding proceeds in dance, as the body and the mind assimilate the information that leads to increasing physical mastery of the dancing body.

THE SCIENTIFIC METHOD

This entire scenario, really the scientific method of proffering and testing a hypothesis, can be read as an outline for H'Doubler's classroom systems. She was notorious for never demonstrating for her students, for teaching in a manner absolutely antithetical to the follow-along dance methods she had so disliked in the prevailing Sargent School and Chalif systems. This was the dance equivalent of giving them "a genuine situation of experience," a "continuous activity in which (s)he is interested for its own sake."[11] For H'Doubler this would eventually mean her students' individual testing on their own bodies of a certain movement impulse and their private discovery of how the activity this investigation inspired might lead them across the floor or into cutting a wide swath of movement through the space of the dance studio. "You are the only recipient of your own impressions," she was fond of telling her students.[12]

H'Doubler also always posed "genuine problems that developed within this situation as a stimulus to thought," prodding the students to test more fully the kind of movements they might improvise within the spatial, rhythmic, and stylistic parameters she had set. Finally, each student arrived at movement solutions suggested by her experimentation, ideas that were repeatedly tested in the studio to see if and how they answered the movement problem H'Doubler had initially posed. H'Doubler thus shaped her methodology of dance education into a Deweyan process of experience. Far more than just a teaching method, however, Dewey's framing of experience and aesthetics suggested to H'Doubler how dance could be similarly taught and shifted from the realm of exercise into the aesthetic: "Because experience is the fulfillment of an organism in its struggles and achievements in a world of things, it is art in germ. Even in its rudimentary forms, it contains the promise of that delightful perception which is esthetic experience."[13] For an educator in search of a dance content with an educational force, a dance that could become a free and universal form of communication, Dewey's reassignment of where the value in art and education lay was foundational.

H'Doubler understood that Dewey's points in the 1916 *Democracy and Education* had the profound simplicity of educational truths that extend beyond mere discipline boundaries. For example, Dewey's elucidation of the educator's role fits perfectly with how H'Doubler constructed her role in the dance studio: "The educator's part in the enterprise of education is to furnish the environment which stimulates responses and directs the learner's course. In the last analysis, *all* that the educator can do is modify stimuli so that response will as surely as is possible result in the formation of desirable intellectual and emotional dispositions."[14] H'Doubler's entire classroom posture, in fact, was built around this notion of furnishing a stimulating environment, with the students self-correcting as they responded to movement problems and kinesthetic dilemmas posed to them by H'Doubler. In large measure she was leading students into discovering how they could use their own bodies as stimuli and modulate their physical responses to the essential limitations nature exercises on bodies in motion. This heightened attention to the effect of internal mental stimulation on the external movement of the body also prompted an awareness of the fundamental integration between the dancer's intellect and her responding body. To make the body expressive, one first had to reestablish these forgotten paths of communication.

While H'Doubler was attending Dewey's seminar, Dewey himself was beginning to work with movement analyst Dr. F. Matthias Alexander, an Australian who had an unusual and interesting theory as to the cause of most contemporary ailments. More important, Alexander also had a technique for treating them. Dewey reportedly was deeply impressed by the practical benefits and soundness of Alexander's teaching. He soon began regular lessons in Alexander Technique and continued to have them at intervals for many years.[15] This experience seems to have been pivotal in confirming his belief in the deep connection between the psychological and physical dimensions of existence. "Education is the only sure method which mankind possesses for directing its own course," Dewey wrote in his preface to Alexander's third book, *The Use of the Self*. "But we have been involved in a vicious circle. Without knowledge of what constitutes a truly normal and healthy psycho-physical life, our professed education is likely to be mis-education."[16] Here was Dewey's philosophy, ready-made for H'Doubler's linking of emotions and motion.

Dewey's flirtation with movement as a student and client of Alexander Technique was the closest he ever came to actual movement training. It suggests interesting parallels with H'Doubler's own light sampling of movement firsthand. One imagines that, had Dewey addressed the subject of dance directly (he omits it entirely from his discussion of individual arts in *Art as Experience*), these are the kinds of things he might have said.

Dewey did, however, envision a place for dance in his Laboratory School in Chicago, where he placed studies under three categories. In the first group were all active pursuits or occupations—modes of activity, both play and work, that appeal to children for their own sake and yet lend themselves to educative ends. Here is where dance would be found, and indeed, in 1904, the last year he was at the Lab School, "after it had moved into the School of Education Buildings and there was adequate and suitable space for such experimentation," the first steps were taken toward developing interpretive dance classes there.[17]

THE MECHANICS OF THINKING

Dewey's notion of the mechanics of thinking and the links between cognition and education offers a persuasive, if recondite, rationale for the value of the arts in education and art in science. In *Democracy and Education* Dewey argues for a broad view of thinking, one grounded in precisely the kind of creative problem solving that is essential to discovery and insight in the arts and sciences. Contained within the major educational objectives Dewey outlines are the erasing of dualisms, a linking of the scientific method and invention in the arts, and a fresh appreciation for experience as integral to thinking and learning. This shift to valuing the process over the product was one of Dewey's ideas that underlay H'Doubler's whole philosophy of dance education.

Within this process Dewey pinpointed the thinking skills that are cultivated as being particularly valuable. It was his underlying conviction that, because the learning process is the thinking process, for a student to learn she must first be taught to think. For Dewey at this early stage of work, thinking was best exemplified in the scientist's attitudes of mind and habits of thought, yet science would soon be joined by the arts as an equally potent model. H'Doubler's writings reveal her poised between these two Deweyan tenets—the scientific and the aesthetic models of inquiry.

In talking about "learning," "understanding," and "intelligence," there is a tendency to locate these activities as the products of exclusively "mental" activity or activity that belongs only in the domain of the sciences. Only recently have notions of "bodily intelligence," and an appreciation of how fully integrated physical and conceptual understandings are, permeated educational discourse. Here again Dewey's understanding guided H'Doubler, particularly in regard to the notion of how action must precede ideas. "Only when a man can already perform an act of standing straight does he know what it is like to have a right posture and only then can he summon the idea required for proper execution. The act must come before the thought, and a habit before an ability to evoke the thought at will. Ordinary psychology reverses the actual state of affairs," Dewey wrote in one of three introductions he drafted for Alexander's books.[18]

FALSE DUALISMS

The arts are prime exemplars of activities that thwart facile separations, what Dewey regarded as the false dualisms that plague much educational theory. Ironically, it may well have been Dewey's long-standing dislike for dualisms that led him to use the arts as a model for education. For it is in the arts that dualisms get resolved, where "means and ends, the instrumental and the consummatory, process and product, the contingent and the necessary, the irregular and the settled, the precarious and the stable, the subjective and the objective, no longer work at cross purposes, but mingle in harmony until consummation is achieved."[19] *Art as Experience* was still decades away from being written at this point, but *Democracy and Education* is replete with important ideas about how understanding and education proceed. These ideas deftly outline the fundamental stages of discovery, invention, and understanding in the arts, stages that correspond closely to scientific discovery.

This "soft sell" makes Dewey's arguments all the more persuasive, for in not attempting to be an advocate for the arts, Dewey emerges as their paramount champion, someone who articulates what they do almost without naming them. It is similar to the salutary outsider role H'Doubler assumed in the wing of education she reformed. Indeed, the persuasiveness of Dewey's observations about thinking in education stem from the placement of his focus steadily on experience. He alludes to the process of the arts essentially as a means of reinforcing his own theories about what he calls "intellectual productiveness," the method by which understanding proceeds.

Dewey establishes well his dislike of dualisms as he argues for a broadly defined notion of learning as the product of several stages of understanding. His use of artistic insight and creation as models for all education in fact anchors them far more firmly and paradigmatically as an essential part of the curriculum than if he were to have advocated directly for them. Similarly H'Doubler, in part because she was not a performing artist and did not have the stage in mind as the ideal end of dance education, was able to focus on what no one else had up until this point. Specifically, she was able to give students experiences, structured investigations in dance, so they came to understand themselves and their surroundings and to wonder at the world while making meanings through sensory information.

H'Doubler was knitting educational theory and classroom practice together, testing her educational themes in practice. If there was a single great idea behind H'Doubler's view of dance education, it was that the practice of dance in schools could be shaped and defined by educational theories.

DUALISMS AND H'DOUBLER

The arts, particularly the performing arts, defy dualisms, especially the splits between the "mind" and the "body" and between experience and thought. This is perhaps why the one dualism H'Doubler tried to split, but never really succeeded in, was that between movement training in dance and the performance of dance. Initially H'Doubler was only interested in giving her students the opportunity to explore dance movement. Eventually her students pushed her to allow for a modest, and at first fairly private, performance group of dancers.

H'Doubler used Dewey's insights to look more closely at how dance might be reconceptualized for education, while Dewey in turn was looking at the arts to see how education might be rethought along with our approach to thinking and knowledge acquisition. In this respect the arts are the implicit models that lie behind many of Dewey's observations about how the human organism learns, as well as his revelations of the false assumptions clouding much educational practice. Dewey, in fact, may have initially chosen the arts as a model for educational process because he knew so little about them firsthand. Consequently, he might have had a naive view of the arts as being a holdover from mankind's "simpler days," when everything was spiritually and practically functional. Whatever his personal understanding, however, the insights Dewey had into the functioning of artistic understanding were masterful because of their profound simplicity.

Implicit in Dewey's *Democracy and Education* is a broad and fundamental notion of creativity, knowledge, and thinking, a notion that spans both the humanities and sciences. "The operation is novel, not the materials out of which it is constructed," Dewey wrote of Newton's devising of his theory of gravitation. Noting that Newton's originality lay in the novel use to which he put familiar understandings by placing them in an unfamiliar context, Dewey concludes with apposite profundity, "The same is true of every striking scientific discovery, every great invention, every admirable artistic production."[20]

In acknowledging that invention, indeed creativity in the broadest and also most specific sense, lies in this "reframing" of the familiar, Dewey draws important links between the sciences, where invention is celebrated, and the arts, where invention is also fundamental yet often cloaked as something almost accidental rather than intelligently insightful. While this dimension of the arts did not particularly concern H'Doubler, she did incorporate improvisation into her dance classes as an important method for gaining experience in movement. Every aspect of dance she used echoed her belief in the intelligent insight all educational dance provides. While H'Doubler did not emphasize the term *creativity*, she clearly valued the creative art and gave it a significant portion of class time.

Intelligence is the fuel for scientific creativity, yet *talent* is often the term applied to this same act of originality and insight when it occurs in the arts. Dewey, rather than trying to argue for the similarity between the arts and sciences, merely conflates the processes and methods that are key to both. In doing so, he shows that on a fundamental level education is about magnifying the stages of this process of invention and making them into something predictable, repeatable, and ultimately teachable.

As he argues this point, Dewey repeatedly has to debunk many of the myths surrounding both art and science. "Only silly folk identify creative originality with the extraordinary and fanciful," he asserts; "others recognize that its measure lies in putting everyday things to uses which had not occurred to others. The operation is novel, not the materials out of which it is constructed."[21] Within this statement Dewey links the often perceived "frivolity" of art with the "hard" discovery of science. In so doing, he not only aligns the two domains but underlines the fundamental similarity of their methods and insights. Both make the familiar strange in the process of discovery.

For Dewey the goal of all education is to wrestle with the conditions of a problem firsthand, thinking as one "seeks" and "finds" his "way out." In much the same way that he roots his understanding of man's nature in a biological model, Dewey repeatedly uses the model of the arts as a similar kind of paradigm for how humans interact with and order their world. We tend to see objects and events not for their functions but for the use we can make of them in the furtherance of our own ends. "What the arts help us recover," according to Dewey, "is not prior knowledge, but instead prior experience, the world we once grasped in all its immediate glory."[22] The result is that on this level one gets a fundamental linking between the world of naturally occurring phenomena (the sciences) and the world of man-made phenomena (the arts).

A. A. Leath, a University of Wisconsin graduate student in biology who took classes from H'Doubler from 1949 to 1951, was one of H'Doubler's leading male students. Leath, who had a background in athletics, said it was apparent from how H'Doubler taught dance that she had taught sports first and also that she had a natural science background. "She had been a basketball teacher and there she taught the movements of basketball first. For example, before she would put the ball in your hands, you practiced the gesture of throwing the ball into the basket. She did the same thing in dance, had people lie down on the floor and begin moving there where they didn't have to worry about gravity or balance. Of course it was right up my alley, being a scientist. The scientist looks for what's there and appreciates it."[23]

H'Doubler's approach blended aspects of a scientific method with the kind of training through repetition and reflexive muscle response advocated by turn-of-the-century playground reformers, together with Dewey's emphasis on learning through doing.[24] In fact, in his chapter "Theories of Knowledge," Dewey attacks the dualism of activity and passivity in knowing, illuminating its flaws by referring to the biological basis of the brain as an organ of knowing that is tightly connected to the organs of motor responses. Linking this up directly with the notion of another false dualism, that between "purely physical" things and "purely empirical" ones, Dewey argues for the idea of continuity, for a connection of mental activity with the activity of the nervous system. "The older dualism of mind and body has been replaced by that of the brain and the rest of the body," he states, decrying both.[25]

Indeed, here Dewey depicts the brain as an adaptive organ linked to the environment via sensory stimulation. Experience is the transformative and educational force in both domains. In Dewey's model the studio and the laboratory begin to look very similar in their roles in fostering problem-solving thinking. "Only by wrestling within the conditions of the problem at first hand, seeking and finding his own way out, does [he] think," Dewey tells us about the individual. Without this vital dynamic exchange, Dewey cautions, "the attitudes which spring from getting used to and accepting half-understood and ill-digested material weaken vigor and efficiency of thought."[26] The arts and sciences are two domains where vigorous and efficient thought is kept alive through precisely the means of discovery and thinking that Dewey outlines and that H'Doubler subscribed to so systematically.

H'DOUBLER'S CLASSROOM AND THE EARLY INFLUENCE OF DEWEY

Was it just a happy accident that H'Doubler found such fertile theory as Dewey's for her first dance class? Probably not, for his Progressive Education ideas were a natural fit with creative dance—provided an educator like H'Doubler was willing to reshape her "lab" to test, in practice, what Dewey's key ideas of education were in theory. When Dewey left his Laboratory School in Chicago in 1904, interpretive dance was a significant curricular innovation on the horizon. Mayhew and Edwards, writing in 1936 in their comprehensive history of the Dewey School, noted: "The department of physical education in this school never fully carried the finer extensions of its meanings to their expression in the art of rhythmic movement as now developed in the esthetic and interpretative dance."[27]

In her first major book, *The Dance, and Its Place in Education*, written in 1925, H'Doubler outlines what she sees as the value of dance in education, and one may assume much of her argument here was based on points she used in persuading the university to offer a dance major the following year. That H'Doubler became the leading spokesperson for dance in education without ever having significant firsthand dance experience herself is, in some ways, analogous to the situation of John Dewey; like her, he had limited direct experience in the arts, yet he wrote with far-reaching perception about the larger issues of aesthetic experience.

The focus of *The Dance, and Its Place in Education* seems to be to bleed dance of as many of its "art" connotations as possible in order to stress its educational value, something a dancer would have had a very hard time doing. *Expressiveness, artistic,* and *aesthetic* are words studiously avoided in this book. Technical mastery and preparation for performing are also carefully skirted as goals, because they would have linked university dance too closely with professional theatrical dance of the time. Ballet was assiduously circumvented as well, possibly for the same reasons and also because it was the dance form of outdated European aristocracy as far as most Americans at the time were concerned. This new dance that was entering the universities had a more egalitarian ideal, the creation of a fully awakened contemporary individual.

Instead of borrowing one of these existing dance styles, H'Doubler fastened on her own hybrid of interpretive dance, gleaned from her observations of watching others teach. She joined the University of Wisconsin's dean of women in initially lauding dance as central to university education because of its ability to "give college women a habit that will carry beyond their campus days, a resource for happy living that can be done anywhere and without special equipment." H'Doubler in particular emphasized dance's virtue as a noncompetitive physical activity and as a means toward "developing a free and full individual." "Our real purpose is to teach boys and girls a philosophy of life," she wrote in her book. "The problem is how to keep alive the creative impulse in the child and help carry it over into the realities of adult life."[28]

As a result of H'Doubler's desire to teach a philosophy of life through dance, in *The Dance, and Its Place in Education* she tries to link dance with larger goals and values in society while ignoring its artistic attributes. She does not fully succeed at either. "The greatest contribution of dance is it frees man from jealousy and releases his energies for co-operation and appreciation of beauty," she writes in the book's concluding remarks. That this is a tangential rather than a primary goal of dance she seems not to have noticed. H'Doubler had become, in eight years, a passionate supporter of dance in education. It remained for the later philosophical writings of John Dewey to provide her with the larger rationale she would use in her next book to argue for the unique contributions the arts can make toward a democratic education, a democratic nation, and a democratic citizen.

Dewey saw art as "a record and celebration of the life of a civilization" because of its capacity to embody "the consummatory experiences of a people."[29] He saw aesthetic experience in particular as a great model, the kind of experience in which philosophers could discover the essence of experience as a "prolonged and continuous" interaction between an individual and her environment: "Art is neither merely internal nor merely external; merely mental nor merely physical. Like every mode of action, it brings about changes in the world."[30] In her classroom H'Doubler taught dance in the spirit Dewey suggests, as if it were one of the most vital subjects in the university. Her students believed it as well, and they frequently wrote papers on dance for their other academic classes, using the insights of their experience with H'Doubler as a springboard linking the physical and emotional with thinking and knowledge.[31]

ARTICULATING THE LINKS BETWEEN EXPERIENCE AND ART

The period of 1930 to 1940, the second decade of the dance degree program H'Doubler developed for the University of Wisconsin, was a momentous time for ideas about dance and education in America. It was also a significant period for the fledgling efforts that were beginning to secure a place for dance in the nation's universities. By 1936, graduates of the University of Wisconsin were teaching dance in fourteen universities, five teachers' colleges, six women's colleges, and many public schools throughout the United States.[32] A few years later, in the mid-1940s, almost all the heads of dance sections and divisions in the nation's universities and colleges were H'Doubler's former students. In less than twenty years since she started, H'Doubler would succeed in franchising dance education across America.

In 1940, six years after the publication of John Dewey's landmark aesthetic treatise, *Art as Experience,* H'Doubler published *her* definitive book on the subject of dance education, *Dance: A Creative Art Experience.* Beginning with its title, this book is permeated with Deweyan ideals and rhetoric. In Dewey's essays on art H'Doubler had finally found a vision for establishing dance's larger service to society. "This book is designed to show that dance is available to all if they desire it and that it is an activity in which some degree of enjoyment and aesthetic satisfaction for all may be found," she writes in the preface. "The future of dance as a democratic art activity rests with our educational system," she continues in her introduction.[33]

How openly did H'Doubler acknowledge Dewey's influence? In her first book H'Doubler had listed *Democracy and Education* as the only Dewey book in her bibliography. By 1940, however, her single Dewey reference was *Art as Experience.* Her bibliography annotation for this item contains only the following three cursory sentences: "The author relates art to all forms of living, government and democracy. The chapters 'The Natural History of Form' and 'Organization of Energies' and the discussions of abstraction and rhythm are of special interest to the study of dance. It is of great value for anyone concerned with any art."[34]

The more closely one reads both Dewey and H'Doubler, however, the more one realizes how, even though it was at times partially assimilated and contradictory, H'Doubler's understanding of Dewey was essential to her efforts to establish dance firmly in education. This is substantiated by H'Doubler's students and colleagues. Although none can recall her ever directly lecturing on Dewey, they agree that her esteem for his theories would come up repeatedly in her spontaneous discussions with students. Hermine Sauthoff Davidson, who was a student of H'Doubler's from

1928 to 1932, remembers having a slim, brown-covered copy of Dewey's writings. "It excited me to read it, and I carried it around with my other stuff," she said. "I don't know if it was required reading, but John Dewey was present and accounted for in our dance experience."[35]

Dewey's notion of encouraging the human personality according to its natural capacities and energies and in so doing "clos[ing] the gap between the organism and the environment" seems to have particularly appealed to H'Doubler.[36] H'Doubler introduced dance's capacity to do precisely this. Echoing Dewey, H'Doubler, according to Judith Alter, "believed that the fusion of inner and outer experience produces the fullest meaning in an art form. In dance she saw the creative process requiring the mind's expressive faculty to organize the motor and emotional impulses."[37]

H'Doubler begins her seminal *Dance: A Creative Art Experience* with two chapters that deal broadly with dance as an expression of society's and the individual's innate physical and emotional ways of understanding the world. It is a beginning reminiscent of Dewey's first two essays on the Live Creature in *Art as Experience*. Half of the remainder of H'Doubler's book, encompassing two chapters, is devoted to a discussion of form as the way in which experience in dance is organized; Dewey, too, devotes two chapters to form. However, in her efforts H'Doubler ends up narrowing the very definitions Dewey seeks to broaden. For example, this is what H'Doubler says about the appeal of the arts: "People go to the theatre to partake of emotional experience, to have their concentration on everyday affairs broken down and to be made to concentrate with the artists and live their experiences."[38] H'Doubler interprets Dewey far too literally here; his point about experience is that it is the "reward" of an interaction between a person and an environment and that it involves participation and communication for each individual. The experiences of others cannot be "lived" as H'Doubler suggests; they must be freshly undergone by each perceiver.

One of Dewey's main points in *Art as Experience* is that aesthetic experience resides *within* the context of our ordinary life experience. In these essays he is seeking to restore the continuity of aesthetic experience with normal processes of living. He expounds a theory arguing that experience that is unifying and fulfilling is, or can be, a product of all aspects of life, not just the fine arts.[39] So it is not, as H'Doubler infers, exclusively the *artist's* experiences audiences are living, but their own as well, stimulated by contact with the artist's work. In Dewey's words, "The work of aesthetic art satisfies many ends, none of which is laid down in advance. It serves life rather than prescribing a defined and limited mode of living." Dewey continues:

For to perceive, a beholder must *create* his own experience. And his creation must include relations comparable to those which the original producer underwent. They are not the same in any literal sense. But with the perceiver, as with the artist, there must be an ordering of the elements of the whole that is in form, although not in details, the same as the process of organization the creator of the work consciously experienced. Without an act of recreation, the object is not perceived as a work of art.[40]

Dewey's idea of perception is very complex. It suggests that the act of the connoisseur can be as rich with differentiation as that of the artist. H'Doubler's interest was more focused on the experience of the student as artist; critical perception and analysis of dance were never as important to her. Another key place where H'Doubler misreads Dewey is in discussing the essentiality of dance in education. In *Dance: A Creative Art Experience,* H'Doubler says there are two aspects to education, "one, the capacity to take in, to become impressed; the other, the capacity to give out, to express." This is a core concept for her, but again it is based on an incomplete understanding of Dewey's notion of the act of expression. "To know is the essential first step, but it is the expression of what we know that develops character and a sense of values," she continues. "It is through perception, intuition, feeling and conception that our personalities assimilate experience and work it up into our own substance and the world of thought, emotion and will. *Without this metabolism of experience damage is done to the emerging personality* [emphasis added]."[41]

H'Doubler makes it sound as if psychosis might be the inevitable consequence of thwarted art making, when in fact Dewey's point about expression is not this at all. For him the expressive object does not represent or stand for things in the sense of literal imitation; rather it "re-presents" meanings in experience. H'Doubler misses the subtlety of this point. "The real work of art is the building up of an integral experience out of the interaction of environmental conditions and energies," Dewey writes in *Art as Experience,* "The thing *expressed* is wrung from the producer by the pressure exercised by objective things upon natural impulses and tendencies. The act of expression that constitutes a work of art is a construction in time, not an instantaneous emission."[42]

Just as she takes the whole notion of expression and experience too literally according to Dewey's model, H'Doubler also views rhythm in dance almost exclusively in its strict musical meaning. Dewey's notion of rhythm in art belongs to the much larger sense, a biological sense, of "the ebb and flow of doing and undergoing."[43]

Yet even with these inconsistencies, H'Doubler's effort at being philosophical about dance in education marked a major breakthrough for herself as an educator. Her theorizing in *Dance: A Creative Art Experience* also indicated a breakthrough in the larger task she had given herself of seeing dance situated firmly in the university as a subject of both practice and theory. "I don't think H'Doubler was really ready for Dewey," her former student Margaret Mullen remarked. "She had a certain anti-intellectual side and that, mixed with her yearning to be respected, I think contributed [to the confusions in *Dance: A Creative Art Experience*]."[44]

For the next three decades H'Doubler's book was to be looked to as the mission statement for the nation's college and university dance programs. Its Deweyan rhetoric and emphasis on dance as experience rather than a means toward the product of a performance endeared it to academics, particularly dance educators. These individuals wanted a physical activity for women free from the masculine taint of competition and the moral equivocalness of the stage, yet at the same time rich with aesthetic value of the kind Dewey advocated.

H'Doubler's use of Dewey's ideas gave her approach to dance education a theoretical base that distinguished it from other fledgling attempts to situate dance in academia. H'Doubler was also distinctive in not focusing on performance and in making the development of self her steady focus, and she shunned the older formal, authoritarian, and militaristic models of gymnastic dance and mass calisthenic drills while other movement educators were incorporating them.[45]

Economically and socially America was in an unprecedented upheaval during this decade that saw the publication of *Dance: A Creative Art Experience* and *Art as Experience*. The Great Depression from 1929 to 1933 challenged American society to redefine itself. As one result, a new esteem was accorded the role of artists and the arts. Art was beginning to be seen as central not only to American culture but also to a changing and new American civilization.

Society at large supported this change, and in all the art forms new energies began stirring. Art was no longer presumed to be a monopoly of older civilizations or the wealthy. As Charles and Mary Beard noted in their influential historical overview of the period, the aesthetic quest was merging with the social quest, and the words *art, democracy,* and *culture* became more associated: "The image of a perfect society was not that of aesthetes in a museum, but of artists at their work. The discussion of art and beauty widened out to the schools of philosophy and the very nature of the aesthetic sense. Its sources and manifestations were plumbed."[46] This broader merging of aesthetic, social, and political discourses considerably facilitated dance's entry into the university.

This climate made for unique and lasting alliances between the arts and higher education. Not only the body politic but bodies themselves were the subjects of a new philosophy of organic unity. Long-standing hierarchical and, in the case of the body, puritanical beliefs about social order, male prerogatives, and the superiority of the intellectual over the corporeal, began to be challenged. Again dance was seen as the ideal way to combine physical and mental fitness. Throughout the 1920s and early 1930s the newly democratic art form of modern dance had also emerged in the concert halls. It was a distinctively American dance form that depended upon a personal movement vocabulary developed primarily by young women choreographers to express their unique identities as sentient individuals.

DEWEY AND MOVEMENT: THE ALEXANDER TECHNIQUE

As if literally enacting this notion of a newly integrated mind and body in himself, Dewey, a man emblematic of a finely tuned intellect, had become involved in a movement discipline known as Alexander Technique. In 1916, the same year H'Doubler encountered him, Dewey began experiencing a series of physical symptoms—stiff, sore shoulder and neck muscles and eye fatigue. Dewey scholar George Dykhuizen reports that from friends Dewey learned of Dr. F. Matthias Alexander. "Alexander believed that the development of man's body had failed to keep pace with that of his brain and nervous system. Brains were becoming very complex and bodies were as they had been when they served a much less complicated brain and nervous system."[47] The solution, according to Alexander, was to create bodily habits, including participation in sports, that could better serve a nervous system already adapted to the complexities of civilization. Dewey worked with the Alexander Technique a few years before he gave the series of lectures later published as *Art as Experience,* the thinking that so resonated with H'Doubler's ambitions. Dewey sensed physical truth when he saw it and, in the case of the Alexander Technique, when he experienced it firsthand; thus he agreed to write about it in these introductions to Alexander's writings.[48]

The premise of the Alexander Technique was that modern man's brain and nervous system were in disharmony because of what Dewey called the development of conscious intelligence. "The remedy is to let intelligence sleep," he wrote in the introduction to Alexander's first book, which outlined Alexander's method for retooling the balance between the brain and the nervous system through exercises to correct one's posture and balance.[49] Dewey was so impressed by the practical benefits and soundness of Alexander's teaching that he wrote introductions to Alexander's next two books. Dewey also readily acknowledged that he owed the concrete form of certain of his ideas to his experience of this movement training. Basic among these ideas was a thoroughgoing acceptance of the principle of mind-body unity. Dewey, like Alexander, believed this was the missing link in the current theories of both physiologists and psychologists.[50]

"Men are afraid, without even being aware of their fear, to recognize the most wonderful of all structures of the vast universe is the human body. They have been led to think that a serious notice and regard would somehow involve disloyalty to man's higher life," Dewey wrote in his introduction to Alexander's first book. He stressed, however, the need to link this training in free physical action and the corresponding expression of emotions to the intellect: "[The exercises in physical action and emotional expression] are means, not ends, and as means they are justified only in so far as they are used as conditions for developing power of intelligence."[51] Here was a movement-based exploration of Dewey's philosophy, which anticipated H'Doubler's fuller linking of emotions, dance motion, and intelligence.

Dewey's theories articulated issues about art in a way that provided the blueprint and theoretical basis for H'Doubler's vision of dance's place in the university. Had he set out deliberately to champion dance, Dewey could not have done a better job, for it was precisely because of the broad and sweeping scope of his rationale that it worked as well as it did. While his focus may have initially been to explore the inadequacies in philosophers' regard of art, he also spoke to another just-emerging audience eager for a means to make dance more central to American education now that the last encumbrances of Victorian Puritanism were fading away.

In positing aesthetic experience not as the passive contemplation of art but rather as active and dynamic, Dewey dignified the essence of art not as artifact but as action. Suddenly the developing and experimental activity that surrounds creation and perception in the arts became the focus, and the links between the physical and intellectual became tangible. This is an emphasis in which dance, which leaves no lasting artifact, is particularly well served.

Writing in response to a strongly voiced criticism of *Art as Experience* in a review by Benedetto Croce in the *Journal of Aesthetics and Art Criticism*, Dewey noted the following, revealing something of his larger objective: "I have learned little from what has been written in the name of the philosophy of art and aesthetics, since it has seemed to me to subordinate art to philosophy, instead of using philosophy as an incidental aid in appreciation of art in its own language."[52] Indeed, in choosing not to subordinate art to philosophy but rather to do precisely the opposite, Dewey imparted a tone of generosity to his discussion, which allowed his ideas to be applied to dance—a situation that was particularly important given the long-standing neglect of dance by traditional aesthetics. Ironically, H'Doubler, in using Dewey's ideas, took things back a step, subordinating dance to philosophy, albeit Dewey's, more than she realized. Her impulse in this regard was the inverse of that of Dewey, who opened the Laboratory School because he wanted precisely what its name suggests, a laboratory situation where he could test in practice the psychological theories that influenced his experimental school idea. As Laurel Tanner notes in her study of the Laboratory School, others were also influenced by these ideas, but it was Dewey who felt keenly the need to test them in practice.[53]

The closest experience Dewey seems to have had with actual dance training was through his children's study with Mary Wood Hinman, a pioneer importer of national folk dances. Hinman ran a dance school in her family's large home in the same suburb of Chicago where Dewey and his family lived. She reportedly looked up one day to see Dewey standing in the doorway watching her teach. He explained that he "thought he'd see what was going on here. I can't keep my children away and it's the first time they've taken to any sort of study." He formally enrolled his trespassing children in her dance classes. Later he told Hinman she had "hit upon a big thing in education" and offered her a more professional teaching post.[54]

A RATIONALE FOR DANCE EDUCATION

Dewey was the first to describe the "forest" of art in terms clear and universal enough so that others, particularly those outside philosophy, could go in and describe the "trees" of specific art forms in relationship to educational goals. Dewey's vantage point in *Art as Experience* is that of someone interested in showing what aesthetics shares with other cultural subjects and functions such as science, religion, and technology.[55] Perhaps because he was not speaking directly *to* the arts, arts professionals listened all the more closely to him.

In removing separations and emphasizing instead the "common substance" that all the arts, and indeed all cultural subjects, share, Dewey provided a rationale that dance could use to establish itself in the university. What gave Dewey's ideas such utility for early dance educators was that he endorsed the need for a general logic of experience. For Dewey the aesthetic was a paradigmatic form of experience. He saw the creative act as the experience that best exemplifies not only the nature of man's encounter with existence but, more important, the successful culmination of this encounter.[56] Dance, because it is a temporal art form, has always been difficult to discuss in object-centered aesthetic theories.

Dewey was looking for an explanation of art, but more important to him was finding a way people could achieve self-realization through interaction with nature. Art for him provided the conditions in which humans could attain their highest fulfillment, an achievement necessary for the peoples of a mature civilization.[57] One way Dewey established his theory of self-realization through aesthetic experience was to explore the question of what function art served and then designate the pervasive quality that gave to experience the unity, order, and definiteness of character that we identify as "aesthetic." Through Dewey's direct articulation of what was fundamental in all forms of experience, dance could at last argue for respected status from the standpoint of being central to human experience rather than peripheral, different, separate, and isolated, as had been the case for so long. Dance would now lay claim to a unique ability to contribute to building the new social individual, well rounded and with flexible strength.

H'Doubler constructed the bridge between Dewey's philosophical ideas and higher education by writing her most important treatise, *Dance: A Creative Art Experience,* in the shadow of Dewey's *Art as Experience.* In so doing, she created a persuasive argument for the place of dance in American colleges and universities, taking Dewey's ideas from the realm of the general to the practical and specific in education. H'Doubler embraced Dewey's general approach, interpreting it most immediately as a focus on process over product. She also echoed his Laboratory School hypotheses: that freedom to express in action is a necessary condition of growth and that the test of learning is the student's increasing ability to meet new situations through habits of considered action that are social in character.[58]

H'Doubler's *Dance: A Creative Art Experience* is the first major argument for a consideration of dance as more than a mere subset of physical education. She posited dance as a key educational tool for learning about oneself, creative expression, and human behavior. *Dance: A Creative Art Experience,* while written in the new optimism of its time, sold more than thirty-six thousand copies, a record for any dance education book, in the forty years it dominated the literature of dance education.

Written just four years earlier, Dewey's *Art as Experience* reflects on art with his signature humanism and profound learning, relating it to ways of social life and forms of government, ultimately democracy. While he rarely used specific examples from art, Dewey, like H'Doubler, was creating a theory of art in a historical moment saturated with new models of what art and its role in society should be.

Dewey defined the artist as a person with a mind influenced by values and interests arising out of his society. With deft economy he sketched out art and the artist in their political and social context. Most important for H'Doubler and dance, Dewey identified the educative potency of the arts as their capacity to provide experiences that are exemplary in the consummatory pleasures they yield.[59] Historian Charles Beard regards Dewey's achievement as a momentous breakthrough: "Thus Dewey drew art into the mainstream of American history and philosophy, broke through the restraints of class and gave aesthetics an organic connection with the humanistic aspiration of society."[60] At few points in contemporary history has art been viewed as so central to American ideals. At few points could H'Doubler have found a moment so propitious for her ambitions and a philosophical base so perfect for dance in education.

A DEWEYAN APPROACH TO DANCE EDUCATION

The model H'Doubler created for dance in American higher education, shaped by Dewey's theories, dominated the field for nearly forty years. Even into the 1990s, many aspects of the dance curriculum she inaugurated continued to inform a number of the nation's college and university dance programs and the very identity of dance in higher education.

Among the most lasting of H'Doubler's Deweyan innovations was her shaping of dance education to focus on the qualitative immediacy of experience in dance. Instead of emphasizing preparation for a performance, or the methodical acquisition of rote skills, H'Doubler followed Dewey's lead and made broad, openly structured explorations in dance the priority of her classroom. She experimented with methods to make students attend to the qualitative experiences they had while dancing and while watching others dance, and then "try on" others' movements and reflect in a group on those experiences.

H'Doubler was trying to establish a model of dance education that could teach students to attend to the experience of "doing and undergoing" as they wrestled with movement problems. As part of this she was particularly sensitive to the use of classroom time, allowing the dance explorations she led the students into to unfold and resolve as needed. Dance classes in the university still generally stretch well beyond the standard fifty-minute class unit, often continuing for ninety minutes or, in the case of composition and improvisation classes, extending as long as two or three hours, so that students can explore material until they reach a satisfying culmination.[61]

As an educator H'Doubler also continually looked for ways to make the immediacy of dance educational experiences as intense and vivid as possible for her students. The studio itself was decorated like a Victorian parlor, but without furniture or mirrors. Long drapes lined the walls, ornate chandeliers hung from the ceiling, and pedestals stood in the corners. The idea seems to have been to create an environment to transport the students out of the ordinary, to lead them into a marked-off space where how the dance movements *felt* to each student was more important than how they looked.

To this day modern dance studios in colleges generally do not emphasize looking at oneself in the mirror nearly as much as ballet classes do, and often those university dance studios that do have mirrors have curtains that can be pulled across them. H'Doubler would have been gratified to know that today the notion of dance training as preparation for a performance continues to be the exception rather than the rule for most higher education dance classes. "[Just] because we teach a child to saw or plane, it does not follow that we expect the child to be a carpenter," Dewey once commented. "What we do wish is to make the child think—to question, to wonder."[62]

H'Doubler also initiated the educational practice of using dance to attune students to the expressive dimensions of life outside the studio. She was fond of telling her students that the best index she would have as to the efficacy of her dance teaching would be to contact them when they were fifty years old and see what effect the experiences of her dance classroom had had on their lives.

7

Structuring Experience
in the Classroom

Margaret H'Doubler Brings Dance
to the University, 1917–1926

A dance is the observable form of what the mind has created.
Margaret H'Doubler, University of Wisconsin classroom handout,
1953

WHEN H'DOUBLER INSTITUTED THE NATION'S FIRST DANCE CLASS in higher education, she had watched a few dance classes, sampled a couple, and felt bolstered, ironically, by the fact that she herself had never really studied dance, much less performed it. Like her theatrical contemporary Isadora Duncan, H'Doubler as a dance teacher is both a mystery and a legend. The respective artistic and educational breakthroughs both women's work initiated are established, but precisely how that work *looked* remains vague.[1] Like dance, the *performance* of teaching essentially vanishes the instant it is created, and it was in the act of teaching, and in the quality of the studio climate she created, that H'Doubler's impact began. In effect, then, the dance education researcher's challenge is to reconstruct a teaching "performance" that left behind few, if any, of the normal tangible artifacts of the performing arts, like critical reviews, essays, or photographs.

In addition to dance, H'Doubler's classroom was also where the major themes of late nineteenth- and early twentieth-century women's health, freedom, physicality, and public image became visible as a curricular force. Here in the classroom, in the exchange between teacher and her female students, these emerging issues about social identity and women's efficacy would be richly explored; they were the subtext for what transpired in that dance studio high up in Lathrop Hall. That larger context having been examined, this chapter will focus on the more specific issues between teacher and student as a still point in a rapidly changing new world.

The one aspect of H'Doubler's classes for which there is ample data is that of the educational transformation initiated in students. This transformation has been attested to by many of H'Doubler's students and colleagues in a general sense, while the step-by-step activities of an actual lesson remain elusive. As educator and psychologist Philip Jackson has noted, however, some of the most valuable educational exchanges involve "untaught lessons":

We all at some level are convinced that teaching makes a difference, often a huge difference in students' lives. . . . Yet we often have a hard time convincing others of that fact. As a result when it comes time to talk about how effectively our schools are functioning *or how well a particular group of teachers are doing their job we seem to forget what we know from personal experience* [emphasis added] and we wind up relying on evidence, such as achievement test scores, that completely ignores almost everything [meaningful] I have been talking about and alluding to here.[2]

Jackson's argument has particular importance in considering Margaret H'Doubler's classroom because, by her student's accounts, so much of her effective teaching happened outside of traditionally planned lessons and without producing test scores. Instead it crystallized in the individual experiences each student took away. While it is difficult to label them all "untaught lessons," because H'Doubler's planning customarily allowed for a certain amount of students' spontaneous responses to her initial instructions, much of what was learned was not part of an explicit lesson plan with anticipated outcomes.

This is not to say that H'Doubler did not have a *curriculum*, because she most definitely did. She had a curriculum in the broad sense in which Elliot Eisner defines it, as a series of planned events with "some aim, purpose, goal or objective even though it might be highly diffuse or general." H'Doubler practiced what Eisner and Dewey have called "flexible purposing," teaching by following what emerges in the classroom rather than by imposing a strict sequence of information to be transferred to the students.[3]

This chapter begins by looking at what Eisner calls "the operational curriculum," that is, what actually transpired in H'Doubler's classroom, but without the benefit of the live, direct classroom observation Eisner advocates. A relevant component to consider is the actual physical space of the dance studio—its appearance and ambience—as well as the special attire H'Doubler specified that her dance students wear. Additional aspects of this operational curriculum to be discussed are the student examinations H'Doubler administered as well as the extracurricular student performing group, Orchesis, which the dance students initiated. Finally, we conclude with what H'Doubler's students saw as enduring, several decades later, from this experience of dance education.

THE STUDENT VOICES: THE OPERATIONAL CURRICULUM

Ellen Moore studied under H'Doubler as a graduate student from 1949 to 1951, during the final years H'Doubler directed the dance program at Madison. She is apparently the only student of H'Doubler's to have made a detailed written description of a typical class, and as such her account makes a good starting point from which to explore H'Doubler's classroom.[4] The descriptions below are taken from two specific classes, H'Doubler's "Theory and Practice of Dance Technique," a ninety-minute class that met twice a week, and her "Movement and Its Rhythmic Structure," a fifty-minute class meeting three times a week. Both classes were for undergraduate and graduate students. As Moore describes it, H'Doubler's classes unfolded with the students being coaxed to teach themselves by solving a series of problems she gradually fed to them.[5]

Among the rare photographic images of H'Doubler in dance attire are two that likely date from 1917, the first summer she introduced interpretive dance classes (figures 2 and 3, pp. 17, 18). Wearing a heavy dark tunic that falls straight from her shoulders, with a tuck at the waist and extending to several inches below her knees, H'Doubler stands in a woodsy clearing barelegged and barefooted, her weight striding forward onto her right foot. In one photo both her arms are raised upward, slightly rounded at the elbow, and she tilts her head happily to the side as she gazes upward and out at some distant figure she might be greeting. In the second she appears in profile, one arm held at shoulder height as she gazes off to the side, her knees bent and her heels lifted slightly off the ground. The first image seems clearly posed and, given its date, was likely created to publicize the addition of this new subject, dance, to the curriculum. The second, however, looks as if it were taken in the midst of a simple exercise sequence; it is not about a pose but rather an action snapped in an instant of real physical motion. H'Doubler reportedly enjoyed taking her students outdoors to dance "in harmony with nature."[6] This must have complemented her Deweyan vision of man's biological drive to synthesize experience. It also echoed the Victorian linking of women with the natural world in a gesture at once risqué, because the women are wearing only their flimsy dance tunics in such a public place, and traditional, because their poses echo Greek statues and Isadora Duncan.

Actually, the most famous image of H'Doubler in the classroom was

Figure 24. Margaret H'Doubler, chalk in hand, lecturing to a class at the University of Wisconsin. She is standing next to the skeleton she always used when teaching. (Courtesy University of Wisconsin–Madison Archives)

taken much later; it dates from what is only referred to as "the 1960s." It shows H'Doubler dressed in a dark, conservative dress, with heavy metal bracelets slid up on each bony forearm as she gestures in front of a marked-up blackboard while holding a piece of chalk in her extended right hand (figure 24). Looking on attentively from the right, his profile exactly paralleling hers, is a human skeleton wired together and suspended from a hook.[7] As the typical image of H'Doubler the dance educator, this photograph of her in the classroom with a skeleton suggests the prominence of anatomy in her method of dance instruction. The image this photograph conveys is one of dance instruction as a serious, and very academic, pursuit. H'Doubler looks proper, even prim, as if this were a lecture class on physiology rather than a seminar on an art form that uses the unencumbered moving human body as its medium.

Figure 25. Margaret H'Doubler demonstrating in front of a skeleton in a master class at Mills College, Oakland, California, in the 1960s (Courtesy University of Wisconsin–Madison Archives)

As much as she may have been a budding educational pragmatist, however, H'Doubler was first and foremost a trained biologist from her undergraduate work, and her dance classes commenced with a detailed anatomical observation. H'Doubler would direct the students' attention to the model skeleton (figure 25). Before the students ever started moving she would ask them to observe the skeleton as she manipulated it through a certain action, such as the extension of the head into a backward arch. The students were asked to notice how all the adjacent movable joints were affected by the movement of this one part.

Anna Schuman Halprin, a leading H'Doubler protégé and her student in the early 1940s, said that H'Doubler might begin class by asking the students to look at the skeleton and observe the different ranges of movement that had to do with hyperextension, extension, and flexion. "And so we might look at the scapula and she might talk about the trapezius muscle that goes over the scapula. Then she would go to a muscle chart and talk about the three sections of the trapezius muscle and she would show us that when you contracted the muscle fibers they contracted diagonally into the vertebra. When you were done you would have a clear image of how the scapula supports your head and when you did it you would be working your body in the right way so it was very comfortable, natural, and right."[8]

Ellen Moore also recalls her fascination with how H'Doubler moved the skeleton's bones, noting that at times H'Doubler would show this same action of the joint on her own body, never as a model for the students to mimic, but rather as a way of offering "visual cues" for the students to formulate their own responses. H'Doubler's use of the skeleton in the dance studio seems to have been purely her own invention, likely a carryover from her anatomy classes.

With the problem thus presented, the students were next instructed to lie on their backs on the floor where, free from worries about balancing, they could test out specific joint actions in their own bodies, rotating each of their own arms, spines, or hips and notice how it affected the rest of their bodies. Moore, like several of H'Doubler's students, had dance training before coming to the University of Wisconsin. She notes of these experiments:

Our bodies often felt awkward and unknowing in the careful searching, despite our previous dance experiences. In familiar and natural movement patterns, we discovered new and often subtle choices of movements. We gathered information which caused us to have a new regard for these movements as materials of dance.[9]

Rather than seeming overly simplistic, this process of finding dance in the physical laws of the body generally seemed to appeal to the outright novice and more experienced dance student equally. Halprin still recalled with delight, sixty years later, the richness she discovered in the nuances of crawling, one of H'Doubler's favorite exercises. Giving her students kneepads, H'Doubler would instruct them to crawl at various tempos around the studio and in the process to attend to how the body adjusted. Halprin still sees this as revolutionary. "What other dancer at that time in history ever had anyone get down and crawl?" Halprin asked rhetorically. "That action is such a vital movement because it deals with coordination. It's the whole thing" (figure 26).[10]

In the initial years of H'Doubler's dance teaching there was little good dance training available anywhere in America, but by the late 1940s, when Moore arrived in New York, the dance scene was thriving with many excellent teachers such as Hanya Holm, Doris Humphrey, Charles Weidman, and Martha Graham teaching in their private studios. For those students, like Moore, who came to Wisconsin after studying with Graham, the initial contrast could be dramatic. Moore notes:

I was at first shocked and annoyed to have to stop, think, explore and dance without a model to watch. I did not want to give up the exciting speed (and anxiety) of a follow-the-demonstrator class. But the pleasure and relief of being able to put my concentration into my own rendering of a dance movement rather than an exact copy of someone else's movement gradually pulled me into the intricacies of Margaret H'Doubler's environment for learning.[11]

Moore's statement here about "the pleasure and relief of being able to put my concentration into my own rendering of a dance movement" captures well H'Doubler's approach to dance as an avenue for personal, but never free-form, expression. H'Doubler was in fact critical of some professional modern dancers, including Martha Graham, for using precisely too much of this "follow-the-demonstrator" teaching; she saw their work as inviting a slavish imitation of the director's personal style rather than cultivating each dancer's individuality. Halprin concurred: "New York studio training was about imitating movement. It's like brainwashing so you respond automatically. H'Doubler always thought that one dancer imposing her movement on another was autocratic to the psyche. She fiercely defended the right of each person to have their own individual expression—that was the core of her philosophy."[12]

As Halprin's statement suggests, in her classes H'Doubler was striving to draw out the distinctiveness inside each student. She began by working with a reduction to essentials that somehow caught that stage of innocence the poet William Blake regarded as simultaneously a beginning and an end.[13] In fact, in the arts a call for a return to fundamentals has often presaged innovation. Particularly in dance, some of the major experimental departures of the twentieth century have been initiated by a stripping away of stylistic mannerisms and a return to the essential movements of the body.[14]

THE CRAWL (FORWARD)

Figure 26. Sketches of one of Margaret H'Doubler's basic dance-class exercises—the forward and backward crawl. This figure drawing is one of a series by Bernice Oehler. Oehler developed her drawings from quick-action sketches she made of dancers in H'Doubler's class. (*The Dance, and Its Place in Education*, 1925)

(The last position of the backward crawl is the same as that of Fig. 1 with leg position reversed.)

Thus H'Doubler's use of a skeleton may well have also been a way of reintroducing her post-Victorian female students to their bodies. Becoming aware of something that has been slumbering for decades can be extremely difficult, yet visualizing it first can make it easier. At the time H'Doubler first began using the skeleton in her dance class, skeletons still had a curious iconography left over from the Victorian era. In antidance literature they were frequently used as images representing contagion and death from licentious social dance. They were also used as models in life drawing and painting academies of the time, one of the few socially acceptable means for visual artists, particularly women, to study the body accurately. Curiously, H'Doubler seems intuitively to have used the skeleton as a safe means into the risky territory of women's discovery and self-possession of their bodies. How interesting to turn a signifier of the forbidden into an emblem of progressive enlightenment!

H'Doubler's larger strategy was to use the mind as a conduit to the body. For example, she would have students work from watching a demonstration of hip rotation to feeling this action and then "seeing it" in their mind's eye on their own bodies. For her, dance's educational importance was its capacity to make individuals increasingly aware of movement principles and their sensations rather than training students for precise techniques. Davidson remembered that "the experience of anatomy class was persuasive. The body became a precious and remarkable tool, something to honor and respect, not only your own body, but anybody else's body whom you might have the responsibility to teach." Thus her class might be said to be a first step toward personal and social authority. In H'Doubler's model, movement expression results from the mover's concentration of physical and emotional energy.[15] While H'Doubler and her students never made this assertion directly, the links between behavior and emotions as related to the body and self-worth *were* talked about frequently in other contexts of H'Doubler's teaching. The following are representative statements from her own writing:

The body considered as the outer aspect of personality should be given as careful a study, as high a perfection of technique as the associated processes of thought and feeling. The most completely developed an individual is the one who has trained all his powers with equal dignity and consideration that he may be physically, intellectually and emotionally integrated.[16]

To integrate oneself within a group, and to cooperate intelligently with his fellow men, one first must feel the security and self-value which comes from integration within the self.[17]

This capacity of dance to allow individuals to know themselves is a recurrent theme in H'Doubler's teaching. It seems to have been one of the most enduring legacies she left her students. For those like Marion

Bigelow, who spent thirty-three years teaching in the dance program at California State University, Fresno, and Hermine Sauthoff Davidson, who joined the faculty of Ohio State University immediately after graduating as one of five dance majors in 1932 and who, at the age of seventy-eight, after decades of teaching dance, was elected to the Madison school board, in between competitive sailing and downhill skiing, the lasting lesson of H'Doubler's class was this discovery of personal strength and the efficacy it initiated in each of these remarkable women.

On rare occasions H'Doubler would herself demonstrate the action she wanted the students to explore. "Marge moved with a certain abandon, which was fun," Hermine Sauthoff Davidson remembers. "When she would feel like demonstrating a little bit (and she would never do it for more than eight or ten counts of anything), she was charming. She had this native energy and remarkable coordination, yet she never would have called herself a dancer."[18]

More often, however, H'Doubler would demonstrate on a student's body—for example, grabbing hold of a student's leg and, with what Moore remembers as a gentle but firm twist, rolling the student over in a matter of seconds from face up to face down as each part of her body responded in succession to the twist. "Amazed, we attempted in partners this curious feat," Moore writes. "We found out how much energy it took to flip the other person's weight and how much we could relax to be flipped, and were resoundingly convinced that a rotating leg could cause the hips, spine, shoulders and head to roll 180 degrees."[19] At the age of seventy-nine Anna Halprin still clearly recalled this exercise and demonstrated the magical successional linkage of body parts a movement initiated by the crossing over of a foot might trigger.[20] Hermine Sauthoff Davidson suggested that this emphasis on physically resolving a movement impulse in the body came directly from the children's movement classes H'Doubler had observed Bird Larson and Alys Bentley teaching in New York. "I don't know what she learned there, except for being convinced that there was a need to do a follow through, that movement initiated had to be pursued through the structure of the body from whatever the initiation point. And that was the whole basis of the stuff we did."[21]

So much of what H'Doubler used both as theoretical and practical information in her early years as a dance teacher came very directly from things she had just learned herself. The whole structure of her technique class, having the students lie on the floor and explore sequential motion in their bodies, harkened back to what she had seen in New York. The theoretical underpinnings of her rationale for how dance could be made an educational part of the curriculum came from John Dewey's theories about education, art, and experience. It seems H'Doubler had neither the time nor, initially, the inclination to thoroughly digest or completely

Figure 27. Two of Margaret H'Doubler's students, Julia Post and Lucille Everett, in "The Bee and the Rose," part of H'Doubler's first Dance Drama, 1918 (State Historical Society of Wisconsin. WHi (X3) 29037)

reinterpret these ideas. Perhaps this was why she was able to preserve such excitement about what she was doing. At least for the first several years of her teaching, this information was still essentially as fresh for her as it was for her students (figure 27).

When H'Doubler introduced a sequential roll by grabbing a student's leg as a model, the next step would be for students to try to replicate this fluid roll themselves by lifting one leg twelve inches off the floor and repeating the roll. H'Doubler would instruct them to notice how their shoulders, head, and pelvis dropped in response to gravity and how what she called the "feeling tone" or quality changed as they sped up or slowed down their actions. Apparently the students learned in this way to attend with minute detail to anatomical shifts. As Moore notes:

Moving very deliberately, we examined the mechanics of the roll in more detail. We observed that no lift of any body part was possible without downward pressure: lifting the right leg initiated downward pressure of the other leg; rotating the right thigh could not cause the weight of the pelvis to tilt without very strong downward pressure in the left leg. We felt strong contractions of left gluteal muscles pulling the left hip joint open and the left thigh down hard at the moment of greatest lift of the right side of the pelvis.[22]

Describing movement muscle by muscle like this makes for tedious reading because it translates a few seconds of activity into a string of imprecise and difficult-to-visualize words. However, the point Moore makes, after several paragraphs of painstaking description, is that H'Doubler's larger goal was to arrive at a pace in class where students' "intellects, feelings and motor responses could progress together so that they could enjoy as much as possible what she called an integrated response."[23]

Moore's recording feat attests to H'Doubler's effectiveness in getting students to attend to and recall movement detail in this way. Yet it is interesting that H'Doubler, in her quest for naturalness in the body, would aim for a certain *un*naturalness through this synchronization of three levels of awareness—intellect, feelings, and motor responses—that are customarily presented as distinct by the dominant culture. Five decades later one of H'Doubler's major disciples, Anna Halprin, would marry synchronized awareness with the psychological aesthetic, prevalent in the 1960s, of being present in the moment. For H'Doubler in the post-Victorian Midwest, however, this meshing of awareness was biological in the extreme. She often spoke to her dance students about the chain of command between nerve impulses and understanding, of what she called "transmission of nerve impulse into conception, motor response, kinesthetic feedback, perception, comprehension, evaluation and initiation of new motor response."[24]

Science rather than art seems the context and means of justification H'Doubler was using for dance education. Her rationale could have been complicated: the scientific model was the standard by which academic legitimacy was conferred at the time; John Dewey's discussion of aesthetic experience was grounded in biology, H'Doubler's own undergraduate field of study; and H'Doubler was repeatedly replicating, in her teaching, a scientific path of inductive discovery. After all, it had been in watching Alys Bentley's students experiment on the floor that H'Doubler first saw the possibilities of creative dance for college women: they could make discoveries about the kinesthetic possibilities of their own bodies. Rendering the private public in this way makes for an empirically grounded and uniquely persuasive pedagogy.

Lacking any real dance training herself, H'Doubler also created novel means to help students attend to movement in their bodies. After initial physical explorations on the floor, H'Doubler would give each student a blindfold and have them execute different movement instructions without seeing. Like her use of the skeleton as a demonstrator, H'Doubler's blindfolding of her students was another means to develop these women's awareness *inside* their bodies, to render women's bodies, so long experienced as objective, subjective. She was also, although not consciously, suggesting that learning could be physicalized and that the place of the student *body* in American higher education could be looked at in a new regard. Indeed, Moore recalls that H'Doubler's sensitizing of our "kinesthetic sense soon made it as important to me as my eyesight," and that by eliminating visual data one attended more closely to kinesthetic information about movement:

The kinesthetic data from the proprioceptors in our muscles, tendons and joints told us the intensity, duration, location, direction and amplitude of our energy release. Part of the process in class was constantly to compare this data with our understanding of the verbal directions, then to adjust our movements until we were satisfied that they were our most accurate response to the directions. In this way, we learned to analyze and describe motor response and to practice evaluating objectively the details of our own performance. We gained confidence in our judgments and came to relish the complex kinesthetic symphonies from our muscles, tendons and joints when they were being moved sensitively.[25]

The concentration and respect H'Doubler was able to elicit from her students must have been extraordinary. It is difficult to imagine even the most devoted dance students today "relishing the complex kinesthetic symphonies from their muscles, tendons and joints" for even a few minutes, let alone for nearly three hours of weekly class meetings. Helen M. Niehoff, who had been teaching dance at the University of Nebraska, came to the University of Wisconsin to work under H'Doubler in the late 1920s, and later went on to teach dance at the University of Chicago, recalls little of the specifics of H'Doubler's teaching, but like many other alumnae she retains a vivid anecdotal memory of H'Doubler's enthusiasm for dance and its value in everyone's life:

One evening three of us dance majors who were rooming together in very simple quarters, invited Miss H'Doubler to come have supper with us . . . and she was so full of life and fun she would finally realize it had passed midnight, and when she got home and realized the time it was, she called us to apologize to all of us who were still in seventh heaven from her lovely, generous, sharing of her joy of living! I get choked up thinking back of many, many ways this wonderful woman shared her wisdom, her belief in dance for a good life and her joy of living![26]

The content of one's teaching is of course important, but the repeated sentiment that it was H'Doubler's persona that made her lessons extraordinary comes through again and again in the accounts of her students. It may well be that in a discipline like the performing arts, one that requires personal risk-taking on the part of each student, and at a time of high-risk innovation when such a subject is just entering the curriculum, this kind of charismatic leadership and dedication is essential. Jane Eastham, who studied under H'Doubler in the 1940s and continued a close friendship with her up until her death in 1982, recalled with amusement H'Doubler's indomitable spirit. "I remember once we all dragged into dance class very droopy and tired and Miss H'Doubler was so annoyed," Eastham said.

"She ordered us all to exit immediately and come back in again energized and ready to dance!"[27]

"To work under Miss H'Doubler, it was just inspirational," recalls Edith Boys Enos, who studied with H'Doubler from 1922 to 1926 for her bachelor's degree and in 1932–33 for her master's:

Anyone who studied with her would probably say that she was really the greatest professional inspiration that anyone had come in contact with. . . . She wasn't the kind of teacher who was just in the classroom and then good-bye, you never saw her again. We saw her all kinds of times a day, and we'd run into her in the hall, and she'd say, "Oh, by the way I just thought of something," and she'd give us an idea that had come to her.[28]

H'Doubler apparently ruminated on her dance classes continuously, stopping students to follow up on something from an earlier class, as Enos says, and at other times appearing lost in thought about a movement exercise as she walked across campus. Setting up the conditions for making student investigations physically safe was also always a concern for H'Doubler, so kneepads were distributed and all students were instructed to wear them. Moore reports that as much as students complained about their kneepads continually coming untied, H'Doubler insisted they be worn for safety during floor explorations, like the crawling exercise Halprin described.

It was only after a good portion of class time had been given over to these kinesthetic investigations that H'Doubler turned to what could be more readily recognized as dance. Here, with the masterful improvisatory musical support of accompanists such as Beatrice Hellebrandt, Norma Behrens, Joe Hawes, or Shirley Genther, played from a grand piano in a corner of the studio, H'Doubler would direct the students.[29] She would tell them to execute a rotary action and to remember the way muscles and joints worked in this action on the floor. Then the students were told to continue the gesture through the spine and shoulders until they could wind into and away from the floor, varying their speed at will as they made the movement a fluid and almost reflexive response to the music, freezing suddenly in midmotion when H'Doubler shouted, "Hold!"

Although her experience as a choreographer was even less than her minimal experience as a dance student, H'Doubler would direct the class into the choreographic shaping of dance phrases after the floor explorations. Watching the students manipulating this structure, she would ask them to determine the moments in the phrase they had been executing when "their efforts were strongest."[30] These moments then became the beginning of the sequence. Continuing the same process based on student findings, H'Doubler would next ask the students to count the number of beats their version of this phrase consumed until finally, after the students had told her how many, she chose one of those lengths of phrases for the whole class to learn. By Moore's account this imposed order was as enjoyable as the freedom had been earlier: "We discovered the satisfaction of staying within the established timing of each movement as we performed the phrase to the music."[31] It takes substantial leadership by a teacher to shift goals suddenly from open-ended to narrowly defined exercises and keep the students actively involved and appreciative of the virtues of both. H'Doubler seems to have succeeded at this repeatedly.

After encouraging the students to practice again and again the translation of the original floor exercise into a standing and vertical dance phrase, H'Doubler would select one of the student's phrases and note its rhythmic and locomotor patterns on the board. She abbreviated the dance phrase into a system of movement shorthand she devised, indicating what the legs were doing, the counts, accents, weight change, and the general locomotor actions.[32] To this day a grid of H'Doubler's chart is affixed to the chalkboard in the fifth-floor dance studio in Lathrop Hall, a testament to how institutionalized her method of teaching became at the university. While this chart makes little sense to those unfamiliar with H'Doubler's system, Moore credits it with helping H'Doubler achieve her goal of assisting the student dancer's mind and body to work together.

Marge was absolutely integrated in endlessly teaching the whole package as she went along; what the anatomy is doing, how the laws of motion and gravity affect it, how that works in the body, and how it makes us feel.[33]

When she did not have an accompanist, H'Doubler would use records, Davidson says. "We did a lot with Chopin or Brahms or Bach suites. She also used folk-dance materials, and I later realized these may have come from Burchenal." H'Doubler recognized the importance of music in dance education classes early on, teaching a special class in rhythmic analysis for dancers, but here again Davidson reports her use of it could be idiosyncratic.

[Rhythmic Analysis] was based on musical analysis, except Marge didn't use notes. I always faulted her for this, because all of us had some musical training either in school or in music lessons and were used to quarter notes, half notes, and bar lines and musical signatures. But Marge felt that a visual system using dots and dashes was more meaningful. But the minute I left Madison I never used it again.[34]

Halprin, however, calls H'Doubler's rhythmic analysis "ingenious." "I used her way of rhythm—dots and dashes on paper or chalkboard— forever," Halprin says. "She would talk about the beat and then have us take a partner and tap out the rhythm on a partner and feel it in our own body. It was incredible how she always related rhythmic analysis to movement."[35]

The next stage of H'Doubler's class—and this corresponds to the standard progression of most dance classes in the late twentieth century—

was to have the students cross the floor, performing the agreed-upon pattern with the addition of greater flexion in the leg to add height to the hop, better extension of the other leg, and perhaps covering more space by stepping out. The methodicalness of this progression reportedly erased much of the anxiety usually associated with this "going across the floor" section of class. Students were so involved with stretching the parameters of their phrase, says Moore, that the anxiety of being exposed was minimal.

H'Doubler's add-a-challenge method seems to have been expertly timed to maximize student engagement and minimize self-consciousness and self-doubt. The class climaxed with H'Doubler inviting the students to play with moments in the pattern where timing might be varied and to stretch other aspects of the phrase through improvisatory exploration. "As involvement deepened, we lost our fears of trying new things, and [we] were excited with our own improvisations," Moore says. "Our bodies, of course, wanted to go on and on."[36]

Interestingly, H'Doubler customarily wrapped up the class with a verbal discussion of what had transpired. In the course of these conversations the achievements of the class were summarized, and often H'Doubler said something of her underlying educational philosophy. "Miss H'Doubler didn't want our education to be piecemeal," Edith Boys Enos says. "She wanted everything to be related. In other words she wanted dance to be related to us and to life and to history. She was fond of saying, 'There's the philosophy of the dance, there's the theory of the dance, and there's the science of the dance'—those three categories. But she wanted our understanding and interest in the dance to be related to our own lives and to the education that we were getting." Moore recounts that after this kind of philosophizing the class ended with mutual applause.[37]

This idea of allowing time for immediate small- and large-scale reflection is very Deweyan, yet it also parallels the model of how live performances in the arts are usually followed by critical reviews and the evaluative chatter of the audience in the lobby. By all accounts, however, the tone of what H'Doubler said was generally supportive. She tended to summarize what had gone on rather than make aesthetic judgments about the merits of the student efforts. The discussions and the movement exercises were paced in H'Doubler's class in a way that sounds remarkable to someone experiencing it secondhand. Like a conductor shading loud and soft, fast and slow passages, H'Doubler as a teacher seemed to orchestrate the communal mental and group energy in the studio. The challenges of what she was asking the students were substantial, both in terms of mental attention to their bodies and physical submission to sensation, and yet the students trusted and followed her readily.

The loudest dissenting voice among the eleven alumnae interviewed is that of Margaret Jewell Mullen, chair of Dance at Stanford University in the late 1930s, who, interviewed in her eighties, vividly remembered the plight of those for whom H'Doubler's methods were *not* magical. She recalls that H'Doubler's use of improvisation was "very painful for many people who didn't feel that they had enough technical background." She also says that H'Doubler, in telling her students what to do, often selected those whose movement had been very good and offered *them* helpful criticism:

She had a class of physical education majors who were required to take dance. Most of them hated it. They felt awkward, they felt set apart. They simply did not want to dance and didn't want to go in the studio. One day she said, "I want you just to do what you feel; dance what you feel." One of the girls, who was a great soccer star, immediately dropped to all fours and mooed her way behind the drapes. People fell apart and Miss H'Doubler was very angry. She was humorless. . . . She expected people to be enthralled by dance and it was almost impossible for her to recognize the fact that there were people who did not want to dance.[38]

According to Mullen, H'Doubler worked magic with those who were already passionate about dance. "You had to be ready to be dedicated in order to engage her attention," Mullen says. "Otherwise she went ahead with her own business. You could rise or fall on your own."[39] Davidson partially confirms Mullen's memory of the physical education majors' reaction, admitting, "We dance majors were kind of smug. We sort of self-elected ourselves as kings of the kingdom and around Lathrop . . . we thought we were the anointed, because we were doing this rather new thing, and doing it intensely."[40] Commitment to the art form of dance, along with ability, are two essential criteria for success in the world of professional dance as well, and ironically in this regard the elements for success in H'Doubler's educational dance were similar to those in the professional dance world from which she had set herself apart.

Hermine Sauthoff Davidson, in recalling that the challenges of H'Doubler's dance classes were often more philosophical than technical, said simply, "The movement didn't have fire . . . exciting movement is what fires us as dancers and that wasn't a part of Marge's thinking. It wasn't a part of her vision of how to train dancers." In fact Davidson recalls really sweating for the first time in a dance class *after* she left Wisconsin to study at the Graham studio in New York:

The Wisconsin technique was, I thought, a great emphasis on a follow through and on a relaxation technique, not on demanding footwork, not on extending a range of movement. . . . You could have been pushed, had you been made to do the footwork appropriate to jumping, let's say. But it was just not pushed enough. The technique for flexibility was fine, but if you didn't have good flexibility or strength, you weren't encouraged to [develop it]. . . . Any idea of exploring falls, for instance, going into the floor and returning, using the floor as a rebound, were just not part of the thinking.[41]

Reviewing the data on those who studied with H'Doubler reveals that her method of dance teaching may have been best at creating teachers. Certainly hers was a pedagogy that offered a strong model of how one could teach modern dance. Within the first several years of the start of dance in the women's physical education curriculum at the University of Wisconsin, literally hundreds of women studied with H'Doubler, scores became teachers, and only a handful went on to professional careers as dancers and choreographers.[42]

Yet Anna Halprin, who did go on to a very influential career as a teacher, choreographer, and dancer, recalls H'Doubler as being very supportive of her students if their lives did take them into professional dance after leaving Madison. "No one could have supported me more as a performing artist than Miss H'Doubler," Halprin said. Halprin found in H'Doubler's method the seeds of choreographic self-discovery and the honoring of ordinary gestures as the material of dance—two discoveries she would later use to launch one of the nation's most influential workshops for postmodern dancers and dancemakers.[43]

For decades these women of Madison were the pioneers and leaders in the field of American dance education. For H'Doubler this was as it should be. She never saw her program as a stepping-stone to a professional career in theatrical dance. Quite the opposite was true. She once confided to Mary Hinkson, when Hinkson anxiously asked her if it was necessary to be trained as a dancer in order to succeed in dance, "Of *course* you don't have to dance, you can just teach! You can be a wonderful teacher!"[44] This was true for H'Doubler, but she was the rare exception, not the rule.

No other leader in American dance education could have attained professional respectability as H'Doubler did without having studied dance. Almost every alumna interviewed had an anecdote to relate about H'Doubler's active *dis*interest in the world of professional dance. Mary Hinkson recalls the first time she and other Wisconsin students saw the Martha Graham Company perform in Madison:

Miss H'Doubler gathered us around, as she always did, and we had our wonderful discussions, and when she was referring to this performance she encouraged us to share ideas. "Well, girls, what did you think about it?" And everybody had something to say. And Miss H'Doubler listened, and she nodded, and she commented here and there. And finally what I recall her saying, "Well, girls, it was really, really, very interesting, but a little too professional, I think."[45]

Hinkson makes this observation without a trace of criticism or anger. In her equanimity she implies that H'Doubler simply perceived two separate worlds of dance—theatrical and educational—with different goals, different means, different values. During these initial years in particular, H'Doubler maintained a strict divide between those who performed dance professionally and those who taught dance in academia; she saw them as two wholly different enterprises stemming from two distinct approaches to the use of the individual dancer. "Her philosophy was to help us grow as individuals and movement was the medium," Hinkson says.[46] So in the largest sense H'Doubler's accomplishment was not simply to transport dance from the professional stages of New York to the university; rather she *redefined* it, replicating it into a new discipline *for* the university. For H'Doubler the performer was a physical medium for the choreographer, while the educator and the student were authors of their personal statement through movement, a statement reflecting growth and understanding gained through experience.

The one professional modern dance artist whom H'Doubler regarded highly was expressionistic German modern dancer and choreographer Mary Wigman. Just prior to the outbreak of World War II, first H'Doubler, and later several alumnae of her dance program, visited Wigman's school in Germany. H'Doubler seems to have enjoyed in Wigman's dance a similar courting of the individual's voice to that which she emphasized in her own work. While Wigman trained students with a firm eye toward performance, she also pushed them to find their own authentic way of executing a spin or a spiral descent to the floor. Wigman's movement style was highly expressionistic; even the most basic of classroom exercises seemed to speak of deep emotions.

H'Doubler, too, strove for the use of movement as a public vehicle of personal expression. Both women shunned imitators; rather their quest was for innovators in the dance territory they had mapped out. "I imagine the appeal of Wigman for Miss H'Doubler was that she used improvisation and so was open-ended in her approach," Halprin said in explaining H'Doubler's particular affection for this concert dancer. "She disliked choreographers who wanted dancers to mimic them. It contradicted her core philosophy which was 'I heartily defend the right of each person to have their own individual expression.' "[47]

In subsequent years the independent German modern dance artist Harald Kreutzberg visited H'Doubler and her husband (Wayne Claxton and H'Doubler married on August 5, 1934) several times at Waymar (from "Wayne" and "Marge"), their home in Door County, Wisconsin (figure 28). In fact, it is Claxton's several pen-and-ink studies of Kreutzberg that are the male-dancer illustrations in H'Doubler's *Dance: A Creative Art Experience*. Claxton, who was thirteen years H'Doubler's junior, was a respected art educator, first at the University of Wisconsin and then at Wayne State University in Detroit, where he chaired the Art Department from

Figure 28. Wayne L. Claxton, Margaret H'Doubler's husband, and their pet dog, Ronnie, ca. 1940s (Collection of Louise H'Doubler Nagel)

1936 to 1959. He was known for his innovative approach to teaching, which stressed art as a way of life rather than as simply the methodology of making objects; in his life-drawing classes he asked models to dance, providing students a kinesthetic awareness of the human body.

In short order a crossing over between the two types of dance would begin at Wisconsin, with Louise Kloepper, a magnificent dancer with

Hanya Holm, joining the dance faculty at Madison in 1942. Nevertheless, H'Doubler continued to deemphasize the performative side of dance. Few alumnae, however, lived as fully in the world of New York professional dance as did Mary Hinkson, and thus her observations here carry a special insight:

Margaret H'Doubler was not a dancer. I think there was such a separation then— and I realize this is so changed—but there was such a separation at that time between people who were interested in performing as opposed to people who were interested in dance education. I mean, they were totally separate areas. . . . In the Graham company we were rare birds, the three of us who had been to Wisconsin, or even to a university.[48]

The reverse was also true, and once a student of H'Doubler had studied with dance professionals in New York she was viewed with cautious skepticism if she returned to Madison. Hermine Sauthoff Davidson recalls that after she had spent time studying with Martha Graham at the Bennington Summer School and in New York, she was invited to return to Madison to teach dance in the 1940 summer program at the university. "Marge H'Doubler was less enthusiastic than I hoped," Davidson recounts. "It was, I think, Chairman Blanche Trilling who persuaded Marge to invite me to teach. . . . Although Marge was skeptical that I had been indoctrinated by New York we had a good friendship and trust."[49] It is interesting that once she had her dance course "worthy of a college woman's time," Blanche Trilling did not disappear but rather continued as a low-profile force shaping change and growth in Wisconsin's dance program from behind the scenes, intervening when she felt it necessary.

For H'Doubler, sustaining this separation between dance as an educational enterprise, as she practiced it, and dance as a performing art, as emphasized in the professional New York studios, was fundamental. H'Doubler had defined dance education *in opposition* to dance as an art form, and to intermingle the two would have diluted the very values of dance in the university she had worked so hard to espouse. It is no coincidence that her first book is called *The Dance, and Its Place in Education,* for it was precisely inventing and sustaining such a place in education for dance that constituted H'Doubler's lifetime achievement.

In this book H'Doubler devotes almost as much attention to enumerating what is wrong with dance performances as she does to cataloguing the virtues of educational dance. She suggests bluntly that a teacher who focuses on a finished recital as her main objective may turn out a pretty show, but the price will be that she has made dance a "narrowing and stultifying" experience for her students. H'Doubler insists that truth and depth of artistic feeling cannot be gauged by external results. She suggests instead that the teacher of educational dance work to develop a broad appreciation in students for "all that is good and beautiful in life and art." The success of this kind of long-range education, she says, only becomes evident years later. "Dancing should always be an end in itself and the student should devote himself to the joy of this work without any ultimate consideration of whether or not it is ever worked into a public performance," she writes.[50]

H'Doubler's analysis here is only half right. She identifies educational virtues of dance with great insight, yet she is myopic in claiming that they are essentially absent from concert dance. Indeed, during the year H'Doubler was in New York, Isadora Duncan demonstrated in a performance on November 16, 1916, at the Metropolitian Opera House that the truth and depth of an artist's feelings *could* be gauged by external results. Aesthetic insight *can* be made manifest externally; that is precisely what great concert dance aspires to do. Then again, H'Doubler may not have liked Duncan's style of dance because it was too much the opposite extreme of antifrivolous and trivial—it was deeply serious emotionally. H'Doubler complains about dance that "requires much mental effort for its comprehension," claiming that it usually gives far less pleasure than "the simpler dance which leaves the minds of the audience free to enjoy its beauty."[51] Duncan's dance spanned the simple and profound in complex ways.

One problem is that H'Doubler never explains what her reference point is for this perception of concert dance as shallow and dangerous. Is she merely echoing the standard criticisms of the time about recreational and social dance, or has she some real basis for her complaints? It may be possible that H'Doubler the New Woman is eclipsed by H'Doubler the lingering Victorian conservative in this regard. She does go on about the educational and social evils of performing, in this instance for children, insisting that

the wise teacher will remember that a great harm is done to both the child and society when the grace and charm of the pupil are exploited, displayed and admired so that the pride of the parent in his offspring and of the teacher in her pupils may be gratified.[52]

This passage comes from the penultimate chapter of *The Dance, and Its Place in Education,* a section devoted exclusively to "The Problem of the Public Performance." There are valuable lessons here for advocates both of the arts and of educational change, for H'Doubler knew as clearly what she wanted as what she did not want. To effect curricular change in a performing art field, it seems one must know forcefully what one wants and not only tout the virtues of the new discipline but articulate with equal clarity how it differs from the noneducational profile of that activity and why those noneducational qualities are not educationally desirable.

Despite all these reservations about dance as a professional performing art, H'Doubler never retreated from advocating for dance as the means for introducing physical-educational insights in the university. After she discovered dance she never left it; instead she steadily moved away from women's sports until she was exclusively a teacher of dance.

Edith Boys Enos, in noting the difference between dance in the university and dance in the professional world, said: "At the University of Wisconsin, Miss H'Doubler considered dance as a medium of education and individual development, emphasis on the dancer, not the beholder. . . . The studio was never thought of as a stage, but as a space for movement."[53]

What seems more likely is that as a dance educator H'Doubler was neither a converter nor just a guide, but rather something between the two. "Her philosophy was to help us grow as individuals, and the medium that she used was movement," Hinkson says.[54] H'Doubler had arrived at a vision and a notion of the function of dance that she wanted her students to share. Davidson recalls that H'Doubler made clear her displeasure with those who did not: "A lot of us who had been sort of steeped in the idea that education was the use of dance figured we wanted to find out what the rest of the world was doing. And this sort of ticked Marge off."[55]

Margaret Jewell Mullen also ran afoul of H'Doubler, in this instance because she was determined to complete her two-year master's degree program in dance in one year. Mullen almost managed to do it, completing all the required courses by slyly going through the registration line twice and carrying double the normal number of units for two semesters, and H'Doubler never forgave her: movement experience was crucial to achieving the objectives of the master's program for H'Doubler.

She [H'Doubler] was very defensive about the dance major at Wisconsin being a two-year course and she was very strong in her feelings that no one could go for less than two years. I tried to explain my feelings that I had wanted one year. She didn't care for any part of that. . . . When I left at the end of the year, with my master's [in philosophy and the equivalent of a master's in dance courses but without the dance degree] in hand, Miss H'Doubler said that she of course could never recommend me.[56]

Mullen's typification of H'Doubler's classes is similar to Moore's in terms of the mechanics of what went on, but her interpretation of their merits differs significantly. For example, as to H'Doubler's encouragement of individual exploration of movement, Mullen says, "She did more instruction through words than movement. [There was] a great deal of self-expression and musical interpretation . . . it was essentially undisciplined." As to the anchoring of movement in anatomical demonstrations on a skeleton, Mullen states: "It was really very basic. She'd walk over to the skeleton and show you. It was not a sophisticated use of anatomy. . . . For her it was fairly blunt; [for example, the spine] doesn't move laterally."[57]

Judging from her own writings about the skeleton in the classroom, which she began using in 1918, H'Doubler seems to have intended it not as a rigorous technical teaching moment but rather as part of the whole package of making dance educationally meritorious.[58] "Students need to know why they are making movements if they are to make them with any intelligent appreciation of their value and possibilities," H'Doubler writes.[59] She says the lesson will be more comprehensible and interesting if students have the use of muscle charts and, if possible, a skeleton. All of this is in the interest of training the student back toward naturalness, a paradox that is at the heart of H'Doubler's positioning of dance in the classroom.

The drive toward individual excellence both Moore and Halprin remember becomes something different in Mullen's recollections. Mullen recalls an implicit understanding that the dance students "must not be too competent." "You could not get to be too good because then you were emulating men," she said, explaining that this outlook promoted by both H'Doubler and the university resulted in regarding dance performance as "showing off." "You just didn't get to be too good, because that meant you were somehow cheapening the skill," Mullen said. "The link between activity and the art form and creation was totally missed."[60]

Hinkson, who studied with H'Doubler from 1943 to 1948, for both her undergraduate and graduate degrees in dance, bridges Moore's and Mullen's recollections in both time and perception:

Miss H'Doubler could get you stirred up and fired up about whatever, but her philosophy of movement was that "movement belongs to everyone." We live in a world of movement. That's what the whole thing was about—that way human beings can grow, can be nurtured, can be fulfilled, just by experiencing movement. And you do not have to take it to the theatrical level. I think this was a kind of primary thesis with Miss H'Doubler.[61]

If one revisits Moore's remarks, bearing in mind Mullen's reservations, and allowing for a two-decade gap between the women's tenure in the dance program, it is possible to bring a single classroom into focus from their perspectives, incorporating those of Hinkson and Halprin as well. "We had been taught to evaluate our own progress," Moore writes. "It is no wonder that we were awed by our own experience in Margaret H'Doubler's classes, for we not only had participated in an expansive approach to dance, but also had deepened our respect for ourselves as growing, self-directing, potential artists. This for most of us was a unique experience." Speaking on this same subject a few years later, she summed it up: "We went to explore the bones and we bumped into our souls."[62]

A broader outlook suggests that Moore and Mullen are both right: H'Doubler's paramount goal was to bring dance into the university, to reshape it in whatever way possible and to modify it as necessary. She reportedly had a favorite diagram she would often draw on the blackboard depicting two flasks linked by a distillation tube. One flask was labeled "crude"; the other, "personal selectivity guided by knowledge and ideas."[63] The distillation tube was H'Doubler's classroom. In her mind what she was refining was the art form as well as the students.

THE DANCE SPACE AND STUDENT ATTIRE

A series of photographs taken in 1935 of the fifth-floor corner room in Lathrop Hall—H'Doubler's dance studio and classroom—reveals it as what would be called an intensely *feminine* space (figure 29).[64] Although the faint grid of a basketball court's painted markings is still visible on the polished wood floor (and would be until 1998 remodeling), everything else about the original basketball gym has been altered. Tucked away at the end of a drafty narrow walkway in the attic-like space of the top floor, this room is spacious, yet cozy and protected. The four walls, painted the fashionable gray of the 1930s, are all hung with floor-to-ceiling, densely pleated gray curtains that spill on the ground in small pools of material. Victorian lampshades with painted geometric designs and dangling tassels cover the ceiling fixtures; a pair of simple benches, a cloth-draped pedestal,

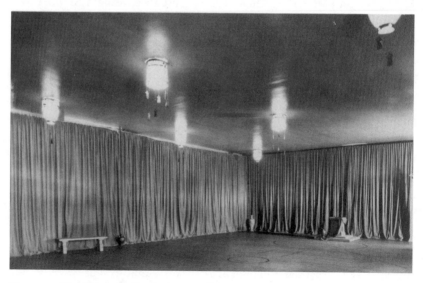

Figure 29. The Dance Studio, Lathrop Hall, 1935 (Courtesy University of Wisconsin–Madison Archives)

and a vase in one corner complete the neoclassical, Grecian decorative details. It was in 1924, shortly after H'Doubler finished her master's degree, that Trilling authorized the painting and decorating of the fifth-floor studio, and the outfitting of it with "rose shades on the light, a flood light, and two lovely statues—Venus de Milo and the Winged Victory of Samothrace."[65]

The room feels like a setting for transformation. There is an important historical intersection here in that for her theatrical performances during this same period, Isadora Duncan's trademark decorations were also long blue-gray velvet curtains, which she always hung as her only scenery wherever she performed. For an outsider the use of curtains in H'Doubler's classroom suggests an illusionistic space, as if every wall might suddenly open onto a proscenium arch and an audience. Given her abhorrence of performance-directed dance, however, this is likely a reference she never intended. Instead H'Doubler's following comment about the use of curtains suggests what may have been Duncan's intent as well—to foster the creation of the spirit of beauty:

A bright airy room is best and if it is hung with curtains in some soft, warm shade, it may become a very real help to the creation of that spirit of beauty that is one of the aims of such a class.[66]

While H'Doubler obviously did not encourage students to think of the stage as their ultimate, or even a desired, goal, her classroom seems to have had about it a sense of each woman presenting herself, perhaps to her female peers, because of the very decorative setting of the studio. By never linking up the study of dance with performance as an objective, however, H'Doubler made strides toward eliminating the surveying generic male, with his "male gaze," as the ubiquitous imagined viewer for her students.[67] In the early years the students' audiences, when they had them, were primarily other female students. Compared to the bare-walled dance studios of today, H'Doubler's space was highly theatrical. At the same time it also felt hushed and private, as if it were a safe environment in which one could take physical risks.

What H'Doubler's students remember most about her studio was the manner in which the curtains on the walls hid the six or eight small, high windows on the three exterior walls, and later the wall of mirrors, added in the 1930s. Julia Brown recounts a popular story about how one day, in the early history of Lathrop Hall, the determined H'Doubler cornered a key administrator in the basement cafeteria; without even waiting for the gentleman to get his lunch, she marched him upstairs to show him the dance studio and to urge him to process the funds for the curtains more quickly. Hermine Sauthoff Davidson recalls that the curtains also hid the storage area for the music and the large Navajo

Indian drum H'Doubler would sometimes beat to give the dancers a simple rhythm.[68]

The use of the drum was a staple of H'Doubler's work. While it may have borrowed from some early physical culture practices, it also echoed the use of the drum in professional dance studios—most notably that of Mary Wigman, who used an elaborate assortment of percussion instruments, including drums, as accompaniment for her teaching. There is a rhythmic essentialness to drums as accompaniment for dance classes: while drumbeats give the student a rhythmic base, they do not do the student's work—one must move between the beats, shading the movement with whatever interpretive qualities are necessary. Hinkson describes her vivid memories of H'Doubler's class:

Even when she taught her special movement classes, those gorgeous mirrors were all covered with drapes. [Just] as she had us work blindfolded. She wanted us to find out what was inside us. She wanted us to avoid being imitative. She wanted to avoid mimicry. She just totally disapproved of everybody looking alike in the class. She wanted us to discover within ourselves what our own movement quality is or was, and to try to elaborate on it. It was very special.[69]

The drums could help ease the dancer into rhythmic responsiveness to a beat without unnecessary self-consciousness. The curtains, too, did not hide the dancer from herself; instead they reinforced the studio climate of encouraging each dancer to turn inward.[70]

For the first several years of her dance classes, H'Doubler specified that her students wear Grecian tunics of her own design as their classroom attire. *The Dance, and Its Place in Education* contains detailed sketches for making these tunics, each of which transforms the wearer into a theatrical vision, her body ringed with her own little "curtains" of pleated material.[71] This information, along with the specifics of lesson plans, was taught to H'Doubler's students so that as they fanned out to teach, H'Doubler's pedagogy exerted an enormous influence on dance teaching across the nation (figure 30).

H'Doubler's studio setting, like much in her teaching of dance, is rife with paradox: a theatrical setting for dance that is not destined for the theater, instruction in dance by a woman who was never a dancer, training in dance as an educational force by using more improvisatory explorations than a set lesson plan. H'Doubler belonged to a new moment of identity creation for dance in America, yet she seemed not to realize that she was a soul mate of Isadora Duncan, Martha Graham, Ruth St. Denis, and other pioneers in performing.

H'Doubler's pedagogy may have been eccentric for dance in education at the time, but it was directly in line with the push toward respectability dance was making in American life. In 1926, two years after H'Doubler

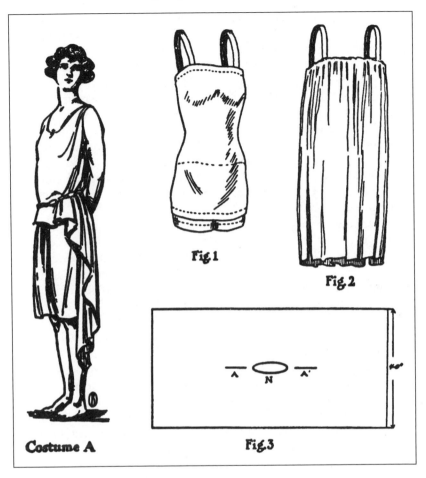

Figure 30. Margaret H'Doubler's designs for student practice costumes. Figure 1 is "a comfortable and practical garment made of silk or cotton jersey that can be worn separately for studio work"; figure 2 is the skirt portion of the costume A; and figure 3 is the over drape, or top, of the costume A. (*The Dance, and Its Place in Education,* 1925)

wrote her treatise on dance education, New York City's three leading dailies—the *World,* the *Herald Tribune,* and the *Times*—hired full-time dance writers. Within a matter of three months, dance criticism in the American daily press had become a specialized field.[72] Also in 1926, Martha Graham gave her first independent concerts. Between 1923 and 1927 two major magazines devoted to dancing, and written for students and teachers, emerged: *Dance Lovers Magazine* and *The American Dancer.* Dance was becoming a visible and legitimate part of American culture.

In the 1920s World War I became the subject of a dance by H'Doubler's students. A series of posed photographs, likely dating from 1919 or 1920, shows a group of seven unidentified women wearing H'Doubler-designed tunics clustered on the shore of a lake, relaxing into "naturalistic" gestures of supplication and sorrow (figure 31).[73] These soft-focus photographs, entitled "Les Miserables: In Remembrance of the Armenian People— World War I," suggest the women as simultaneously noble Grecian forms and reed-like growths along the lakeshore. The contours of their flesh are visible yet muted under their diaphanous tunics. The image is softly erotic, made all the more so by the deep late-afternoon shadows, which erase all individual features of the women's faces, leaving the viewer to study the curve of a gesturing arm or the opened expanse of an uplifted throat for emotional meaning.

Comparing these photographs to one taken on the steps of Lathrop Hall in 1920 depicting the assembled majors in women's physical education, the contrast is striking (figure 32). Standing stiffly, shoulder-to-shoulder in tight rows, these women's bodies are essentially formless, shrouded from neck to toes. Thickly pleated black shirts and bloomers, with black stockings and black lace-up leather shoes, make up these long-sleeved, high-necked uniforms. The only flesh visible is that of the hands and the women's round, smiling faces, each framed by a white collar. These costumes look cumbersome and concealing, and it seems not to matter at all that beyond the first row only faces are visible, since the bodies are so obscured by clothing. Everything is so regimented, and the bodies hold such few clues to individuality, that the women's forms are essentially rendered interchangeable. By comparison H'Doubler's dance tunics invite easy and free body motions; limbs are exposed, legs bare, and the torso unencumbered. The total effect is a bold invitation to dance.

One additional photograph, dated 1930, offers an even more vivid contrast (figure 33). This photo captures two of H'Doubler's tunic-clad students in playful spiraling turns by the lakeshore. The dancer on the right, identified as Elna Mygdal, a member of Orchesis in the late 1920s, curves backward toward the camera, her whole body arcing around to capture a length of scarf that floats perfectly horizontally in the air behind her. Arcing backward toward her is another dancer, tunic-clad and barefoot like Mygdal, who throws her arms and her head in a curving impulse toward the racing Mygdal. It is a splendid dance photograph, capturing a moment of intense and real dance action, with bodies caught in the poetry of spontaneous gesture. The dark trees that frame the women in the background suggest an expansive landscape from which they might have emerged in this gamboling play some time earlier, having lost sight of all responsibilities as they chase one another along the lake's edge. Looking at this image, Isadora Duncan's 1917 essay "Dance and its Inspiration"

Figure 31. "Les Miserables: In remembrance of the Armenian people of World War I," a dance study by Margaret H'Doubler's students (Courtesy University of Wisconsin–Madison Archives)

Figure 32. Women's physical education majors, in P.E. uniforms of the 1920s, photographed on the steps of Lathrop Hall (Courtesy University of Wisconsin–Madison Archives)

Figure 33. Two of Margaret H'Doubler's students dancing lakeside, ca. 1920s (Courtesy University of Wisconsin–Madison Archives)

comes to mind: "I believe here is a wonderful undiscovered inheritance for coming womanhood, the old dance which is to become the new. She shall be sculptor not in clay or marble but in her body, which she shall endeavor to bring to the highest state of plastic beauty."[74]

The vividness of the few dance photographs that exist suggests how remarkably comfortable H'Doubler's dancers appear doing what must have seemed like near-nude gamboling in public (figures 34, 35, 36). Edith Boys Enos, a classmate of Elna Mygdal, voiced H'Doubler's students' sentiments about their independent pride and self-assurance. Enos said that in her small Midwest hometown, where her father was editor of the newspaper, he was teased for permitting his daughter to do such a "sinful thing" as "studying dancing," even before Enos went to Madison. Enos's father was also criticized for "letting his wife wear the pants" because she was a suffragette. Enos, with an equanimity befitting one of H'Doubler's

Figure 34. Five of Margaret H'Doubler's students dancing around a large tree, ca. 1920s (Courtesy University of Wisconsin–Madison Archives)

Figure 35. Five of Margaret H'Doubler's students dancing outdoors in a meadow in tunics of H'Doubler's design, ca. 1920s (Courtesy University of Wisconsin–Madison Archives)

Figure 36. One of Margaret H'Doubler's students dancing lakeside, with a long scarf, a favorite H'Doubler prop, ca. 1920s (Courtesy University of Wisconsin–Madison Archives)

students and the daughter of a suffragette, said her family dismissed these criticisms charitably as "small town gossip that was not worth paying any attention to."[75] One can glimpse in these dance photographs this air of determination in the quest for the loftiest ideals of dance and the dismissal of small-town gossip.

Although H'Doubler's curtains lasted for many years as studio decoration, the tunics did not. Hermine Sauthoff Davidson says that by the early

1930s the dance students routinely wore leotards and tights, often with a long jersey dance skirt as well.[76] The footwear required in H'Doubler's classes evolved from bare feet to leather thongs, and then to skin-colored slippers strapped at the ankle, which served to protect the women's feet from rough wood floors when they demonstrated off campus and also aided in pivoting turns.

H'Doubler herself never wore a leotard and tights; rather, she wore what Mary Hinkson remembers as a special custom-made costume, a form-fitting, one-piece dress with long sleeves, a fitted bodice, and a flared skirt. Despite her not having had dance training, her students remember her graceful and easy walk and her naturally high and elegant carriage. Descriptions and photographs give the impression that she moved like a graceful athlete; she certainly maintained the active lifestyle of one. Edith Boys Enos recalls H'Doubler frequently going for early morning rides before class on her horse, Fire (figure 37).[77] Others recall her striding briskly around campus, absentmindedly testing out the joint rotations for some studio exercise she was planning for her class, with the concentration of an inventor lost in discovery. Indeed, she was just that.

ORCHESIS

Although H'Doubler assiduously avoided any suggestion that she was training performers, her students, apparently feeling strongly the Deweyan impulse to express themselves, appealed to her within the first year of the program for an extra meeting. This meeting, which H'Doubler oversaw, began in the winter of 1918–19 and rapidly grew into a forum for performing. H'Doubler readily agreed to the initial extra class, remarking: "Oh my goodness, yes, how wonderful!"[78]

However, H'Doubler was always cautious about how all student activities were framed. This extra activity would in fact be a student club. In an undated letter to Ellen Moore, who studied with H'Doubler from 1949 to 1951, H'Doubler responded to a paper Moore had written about H'Doubler's work. It is a clear statement of how she continually separated even the *vocabulary* of theatrical dance from her educational form, and it indirectly reveals some of her deeper agendas: "Where you have used *performance* I purposely used *execution* as it did not suggest theatre performance at this stage—but was preparatory for it *if* [emphasis added] performance were the final goal . . . and the last suggestion is I never used the French terms 'plié' etc., etc., English I felt was close to most students."[79]

In fact, *execution* does not suggest movement preparatory for performance at all; rather, it implies the finality of doing a set of proscribed, not necessarily artistic, actions. So, too, H'Doubler's shunning of French

Figure 37. Margaret H'Doubler riding her beloved horse, Fire (Courtesy University of Wisconsin–Madison Archives)

terms, not coincidentally the language of classical ballet, is more than just a gesture toward linguistic practicality.[80] Not using the word *plié*, for example, reclaims the gestures of bending and straightening the knees as a pure action of physical innocence, one that can be reintroduced by H'Doubler's students as a newly expressive *interpretive* dance action.

The incorporation of performing, via Orchesis, into H'Doubler's dance curriculum reflected a similar spirit of starting over with a fresh agenda for an old practice. So began what Enos remembers as "really a great thing." Ellen Moore, describing the ritualistic induction ceremony, became choked with emotion as she recalled being led in a swirling dance run into the darkened, candlelit studio and placed as part of a circle formed by H'Doubler and the established Orchesis members. "It was the closest thing to a pure community I have ever known," she concluded of this experience more than forty years later.[81]

The Lathrop dance studio was available for H'Doubler's Orchesis students on Wednesday evenings. H'Doubler recounted that within the first few weeks of the beginning of this new dance club, professors from other departments on campus were asking if they could come and observe. Often four or five different scientists and faculty from English, philosophy, and physiology would sit on the floor watching and then plying H'Doubler and the students with questions at the evening's end. H'Doubler, no longer reticent about this performing venture of her students, simply enthusiastically recast it as a broader classroom experience for university faculty and her students:

It was a terribly exciting thing. I knew my anatomy and I knew movement. But I read like mad on the nervous system. I could hardly get enough. I discovered for myself, the feedback and the relay systems of the thalamus and how the emotions had got conditioned. . . . The students soon found they were the recipients of the sensation of their own movement and responsible for their responses. It grew and grew.[82]

Interestingly, H'Doubler's comments about Orchesis suggest that her excitement related to its function as a living physiology laboratory far more than as a lab for choreographic creativity. Enos says, in fact, that while she was studying with H'Doubler she never heard her use the word *choreography*; much less did she teach it as a separate subject. Rather, the students just "made up" dances.[83] Here again was the Victorian paradox: the process and actions looked like improvisation and choreography, but for reasons of appearance and emphasis they were called something else.

A single-page class handout from H'Doubler's personal files in the University of Wisconsin–Madison Archives, untitled and dated simply December 1953, contains an example of H'Doubler actually addressing the subject of dance composition, possibly for the senior year "Physical Ed. 165—Dance Composition" course.[84] What is remarkable about this document is that invention, communication, and expression of content to others—in other words, the crucial aesthetic dimensions of dance composition—are barely even mentioned. Rather, the making of a dance is presented as a kind of biological necessity: "A dance is the rhythmic motor expression of feeling states aesthetically valued." "The creation of a dance is born of personality and gives back to personality," H'Doubler also says. H'Doubler's statements invoke the legitimizing influence of science as she recasts choreographing not so much as an aesthetic exercise but rather as a physiological means for achieving mind-body-emotion union. (See appendix 2 for this memo.)

What is remarkable here is the steadfastness with which H'Doubler kept repositioning dance as a means toward personal insight, discovery, and expression while at the same time she just as relentlessly articulated its virtues as being independent from theatrical dance. Yet in Orchesis, she was creating a dance *performance* club. The paradox apparently did not trouble her. She seems not to have ignored many of dance's attributes so much as to have simply moved them, wholesale, into the center of physical education.

H'Doubler initially invited the students to name the dance performance group, which dates its beginning from the 1918–19 academic year. However, she ended up providing *Orchesis* herself, having "saved" the word from her readings about early Greek dance while at Columbia a year earlier:

So in my reading, I ran across this word, "Orchesis," and it was in the description of early Greek dance and it means in translation "the *science* [emphasis added] of movement in action and repose." And it flashed through my mind, wouldn't that be a nice name for a dance club if such a thing should ever happen?[85]

For H'Doubler the virtue of Orchesis as she spoke of it was not that it was a performing outlet for her students but rather the opposite: it offered "a dance experience that can really attain these goals of philosophy of education where the dignity of the self was the main center of the philosophy." The more H'Doubler's club evolved into dance as performance, the more she steadfastly reframed her classes as dance *education*. Yet for all intents her students were developing into an amateur dance troupe. For the first several months H'Doubler was adamant that the purpose of Orchesis was simply to enable members to show their work among themselves "with no thought of appealing to wider circles."[86]

Gradually, however, dance at Madison kept moving toward its essence—a performing art. An art form like dance could be taken into the university and shaped like a sport or other academic discipline, but the more fully the students studied it, the more inevitable its culmination in a performance became. There is the sense of H'Doubler's classroom paralleling the essential evolution of choreographic invention itself, from an activity of individual improvisation into set and rehearsed movement patterns or a progression of phrases. For H'Doubler this seems to have been permissible only because she steadily kept shaping the experience as

educational. For example, she advocated *not* giving corrections to beginning students, something inimical to professional dance. "The beginner
who is doing the work incorrectly should never have his faults called
attention to. It makes them self-conscious," she warned.[87] A yellowed
and undated document from her personal files, entitled "Evaluation of
Dance Composition," however, suggests another approach for the more
advanced students—that of "constructive criticism" framed as a means of
making performance educational. "For the student to gain an educational
advantage from these laboratory Orchesis recitals she must have criticism
of the work she had been trying to do," H'Doubler writes.

Programs from the May 1928 and 1929 Orchesis concerts reveal a
curious tension between the educational and performance approaches to
dance. On the one hand, the programs list only the title of each dance
and the last name of the composer whose music accompanies it. Neither
the person who choreographed the dance nor the people performing it
are identified or acknowledged, save for their inclusion in an alphabetical
listing of "Active Members of Orchesis" at the end of the program. This
practice continued until 1947, when the choreographers were listed for
each work, but the dancers still remained unnamed until the April 1951
program (figure 38).[88]

The practice of not naming the dancers contrasts oddly with the
covers of the 1928, 1929, and 1930 programs, which boldly set forth
the topic of the evening as "The Dance as Interpreted by Members of
Orchesis." This is a very academic way to shape a dance concert: listing
the dancers alphabetically at the end of the program suggests that the focus
is not the dancers—they are just students doing an assignment. There is
also a certain naiveté in the idea that a topic as grand as "The Dance"
could be addressed by seven or eight student dances in an evening-length
concert. "Marge was very protective of the anonymous character of the
dance program," alumna Davidson agrees. "She didn't want to make
any stars."[89]

H'Doubler advocates anonymity on student programs in her guide-
book for dance teachers, *The Dance, and Its Place in Education*, explaining: "[N]o mention is made of individual dancers on the program,
and . . . the names of the entire group are printed in alphabetical order at
the bottom. It is their best tribute to the spirit of the dance that the whole
group cooperates to give the community something of the joy and beauty
they have found with no thought but how they may best do justice to their
purpose."[90] The rationale is that individual egos are to be subservient to
group unity and that the minor and the major contributors share in the
credit for the success of their dance drama equally. This seems another
aspect of H'Doubler's redefining of dance educationally that did not last.
Like not building student recitals into her initial curriculum, H'Doubler's

The Dance

As Interpreted by Members
of
ORCHESIS

Department of Physical Education
University of Wisconsin

May 22 and 23, 1931   Bascom Theatre

Orchesis Members

Norma Anderson
Marion Bigelow
Edith Boys
Katherine Cane
Ruth Clay
Lucille Czarnowski
Barbara Davis
Alice Dieterle
Elizabeth Findley
Elizabeth Foeller
Bernice van Gelder
Helen Gregory
Beatrice Hellebrandt
Delta Hinkel
Vickery Hubbard
Laura Lee Howser
Asenath Ives
Margaret Jewell
Harriet Kroncke
Eileen Logan
Katharine Maple
Agnes McCall
Sarah Ellen Merritt
Orva Mitchell
Helen Morehead
Elna Mygdal
Marion Neilson
Florence Randall
Ruth Riley
Frances Parrette
Hermine Sauthoff
Annamay Smith
Eleanor Sondern
Lucille Sondern
Vera Shaw
Dorothy White
Dorothy Ware
Marie Wettig

1. Orchesis ....*Beatrice Hellebrandt*
2. Waltz .... *Tschaikowsky*
3. Dolor ....*Bach*
4. Song of the Bayou...............................*Bloom*
5. Machine Guns ....*Sound design*
6. Sea Gulls ....*Liszt*
7. Summer is Icumen In ....*John of Fornsete*
   Sung by members of Girls Glee Club
8. Atalanta ....*Beatrice Hellebrandt*

INTERMISSION—THREE MINUTES

9. Sicilienne .... *Schumann*
10. Penguinhood .... *Debussy*
11. Cakewalk .... *Mills*
12. Personages with Long Ears ....*Saint-Saëns*
13. Sing a Song of Sixpence ....*Berta Ochsner*
14. Bal Masque ....*Tschaikowsky*

INTERMISSION—FIVE MINUTES

15. Life's Cycle ....*Beatrice Hellebrandt*
    Birth; strife; triumph
16. Aquarium .... *Saint-Saëns*
17. Impressions ....*Music arranged*
    Watteau; Botticelli, Michaelangelo
18. Bolero .... *Ravel*
19. Polonaise Militaire ....*Chopin*
20. Scarf Study ....*Ravel*
21. Viennese Waltz ....*Mark Wessel*
22. Parados—from Euripedes' Bacchae ....*Beatrice Hellebrandt*
    Translation by Kimon Friar

Baldwin Piano used—Courtesy of Forbes-Meagher Music Co.

Figure 38. A typical Orchesis program, May 1931. Note the alphabetical listing of Orchesis members and the absence of any individual casting information. (Collection of Hermine Sauthoff Davidson)

attempt to structure performances as comparatively anonymous demonstrations would be dismantled by students in the early 1940s.

A program note in the April 6 and 7, 1951, program identifies Orchesis as a "University Dance Club," intended as a "workshop extension of the dance major course . . . [whose] purpose is to develop and maintain as high a standard of artistic integrity and creative effort as is consistent with the student's ability." By this time a Junior Orchesis had also been spawned, a dance club for the less advanced students and open to membership without the required tryouts of Orchesis proper. The creation of Orchesis dance clubs as performing outlets for students was an aspect of the Wisconsin program that H'Doubler's graduates faithfully replicated in the colleges and universities throughout the country where they taught.

The name Orchesis was used by many college dance performing groups until well into the 1950s, while it continued to provide a safe frame for student concerts as educationally artistic enterprises. For all of her framing it as a workshop experience, however, H'Doubler attended to the details of the Orchesis concerts like a professional. Lighting, costumes, props, cues, and, in particular, personal appearance and hygiene greatly concerned her. The concerts were polished public events, rare times for the public to scrutinize what these dancing women were up to. An undated two-page handout H'Doubler distributed before Orchesis concerts contained a checklist of several dozen items to be attended to by each dancer, with the first three focusing on decorous appearance:

#1. Be sure that your legs and armpits are shaved.
#2. Have a suitable deodorant or shields to prevent perspiration from ruining the appearance of the costumes.
#3. Be tightly brassiered![91]

The specter of presenting dancing women who were not "ladylike" was apparently one that haunted H'Doubler and one she continued to refute. For all of her objections to ballet's artifice and her embracing of the honest physicality of movement, H'Doubler's guidelines here suggest the prevailing obsession with disguising the effort of female dancing bodies, which might have bobbing breasts and costumes wetted by perspiration. For feminists today there is an irony in H'Doubler's boldness in forging a new place for the dancing female in higher education while at the same time maintaining a strict and established code of appearances for that body in public.

H'Doubler persisted as a missionary for respectability and legitimacy for dance in the university, steadily building her program as word of her work spread. By the spring of 1919, the second year of H'Doubler's dance teaching, nearly three hundred students were enrolled in her beginning classes and 140 in the intermediate classes.[92] Within seven years she would be offering the nation's first dance major and training dance teachers for colleges and universities around the nation. In 1945, in an article H'Doubler wrote for the dance journal *Dance Observer*, she offered her rationale for dance as an educational force:

The concern of educational dance is the development of expression through the study of dance and not with the development of professional dancers. Its aim is the integration of personality by means of participation in dance as a creative art experience—affording students the opportunity to know dance as a special way of experiencing aesthetic values discovered in reality.[93]

The inaugural years of H'Doubler's dance program at Wisconsin, from approximately 1915 to 1930, comprised a moment when the definition of the liberal arts in general was being considerably broadened in American universities. Dance as a physical art form has always bridged both athletics and these liberal arts domains. Dance needs the facilities of an athletics department—studios and lockers—while as an art form its content belongs with the humanities. By 1932 there were two hundred art departments in American colleges, up from a fraction of that a decade earlier. The spread of dance programs modeled after H'Doubler's was about to start growing at a corresponding rate. The expansion of the curriculum in the visual arts was linked with a democratizing of higher education, a broadening of cultural values and with the future progress of American civilization. "Without the addition of such courses the development of the twentieth-century college would have been arrested," Dean William Leutner at Case Western Reserve argued in the 1930s in regard to the inclusion of liberal and fine arts in the curriculum.[94]

Although it was an extracurricular group, Orchesis was one of the most widely copied academic dance concepts H'Doubler ever produced. Orchesis functioned like a student club, an extremely popular model of the time for extracurricular and particularly performance-oriented activities. A student could apply for membership by demonstrating her proficiency in doing classroom exercises and also by performing a short piece of original choreography. Membership was reserved for the dance elite at the university, and it was conferred in a group initiation ceremony that involved an established member reciting a poem H'Doubler had selected.[95] It was a coveted honor to be invited to apply to Orchesis and, if accepted, to undergo the initiation. Edith Boys Enos recalls: "I know I used to look forward to that Wednesday night meeting of Orchesis, which was the closest thing to a religious experience for most of us."[96]

One can sense some of the challenges exerted on a performing art form in the university through examining the social and administrative pressures about publicity and performing that Orchesis encountered. Under the promise of demonstrating the educational merits of dance,

H'Doubler and her Orchesis group began receiving invitations to bring their studio demonstrations to other colleges and universities. She began by politely declining these invitations, corresponding in written form instead to share her ideas.[97]

While various men's student groups like the Glee Club and Haresfoot frequently toured around representing the University of Wisconsin, no women had been permitted off campus under the aegis of the university. Convinced about the merits of what she was doing, H'Doubler eventually applied for, and received, permission to tour with her students under the auspices of the dean of women, provided that what they presented was "a highly creative presentation."[98] Creative *educationally*, not theatrically. "I'd always write [the schools and universities] and ask that our appearance be under the Dean of Women," H'Doubler said, indicating her concern that how these lecture demonstrations were framed had everything to do with the respect with which she and her students were regarded. Deans of women were generally the most highly placed women in a university administratively, and appearing under their aegis implied that the offering was noble and tasteful and sanctioned by academic women.[99]

Word of H'Doubler's dance touring eventually reached the attention of President Edward A. Birge. Toward the end of 1921, a period in which the university was under close scrutiny by the press for its actions, Birge, a very image-conscious interim president, invited H'Doubler into his office and told her bluntly he would not have the university known as "a dancing school."[100] "So, after nearly three years of popular touring, the last year of which Orchesis visited 42 schools, the trips stopped."[101] H'Doubler was quite sanguine about this cancellation of Orchesis's off-campus performances, however; she simply began accommodating those who were curious about what she was doing as guests in her daily classes on campus. Often visitors would drop in on short notice, so she devised a system of posting calls for last-minute lecture-demonstrations on a downstairs bulletin board, which Orchesis members knew to check several times a day. The annual Christmas and spring Orchesis recitals continued without interruption.

THE DANCE MAJOR

The University of Wisconsin surprised H'Doubler, in her bid for expansion, by granting her initial request for an undergraduate dance major in 1926, the first such dance degree in the nation. H'Doubler had anticipated that it would take two or three attempts before such a radical notion was approved, but Blanche Trilling and the dean of Letters and Science, George C. Sellery, strongly supported it from the start. The institution of a major in dance education further formalized H'Doubler's emphasis on dance as an appropriate educational subject. Classes in teaching dance now became a regular part of the curriculum, with a full session of teaching, usually at a public or private school in Madison, being required of every dance major.

More important, the curriculum for dance majors was now more humanities-based. Enos recalls talking with H'Doubler the morning after the dance major had been approved and remembers H'Doubler's delight that now, at last, the dance students "would be able to have not such a heavy technical course [of study] but would be able to have more time for philosophy or for the humanities and for art and music and things like that instead of the technical and scientific courses."[102] Now that dance had achieved academic legitimacy, H'Doubler could afford to take a more balanced approach to the major curriculum, stressing science only as it truly complemented her notions of cognition and dance movement.

The victory for the humanities was modest by contemporary standards, as courses in physiology, anatomy, kinesiology, and biology or chemistry were all still required. However, thirty to forty credits of philosophy, psychology, speech, music theory and history, and art history classes were now permitted to round out the program of study, a significant departure from the science-based physical education curriculum.

A finished draft of H'Doubler's curriculum for the dance major, approved by the School of Education on October 11, 1926, indicates that of the total of 124 credits required for a bachelor of science degree in physical education, only nineteen *had* to be in dance, although the number of dance credits could range as high as twenty-three.[103] These included one class each in "Rhythmic Form and Analysis," "Dance Composition," "Philosophy of Dancing," and "Folk Dancing" and two in teaching.[104]

On November 12, 1926, the Board of Regents, the final authority, formally approved the new dance major. It was understood that, in keeping with the emphasis of the Physical Education Department as well as the university's broad commitment to service, this degree was focused on creating dance teachers. The 1934 University of Wisconsin catalogue carries two statements, one unsigned but presumably from Trilling, and the other from the dean of the School of Education, John Fowlkes, both stating that the demand for department graduates in dance, as well as women's physical education in general, continued to far exceed the number of graduates. Fowlkes's statement concludes, "For young women, the teaching of general physical education and dance at various educational levels presents a challenging, attractive and altruistic profession for the future."

The 1926–27 roster of students indicates at least fourteen undergraduates and one graduate student were working on the newly established dance major.[105] The following academic year solidified the new major with offerings of new practical and theoretical courses. The graduate major in dance began at the same time, although with much less fanfare.

H'Doubler's annual department report notes simply, "The most significant and far-reaching development in dancing for the year is the addition of the dance major. . . . The degree is a B.S . . . and with the establishment of an M.A. and M.S. in Physical Education, it is possible to get an M.S. in Dance."[106] In 1963 the first Ph.D. in dance would be created, and the following year the first M.F.A. degree in dance would be granted as a terminal degree at Wisconsin. However, from the very first year of the dance program, H'Doubler's graduates apparently found good teaching jobs even with just a bachelor's degree. Marion Bigelow said that when she graduated with a degree in physical education and having taken many dance classes in 1926, on the cusp of the implementation of the dance major, she already had her choice of jobs.[107] Women were thus the beneficiaries in two ways: they found well-paid, satisfying jobs, and these jobs were helping young girls and women acquire good physical health and new capacities of physical expressiveness. Administrators were discovering that qualified instructors of women's dance and physical education remedied problems of women students' health rather than exacerbating them, as untrained instructors could.

THE LESSONS OF H'DOUBLER'S DANCE CLASSROOM

H'Doubler's students seem to have understood almost universally that what she was teaching them was more than just dance. The strongest memories about H'Doubler's dance teaching that emerged in all the interviews are those of her enthusiasm and her conviction that through dance she was equipping these women for life. This may initially sound trivial, but in the context of women in higher education in the early 1900s, a world in which there were still comparatively few rewards for women's success in the public sphere, these were valuable survival strategies and laudable goals. The following quote is from Enos, an undergraduate in dance under H'Doubler from 1922 to 1926, and a graduate student in dance in 1931–32. Interviewed in her nineties, seventy years after she was a student, Enos still communicates a palpable awe for H'Doubler.

Well, she would demonstrate sometimes, yes. But her inspiration was just being there, I think. And she would always come in with an idea. And you know, I can't believe that she ever sat down and wrote a formal lesson plan. She just would kind of come . . . I was going to say "breezing" into the studio, or almost . . . she walked briskly and with rhythm, you know. It was kind of a dance the way she would come in. Then she would get started on some idea. Her face was always aglow . . . it was so exciting, you could hardly wait to get started on it. She just projected . . . I think anyone'll tell you that . . . she just projected the inspiration and belief that she had.[108]

Mary Hinkson also remembers H'Doubler's charismatic dynamism:

Miss H'Doubler was the most encouraging person, I think, in the entire world. She tried to erase all doubts each and every one of us had about ourselves. . . . She just had a way of erasing every worry and every care in the world. She was perhaps the most enthusiastic person, and could find a positive way for one to look at any dark cloud.[109]

Within these observations about H'Doubler are hints about the social and educational time in which she worked. One can read into her energy and enthusiasm a certain kind of cheerleading that may well have helped win student and faculty supporters to the novelty of a performing art in the higher education curriculum. More than a pragmatic strategy, however, H'Doubler's assurance seemed an advertisement for the self-knowledge dance education could give. The following passage from a document H'Doubler prepared, laying forth her argument for dance as a full partner in the academic field, suggests how she boldly linked experience in the physical activity of dance to the broadest goals of education, the creation of mind, a notion well ahead of its time.

To make educational claims for dance it was important to understand education as an inborn drive to seek knowledges and skills with which to make life worth living. . . . What are the contributions that art in general and dance in particular can make to this "job" of spending a life time in "living"? . . .

Mind does not just exist. It evolves out of behavior. It is the conscious phase of the "self-organism's" reaction to its environment. . . . We are not born with a mind, but with a brain. It needs incoming sensorial impressions to stimulate brain activity—to evaluate—to make comparisons—judge them—interpret them—make associations and create new images.[110]

Experience in dance as a valuable part of the development of one's mind continued to be an influential part of the legacy H'Doubler left her students. As is also true of Isadora Duncan, H'Doubler's own writing about her inventions in dance are full of enthusiastic generalizations, while the actual designs and physical "how-to" evolution of a specific dance class are almost never described. In a 1963 interview, for example, H'Doubler recounted the summer class of 1917 that began it all:

So when I came back to teach in summer school, I didn't have a thing but an idea, and no music whatsoever but fortunately the summer group that came to study was a marvelous group, and they too were dissatisfied with this other kind of dancing. . . . Miss Trilling thought that there should be some other kind of dance that would have some vital meaning and could qualify as an art experience and an educational experience for the students. So that summer, it just went beautifully, and things developed, and things resulted, and everybody was so enthusiastic.[111]

H'Doubler's description here is frustratingly vague, but also probably very accurate in that H'Doubler was not initially sure what it was she was doing with dance; she only knew it had worked. It is interesting how in this statement H'Doubler renders herself and the actual mechanics of the class essentially invisible. She becomes a mere catalyst for what is naturally there in her students, waiting to be awakened. There are elements of a Progressive ideal in this posture. There is also the pragmatic strategy of an early modern woman reformer in this tactic of appearing a passive agent of change.

H'Doubler's comment "I didn't have a thing but an idea, and no music whatsoever" is also curious, because H'Doubler apparently had no dance movements to teach either, but what she comments on is her lack of *music*. Music has always been a key atmospheric element for freeing people up in improvisatory dance, and even at this initial stage H'Doubler must have sensed that it would be crucial for her educational aspirations. Indeed, she would promptly enlist talented accompanists for her classes, but the continuing lack of specific dance movements to teach seemed deliberate and not a lack so much as a conscious choice. Ideas and music would be the anchors of her dance studio classes throughout her career. It was in the arc between the two—between an idea and rhythmic music—that H'Doubler's students would each find her own dances.

ASSESSING DANCE LEARNING IN H'DOUBLER'S CLASSROOM

According to Enos, the final examinations H'Doubler gave in her classes prodded the students to make larger life connections to dance in their lives. The 1925 final exam for H'Doubler's "Theory and Philosophy of Dance" class consisted of the following questions:

1. What are the dance's justifications as a physical activity, as a social force and as an educational opportunity? How does it contribute to the refinement of the student and the development of the art spirit [a then-popular term denoting cultural sensitivity]?
2. As long as there are human emotions there will be dance. What is the essential nature of the dance that it has not perished?
3. Discuss this: Rhythm of motion is rhythm of emotion.
4. What are the essential qualifications of the teacher of dance?
5. What is philosophy, theory, science, art, each applied to dance? The art of dancing and dancing as an art?
6. Give the development of instinctive nature to move, to dance, as an art in the individual.
7. What is nature [*sic*] of art, its principles, and relation of all of its branches?[112]

H'Doubler wanted her students to think about dance in their education, and their lives, on a grand scale. Like her prompting of the individual "movement voice" of each student in the studio, these questions asked the dance student to locate herself and her interest in the larger world of intellectual ideas. The external experience may have been gained in the body, but H'Doubler's assessment focused on the traditional elaboration of concepts rather than the articulation of students' recondite experiences. Somatic knowledge was rendered as mental insight.[113]

H'Doubler had to be ready to demonstrate dance's educational and social value with clearly argued reasons for its importance and utility. The body could be positioned as the center of experience, just as Dewey had centralized the mind. The first chapter of Dewey's *The School and Society*, a book H'Doubler strangely does not list in the bibliography of *The Dance, and Its Place in Education,* is, in fact, built on this compelling, and astoundingly obvious, premise, that there should be an articulated relationship between our educational systems and the larger world outside the classroom.[114] For H'Doubler as for Dewey, the school was an embryonic world, embryonic of *real* society and all of its disciplines, the arts included. This was a key lesson in humility *and* relevance, which the students of Margaret H'Doubler carried into American colleges and universities with them.

8

Margaret H'Doubler's Classroom

Educational Progressivism in Theory and Action

> Works of art that are not remote from common life, that are
> widely enjoyed in a community, are signs of a unified collective
> life. But they are also marvelous aids in the creation of such
> a life.
>
> John Dewey, *Art as Experience*, 1934

THE MORE ONE PROBES H'DOUBLER'S CLASSROOM, THE MORE TRUE
it seems to be that she created the conditions for her *students*
to be the real innovators. In this regard Educational Progressivism was a persistent and profound, if unacknowledged, model for
H'Doubler's shaping of her dance classes in the university. The influence of Educational Progressivism, shifts in art education practice and
philosophy, and John Dewey's educational philosophy were forces that
influenced or echoed many of the models H'Doubler was trying to institute in dance education. The following three features that historian
Lawrence Cremin considers hallmarks of Progressive Education are each
also clearly central to H'Doubler's conception of dance in the university.
Cremin writes:

In the minds of Progressives, Progressive Education means: 1.) Broadening the
program and function of the school to include direct concern for health, vocation and the quality of family and community life. 2.) Applying in the classroom the pedagogical principles derived from new scientific research in psychology and the social sciences. 3.) Tailoring instruction more and more to
the different kinds and cases of children being brought into purview of the
school.[1]

An important insight Progressivism initiated with regard to art education, and one H'Doubler extended into the realm of dance education, was this parallel regard for theory and informed practice. "Doing" in the visual, and now performing, arts was seen as producing experiences that were intellectually valuable. Intellectual ideals in the early decades of the twentieth century were now beginning to be linked with physical means. Instead of the arts being used as merely vocational practice for a commercial skill, as had been the case with much visual arts education up to this time, H'Doubler's use of dance was an end in itself, or rather a *means* en route to an end of knowing the self and one's body better. This would come to represent a profound shift in goals for the arts in higher education.

This shift was initially evident in visual art education. Children's art education, from its introduction into the schools on a large scale in the 1820s until the turn of the century, focused on training in industrial drawing. It was not until the tenure of Arthur Wesley Dow, from 1904 to 1922, at Teachers College at Columbia University, that the emphasis in art education, both for teacher training and student learning, shifted from copying to composition and the expression of beauty.[2] Dow could be called the H'Doubler of art education, for his ideas became the model for generations of art educators just as H'Doubler set the prototype for dance.

The changes in art education instigated by Dow occurred while Teachers College was the academic center of H'Doubler's own search for a fresh approach to dance education. As did art educators in their own field, H'Doubler looked for ways to move dance in education from rote drill to artful personal expression. Dow's endorsement of an "art for art's sake" approach to art education strongly anticipates the kinds of sentiments H'Doubler would soon be writing about dance. Both Dow and H'Doubler invested in the same discourse of moving the focus of art in education from rote to inspiration. "The true purpose of art teaching is the education of the whole person for appreciation," Dow wrote.[3]

Dow's sentiments were prevalent in the visual arts educational rationale of the time, namely, that exposure to works of fine art would help students develop spiritual and practical virtues. The roots of this belief actually stretch back to the writings of mid-nineteenth-century German philosophers who argued for a conception of the mind as an active organizer of perception rather than a passive receiver of random perceptions.[4] This paradigm shift resulted in a new perception of the arts as sources of moral insight, resources for constructing the world imaginatively. Certainly this was true for H'Doubler's dance program. Dance involves behavior as a means, not just a result, and H'Doubler stressed morality on both counts. Along with dance, the visual arts, music, and literature were coming to be seen as educational subjects that could lead toward better culture and morality.

While H'Doubler had little interest in the liberal arts per se, her aesthetic certainly seemed in accord with that of British philosopher John Ruskin, who believed that the essence of art was beauty and that the role of the arts was to shift the goals of society to a higher purpose.[5] Many people of Ruskin's time actually believed that great artists were exemplars of high moral character and that exposure to works of fine art could thus help students develop spiritual and practical virtues. The physical corollary of this had already been espoused for some time—that there was a link between physical fitness and mental acuity and intellect.[6] H'Doubler positioned dance as a subject where the physical, emotional, and mental facets of the individual merged and, with the right instruction, blossomed.[7] It was at the crossroads of these concerns with the body, mind, and morality that she created educational dance.

At the turn of the century and into the first two decades of the twentieth century, American art educators were anxious to connect art study with the acquisition of specifically American virtues.[8] In H'Doubler's dance studio the quest for a virtuous, moral, and democratic ideal could be carried out in the dancing body. Over the first few years of her dance classes, H'Doubler would essentially rewrite Cremin's three points with dance at the forefront. The result was that the "concern for health, vocation and the quality of family and community life" of Cremin's first point became a consideration that the presence of good dance teaching in the schools by H'Doubler's graduates could address. More immediately, the dance classes themselves were means toward enhancing the "health and quality of family and community life" of the female university students. Here, too, H'Doubler interpreted the issue of health broadly to encompass mental and emotional as well as physical well-being. As her interest in the nascent field of psychology had shown her, the states of health of all three areas were interconnected.

As for the second point, H'Doubler's shaping of dance in the university was built around pedagogical principles borrowed from current "scientific research in psychology and the social sciences." Although once she established her dance major she deemphasized science courses in her curriculum, the methodology of science always informed her arguments about dance's educational and humanistic validity. This was particularly true of H'Doubler's core belief in the connections between sensory perception in the muscles, joints, and tendons, what she called the proprioceptors, and the sense made of these sensations, what she called the kinesthetic sense.[9] For H'Doubler the "scientific attitude" was essential to arranging the subject matter of dance educationally: this was the structure that enabled her to take a theatrical and artistic practice and make it central to society.

Margaret Jewell Mullen, who was a philosophy major and graduate student in the dance program at Madison in 1930–31, remembers that "the whole [women's physical education] department was swept by the idea of experimental psychology that movement must have a feeling."[10] Other students remembered how professors from the social sciences and psychology departments often stopped in and observed the dance classes in progress, chatting with H'Doubler and the students afterward. Edith Boys Enos recalls these spontaneous seminars vividly:

> Miss H'Doubler was great on having demonstrations, you know, for educational purposes. And she would often have . . . a group of educators or a group of teachers or some people who would be interested in this, and then she would give an informal demonstration and she would have maybe a dozen students or so on the floor demonstrating as she spoke. And because she was just like a disciple of anything, she explained, explained, explained, and explained. Everything has to have a reason and an explanation and a scientific basis and philosophical basis.[11]

In line with Cremin's third point, H'Doubler saw dance as a means for giving the student a new avenue of expression for individuality and difference. In the early 1940s, at a time when there were few, if any, places for African Americans in professional American dance companies, H'Doubler nurtured the dance majors Mary Hinkson and Matt Turney, two young African American women who would go on to become leading dancers with the Martha Graham Dance Company in New York. H'Doubler's dance classes seemed to open up alternatives for young women of all races and backgrounds outside the dominant path of marriage, motherhood, and social invisibility. For Anna Halprin, H'Doubler's dance program provided a forum to explore her Jewish identity—a search she remembers H'Doubler supporting enthusiastically through to her graduation thesis, which focused on Jewish dance. "Her class provided a space for being accepted," Halprin said.[12] This was at a time when many American universities still had strict quotas on the number of Jewish students they would admit.

In looking at what happened inside H'Doubler's studio, it is also important to acknowledge what happened outside. The early years of H'Doubler's association with the women's physical education program at the University of Wisconsin was a period when that university was acknowledged as the leading example of Progressive ideals in higher education, according to Cremin. Wisconsin governor Robert La Follette and university president Charles Van Hise worked together to implement the "Wisconsin Idea" during this period, a belief in the union of academic and practical studies that reflected their shared faith in the university as an active player in public service and public life.[13]

What might be called the Progressive Aesthetic informed H'Doubler's choices and values in the dance studio. The dance classes H'Doubler developed were in many respects textbook models of Cremin's ideal of Progressive Education in their fostering of the individual creator in each student. At the very least there must have been a certain political safety in adopting a Progressive approach in the turn-of-the-century university. At this time the arts existed in the university essentially as courses in specific skills or as recreation. Drawing and painting classes were shaped as practical-skills courses for those seeking jobs in the commercial sector, and instrumental and vocal musical groups were for collegial, social, and recreational needs. H'Doubler's class was radical not only in that it offered movement in the university but also because it was about nuturing individual creativity, about giving students tools for being personally expressive with their bodies. The class material was framed as educational, not social or recreational. For the American university in 1917, *that* was revolutionary.

In developing her methodology H'Doubler borrowed from the one place in the American university where the student's body was addressed, physical education. Using her background as a teacher of basketball for women, H'Doubler's incremental shaping of dance in the studio borrowed directly from early women's physical education. It was the incremental method of teaching women sports at this time, action by action, gradually building up to full-body moves and eventually a full game, that provided the model for H'Doubler in her dance teaching.

H'DOUBLER'S THEORETICAL DEVELOPMENT

H'Doubler's theoretical development as a dance educator is best revealed in the two major books of her career, *The Dance, and Its Place in Education* (1925) and *Dance: A Creative Art Experience* (1940). In the earlier book one sees vividly H'Doubler the scientist in action, looking for what is there and appreciating it in such a way that dance's educational attributes are opened out to a new examination.

After her two introductory chapters exploring "The Problem," that is, the misuse of dance in contemporary times as a mere device of recreation and amusement, and dance's past glory in history, H'Doubler examines the goals of education. Strongly reflecting Progressivist thinking here, H'Doubler posits that education must address "the body and soul and all the beauty of which they are capable." She sees the Progressivist ideal best reflected in "a true democracy where the opportunity to realize man's fullest self is possible. Every child has a right to know how to obtain control of his body so that he may use it to the limits of his abilities."[14]

Building her argument systematically and incrementally, H'Doubler next lists what she considers the six major attributes of an educational task. Dance, she promises, delivers all of them:

> The dance is peculiarly adapted to the purposes of education. It serves all the ends of education—it helps to develop the body, to cultivate the love and appreciation of beauty, to stimulate the imagination and challenge the intellect, to deepen and refine the emotional life, and to broaden the social capacities of the individual that he may at once profit from and serve the greater world without.[15]

Having set up the situation of a need and a possible solution, however, H'Doubler then interjects herself as indispensable, or at least her reconceptualization of dance as indispensable. Dance as it now exists cannot provide these educational experiences, according to H'Doubler; instead it must be redefined in keeping with the following rules she enumerates:

> But it is obvious that if the dance is to realize these possibilities it must take upon itself a form that is natural and educational. It must base its movements on the laws of bodily motion; its technique must be simple enough to afford to those who have comparatively little time to study the dance, an adequate mastery of their medium of expression—the body—and complex enough to prove interesting and valuable to the student who wishes to make the dance his chosen art. The scope of its rhythm must be broad enough to include the various rhythms of the dancers; and it must be flexible enough in forms and content to provide opportunity for widely different types of individuals to express themselves. If it is to be truly educational, it must be elastic so that the growth of the individual will be slow enough to achieve completeness. Above all it must be grounded on definite principles and directed toward a carefully conceived goal.[16]

The value of H'Doubler's philosophy of dance is how thoroughly and consistently she links it to the dominant values in education of the time, the notion of giving expression to things personal and deepening and refining the emotional life of individuals while challenging the intellect. Clearly it was this aspect of her theorizing that won her the greatest following among university administrators in Wisconsin. F. Louise Nardin, the formidable dean of women at Wisconsin, who became one of H'Doubler's most stalwart university supporters, chimed in with the following in her introduction to H'Doubler's *Dance, and Its Place in Education*:

> [In Margaret H'Doubler's classes] physical education was quietly putting these young women into vital relationship with an element of our civilization that is of the spirit as well as of the senses. Body was being made capable in this education of expressing what the mind heard and felt. Body and soul were well at home together in that hour of dancing. . . . There was here no unenlightened paganism bidding the mind to crouch or sleep and inviting the physical to make itself all sufficient and dominant.[17]

Nardin's comment echoes H'Doubler's basic strategy in this book, which is to offer continually her vision of dance as a corrective to the *other* type of dance, empty and socially valueless amusement. By the book's end one is aware that so much of what H'Doubler made valuable in dance was in part determined by the negative qualities in it she had to discount or ameliorate.

H'Doubler's next book, and the one that for decades stood as the definitive work on dance education for American teachers, *Dance: A Creative Art Experience*, presents a softening of some of these more extreme earlier stances. Even its title represents a new appropriation of the aesthetic attributes of dance as educational. In the fifteen years between the books H'Doubler had pulled more and more of the art side of dance under her educational umbrella. Paradoxically, she is much more assertive here about claiming physical education as the real impetus behind the new growth in dance education. If not for the opportunity given dance by physical educators, she insists, it would have had little chance for growth in the United States.

While *Dance: A Creative Art Experience* lacks the sharp originality of H'Doubler's previous book—indeed, whole passages from *The Dance, and Its Place in Education* are repeated verbatim here—the authority of the writing is much clearer. *The Dance, and Its Place in Education* was invaluable as a handbook of dos and don'ts for the young dance teacher. *Dance: A Creative Art Experience* reveals H'Doubler digesting further the educational philosophy of John Dewey as she attempts to forge her own real philosophy of dance education. By the 1940s many of the early Progressivist ideals to which H'Doubler anchored her early ideas of dance education were no longer current. Dewey's philosophy, in contrast, was far more current, particularly in regard to the value of the arts in education, since his *Art and Experience* had just been published six years earlier.

H'Doubler's theory of dance education grew by virtue of the other new philosophies she embraced along the way, and Dewey's work in the 1930s represented the second big leap in her own intellectual growth. Far less a manual than her previous book, *Dance: A Creative Art Experience* offers the first broad-based theory of dance education. The benefits of dance for the individual also take on a new importance here for H'Doubler. Instead of emphasizing how the individual will be made a more fit citizen for society, which is more of a Progressivist ideal for citizens and the tactic H'Doubler took in her first book, H'Doubler begins to tout dance as a means for developing the individual's mind in *Dance: A Creative Art Experience*.

H'Doubler holds on to this new ideal of the development of mind for the individual so adamantly that she begins to criticize theatrical dance anew in *Dance: A Creative Art Experience*, now because it fails to develop the individual in this manner. "Often contemporary dance and modern dance are terms that have come to mean only the personalized manner of contemporary dance artists," she complains.[18] This is the quintessential teacher talking here, for instead of valuing the newly rich capability of dance to reveal the interior life of individuals, as the choreographers Martha Graham and Doris Humphrey had spent the previous decade demonstrating, H'Doubler now faults them for only revealing *their own* interior lives. As if any artist could do more.

What becomes abundantly clear with this second book is how firmly H'Doubler viewed any aspect of dance strictly in educational terms. Subsequent generations of dance educators would be able to see value in dance as both a performing art and an educational pursuit, and in fact would use one as a model for the other. Studying how it is that Martha Graham plumbed, coded, and shaped into public forms dimensions of her existence, often interpreted through myths, holds valuable lessons for dance students. Yet the educational value of this kind of aesthetic analysis of dance eluded H'Doubler.

The analysis of the intellectual life of the artist would be the next frontier H'Doubler's successors would investigate. Evaluations of the other side of the equation of dance creation—that is, the kind of creation of mind that transpires in the perception of a finished work of choreography—lay ahead. It was the dance theorists who began to do this kind of looking at dance in the 1970s. The critics and historians launched the next era of dance education in the university, and in the process they created the field of dance history and criticism as an area of intellectual scholarship. H'Doubler, however, had initiated the method and the model for making dance fit well with higher education. One might generously say that dance has been able to grow as well as it has within the university because the foundation she created was so stable and yet so supportive of growth. She initiated a curriculum and at the same time inaugurated an arts discipline as educational.

9

Margaret H'Doubler's Legacy

Dance and the Performing Body
in the American University

The task is to present the scientific facts of movement, and
of the process of learning, and set up movement experiences
in such a way that movement can become a self-directed
and creative activity rather than a series of super-imposed
stereo-typed movement patterns.

Margaret H'Doubler, University of Wisconsin classroom handout,

1955

IF MARGARET H'DOUBLER HAD BEEN ABLE TO FORECAST THE EVOLU-
tion of dance in the American university beyond her retirement in
1954, she would likely have been more disconcerted than surprised
by what she found. Beginning with the dance boom in the late 1960s,
dance training for performance emerged as the emphasis of most college
programs. By the 1970s dance education had become the poor stepchild of
dance in academia; increasingly college and university dance faculty members were individuals trained in technique, performance, or dance theory
and history rather than dance education, and their curricula reflected this.
What had begun for H'Doubler and Blanche Trilling as a single-class
amendment to Wisconsin's physical education curriculum for women,
and had blossomed rapidly into a change with profound implications
for American higher education, was now finishing out the century as a
bifurcated curriculum with dance education as one small program and
dance as a performing art as the other, much larger one.

For both women the idea of offering dance in the 1917 summer session
must have seemed, at the outset, like a modest curricular addition. Initially
it was probably regarded as no more eventful than adding tennis and an
assistant coach to the women's swimming classes—two changes Trilling

mentioned along with the new dance class in a winter 1917 memo to the chairman of the Physical Education Department. As far back as the 1915 summer session Trilling had offered two sections of "aesthetic dancing" as well as "Singing Games and Folk Dance material for Grades 1–5" and "Folk Dances for Grades 6–8," so obviously the *concept* of offering dance of some kind in the summer program of 1917 was not new.[1] What was novel was the type of dance offered and the manner in which H'Doubler would transform her classroom as she implemented it.

In doing so H'Doubler initiated a complex tradition of continuity and change for dance in academia. Some of the challenges dance addressed explicitly at the outset—the bolstering and affirming of women's physical strength and well-being and the possibility for being feminine *and* physical—faded rapidly as issues. In contrast, others that were initially more recondite became prominent, such as dance's capacity to be a medium for bold social statement, enacted primarily on the female body, and the capacity of dance to model skills for critical problem solving and creative insight. That the former attributes are athletic and the latter aesthetic is significant, for dance, like many of the performing and visual arts, can be a chameleon discipline in higher education, serving social agendas such as promoting athletic opportunities for women and deemphasizing its artistic qualities when necessary.

DANCE IN THE UNIVERSITY EVOLVES

Within fifteen years of H'Doubler's first teaching of a dance class, a new alternative model of dance, dance as a performing art within the university, arose at Bennington College in Vermont.

Well before the German-trained modern dancer Louise Kloepper began teaching at the University of Wisconsin, the field of dance in American higher education had begun to change. In 1932, after ten years of planning, Bennington College opened in North Bennington, Vermont, offering a bachelor of arts degree with a concentration in dance, the first such college degree emphasizing dance as a performing art.[2] In 1936 the first three Bennington dance majors from this program would graduate. John Dewey was one of the many distinguished advisers who had participated in the college's planning, as was William Heard Kilpatrick of Teachers College at Columbia University.[3] The stamp of these Progressive educators from the start was on the curriculum, a curriculum which presented the arts as equal to the other academic subjects. By 1936 dance had been elevated to a separate division within the college.

Despite these educational ideals that valued dance as an art, it was reportedly the need for physical exercise and the lack of a gym that initially led the wife of Bennington president Robert Devore Leigh to suggest that the exercise classes be an art form, dance.[4] At the suggestion of Martha Graham, Martha Hill, a former Graham dancer and then a teacher at New York University, was hired to teach dance two days a week at Bennington. (Hill reportedly turned down a full-time appointment so that she could continue to teach three days a week at New York University.) Trained in physical education, Swedish gymnastics, eurythmics, ballet, and modern dance, Hill had also studied with H'Doubler during the summer of 1927 at the University of Wisconsin, where she had taken some art classes as well.[5]

Hill had then returned to New York, where she graduated with a bachelor's degree from Teachers College at Columbia in 1929, the same year she joined the Martha Graham Dance Group. In a reversal of the manner in which H'Doubler had rejected the theatrical side of the dance classes she found in New York, Hill embraced it, wedding dimensions of dance as a theater form with dance education. The Bennington model Hill would create for dance would become the other major alternative, outside of H'Doubler's, for higher education dance programs:

Taking dance out of the P.E. Department, from a sport to an art form, that was the big accomplishment of 1932. I was brought up to think that theater was something that nice people didn't do. There would be revivalist meetings where you could march up the aisle and say you'd give up dance and drink. . . . So this was absolutely amazing that a New England college [like Bennington] would tolerate dance and the arts. . . . It was further unthinkable that dance, of all the arts, would be backed so thoroughly.[6]

Bennington's emphasis on dance as an art form was cemented with the inauguration, in the summer of 1934, of the Bennington School of the Dance. For the next nine years the Bennington School of the Dance offered the most intensive summer session of dance production and study in the nation, competing significantly with H'Doubler's summer courses for dance teachers. Students, choreographers, dancers, musicians, and other artists participated in the creation of legendary dance works at Bennington by the Big Four, the masters of modern dance: Martha Graham, Hanya Holm, Doris Humphrey, and Charles Weidman.

Many of H'Doubler's students attended summers at Bennington, and H'Doubler herself visited the college in 1934, according to Mills College dance educator Marion Van Tuyl, who remembers H'Doubler's response as being "far from enthusiastic":

In her opinion, the difficulty with modern dance was that it was too closely tied to individual personalities. Impulse for movement from the pelvis was also particularly distasteful to her; Martha Graham's hip thrusts were not beautiful. Except for character impersonations, the curve was more beautiful than the angle for H'Doubler.[7]

In her dislike of angularity and the use of the pelvis in dance movement, H'Doubler once again aligned herself unknowingly with Isadora Duncan. Both women seem to have been forcibly drawing the line between what they saw as the vulgar, ugly, and "primitive" in dance and its sensual, curving, beautiful side. (In this regard their objections to primal forms and images ironically echoed objections to the unattractive and "primitive" images of dancing women in nineteenth-century visual arts.) H'Doubler was a guest lecturer at Bennington during the summer of 1938, but her connection to Bennington's summer dance program essentially began and ended there. The focus on the creation of professional dancers and dances, in the style of the field's leading artists, continued to be antithetical to her interests. The infant field of American dance education was small, and it was now also clearly divided.

The next major university dance program to be established was that at Mills College in Oakland, California, in 1938. As was true of the other college dance programs, the initiation of serious dance classes at Mills dated from the arrival of a charismatic woman dance educator, in this instance Marian Van Tuyl, a graduate of the University of Michigan's physical education program. Beginning there in 1924, Van Tuyl had taken dance classes from Janet Cummings, a recent graduate of H'Doubler's program at the University of Wisconsin. "We could be considered early granddaughters of Margaret H'Doubler," Van Tuyl once remarked of that lineage, and her swift rebellion against it. "Margaret H'Doubler was not bothered by dance being under the Physical Education Department, an administrative and conceptual situation which has frustrated many other dance teachers."[8] From 1928 to 1938 Van Tuyl had taught courses in Martha Graham's modern dance technique, improvisation, and composition at the University of Chicago as well as touring with her own Chicago-based professional group.[9]

Van Tuyl, like Hill, also studied with Martha Graham, attending the Bennington Summer School of Dance from its inception until she went west in 1938 to guest-teach at Mills. Van Tuyl's one-year visit to Mills stretched into a thirty-year permanent position, as she created first a dance major and then a dance department for the college. The dance curriculum Van Tuyl outlined for dance majors at Mills included a balance of dance history, theory, and teaching methods, as well as courses in biological and social sciences, fine arts, philosophy, and languages.[10] By 1941 Van Tuyl had moved dance into its own separate department. Van Tuyl was very conscious of where her interests and those of H'Doubler diverged as dance educators, remarking once, "Anthropology was not one of H'Doubler's fields of interest. Folk dance, ethnic dance, tap dance, she considered lesser forms, always holding her vision of the ideal dance. She was also utterly opposed to ballet of that time, because of its unnatural movement. I remember her once reprimanding a student, 'Your ballet is showing.' "[11]

In 1953 the University of California, Los Angeles hired Alma Hawkins, who had studied H'Doubler's method in the summer of 1926 at Madison, to teach dance and begin to draft the curriculum for its first dance major. Explaining how she knit together a range of influences, Hawkins cited her graduate work at Columbia with Harold Rugg in the School of Education, her awareness of the creative process from Bennington, and her grounding in group process from H'Doubler as all feeding into her concept of what dance in the university should be and what kind of curriculum would best serve it:

I wanted to put the art back in, so students could go where they wanted when they left, to perform or to teach. We were also interested in developing the ethnic forms and ballet.[12]

This hybridization of dance content brought with it problems for academic dance programs. By 1938 a writer in the leading physical education journal, *Journal of Health and Physical Education,* observed:

It is apparent that dancing in physical education has been dominated by the concert stage, with the result that some of our dance teachers have so thoroughly inoculated themselves with the methods and points of view of the concert artist that they find it difficult to make a practical adaptation to the physical education environment. Some of these teachers are guilty of affecting a superior attitude toward the program in physical education and succeed only in developing a resentment among their colleagues which either ignores or openly ridicules the dance.[13]

In many institutions that tried to appease both faculty drawn from the professional world of dance and administrators schooled in physical education, then, the tensions could be destructive. This same article in *JOHPE* went on to bemoan a confusion between the terms *participation* and *performance,* suggesting that the once sharp difference was becoming blurred. This confusion was presented as one of the "fresh dangers presenting themselves as hindrances to continued growth and prestige of dance in education," suggesting that even at this late date there were liabilities if dance appeared *too* much like an art form in some physical education programs.[14]

On the plus side, however, the growing crossover between professional and educational dance in the university resulted in a new diversity of uses for dance facilities in colleges. A network of colleges and universities as performing sites for professional modern dancers sprang up, as the leading modern dance groups toured what came to be known as the College Circuit, performing in college dance studios and theaters across the nation.

Within the next several decades, at least 527 college and university dance programs would be created.[15] These programs would base their identity on how they articulated a distinctive balance between these two poles of dance as a performing art and dance as a medium of physical and art education.

Dance has never been fully at home in the humanities in higher education, however, because until recently it lacked the historical and theoretical scholarship that the other art forms have long possessed. Dance faculties have also not been fully invested in shaping dance as predominantly educational in the way H'Doubler would have liked. There are two main reasons for this: in recent years a substantial portion of university dance faculty have been drawn from the world of professional dance, including performers and critics, and professional dance is no longer seen as a morally dangerous profession that young women must be protected against. So the fundamental tensions remain. Yet within this instability as an academic discipline comes an enviable mobility in the university; physical education, the performing arts, music, and the humanities are some of the fields where dance programs can be found in the university today.

Since that summer of 1917 dance has become much more fully represented as an art form in higher education, with courses in history, criticism, theory, and aesthetic analysis. Having lost a dimension of itself as the initial price of acceptance into the university, it has regained that and maintained its new identity as a medium of education as well.

Initially, the other early modern dance educators shared H'Doubler's dislike of ballet, but by the late 1930s sentiments were changing. In July of 1936 Bennington, which had been conceived as a bastion of modern dance, hosted the first tour of Ballet Caravan, the American ballet troupe organized by Lincoln Kirstein, who three years earlier had brought George Balanchine to America. In October 1937 the *Dance Observer*, the modern dance journal founded by Martha Graham's mentor, Louis Horst, editorialized on the subject of the growing equality between ballet and modern dance as follows:

The modern dance no longer needs the kind of defense we intended. It is no longer a stranger in a hostile country. Both as a mature and a popular art form, the modern dance needs no special nurturing. It stands well alone; walks, runs, and on occasion leaps well enough in a field that is no longer cramped into a couple of seaboard cities.[16]

Here, too, elements that had originally aided H'Doubler in founding her program now loomed as problematical. The splendid isolation of the Midwest, which had initially given H'Doubler such a protected place to launch her experiment in dance education, now made for a certain distance from the rapidly changing world of professional modern dance. In 1922 Isadora Duncan performed in the United States for the last time, and the following year Martha Graham left Denishawn to inaugurate the new order of modern dance, making her New York debut and forming her first concert group in 1926. In the following year, 1927, Duncan would be dead and New York would have three dance critics actively reviewing: John Martin for the *Times*, Mary Watkins for the *Herald Tribune*, and Lucille Marsh for the *World*.

By the mid-1930s American modern dance was becoming an established art form. Martha Graham had received the first Guggenheim Fellowship for choreography in 1932 and was premiering some of her most important dances in New York. The choreographers Helen Tamiris, Lester Horton, Doris Humphrey, Ted Shawn, Hanya Holm, and Anna Sokolow were presenting major new works. In 1932 the governor of New York signed a law permitting dance recitals in theaters on Sunday evenings, a prime performance time for dance, and the following year Black Mountain College opened in North Carolina.[17]

With dance so rapidly becoming a legitimate part of American culture, H'Doubler's dance program did change, but never in such a way as to match this growing emphasis on dance as a theater form. Soon Bennington's Summer School of the Dance was becoming an influential model for the nation's new college dance programs. H'Doubler's influence continued to be present as a starting point for how to work with basic movements and the concept of kinesthetic response, but the sizzle of the aesthetic dimensions of dance was borrowed increasingly from Bennington. Part of the vision of Bennington as a dance summer school was the manner in which it invited analysis of important emerging trends of modern dance, which were studied and investigated both artistically and technically by students who included many present and future dance teachers as well as performers.[18]

Patricia Gumport has posited curricula as "academic knowledge that is always in process or under construction by organizational participants" in her article "Curricula as Signposts of Cultural Change."[19] This is a useful model for looking at H'Doubler's efforts to situate dance in higher education and the subsequent tensions arising from the competing visions from other college dance programs such as those at Bennington, Mills, and the University of California, Los Angeles. Gumport's view suggests the curriculum as a provocatively fluid research environment where not only the methods of looking but also the institution and subject being examined are all in a state of change. This dynamic and constructed view of curricula is important for an investigation of the connections among dance, the university, and society that H'Doubler was advocating, because it suggests a similar state of continual evolution for the discipline.

Gumport cites Ralph Tyler on the idea of continual evolution in particular, quoting him as saying that academic disciplines should be viewed as "not simply a collection of facts . . . but [as] an active effort to make sense out of some portion of the world or of life." Gumport amplifies this:

Similarly, curricula may be seen as that part of the cultural life of academic organizations in which faculty, administrators, and students construct and revise their understandings and in which they negotiate about what counts as valid knowledge, in particular historical and social settings.

For most of the twentieth century the contemporary visual and performing arts have been some of the most contested terrain in American society in terms of what is, or should be, valid knowledge. Gumport cites Clifford Geertz in noting that academic thought can be considered a cultural artifact and that the legitimation of knowledge in higher education is always relative and contingent, not absolute or static. While there is ample evidence of how higher education has responded to societal tensions and the legitimation of knowledge around issues of gender, equity, representation, and race, few realize how equally responsive the arts have historically been in reflecting points of tension in society and consequently in constructing a form of cultural knowledge.[20]

The contemporary art genres, which draw even more thinly the line between the private and public self of the performer, have assumed much of early dance's role as a forum for the disenfranchised. It is only in retrospect that we can now appreciate how profoundly the disenfranchised women of early twentieth-century America were remade into fit, strong, *and feminine* women through efforts like H'Doubler's dance program. H'Doubler was, long before it became a political buzzword, promoting diversity in academia: gender role diversity, forms of intelligence diversity, forms of representing knowledge and learning diversity, race diversity—in other words, image and knowledge diversity.

Carol Vance, an anthropologist at Columbia University, spoke to this issue in an article written as part of the debate over censorship of the arts that raged in the late 1980s; her point has relevance here:

Diversity in images and expression in the public sector nurtures and sustains diversity in private life. When losses are suffered in public arenas, people for whom controversial or minority images are salient and affirming suffer a real defeat. Defending private rights—to behavior, to images, to information—is difficult without a publicly formed and visible community. People deprived of images become demoralized and isolated. . . . For these reasons, the desire to eliminate symbols, images and ideas they do not like from public space is basic to contemporary conservatives' and fundamentalists' politics about sexuality, gender and the family.[21]

H'Doubler not only abetted a dismantling of negative images of women, but, more important, she created a newly visible community of vigorous women and assisted them in fashioning fresh images of women's physical and cognitive vitality.

DANCE IN THE UNIVERSITY: INCREMENTAL CHANGE BECOMES FUNDAMENTAL CHANGE

What was surprising, if not remarkable, about H'Doubler's first dance class was that this initial offering of a higher education dance class— envisioned as a simple incremental addition of a new course—would very rapidly loom as a deeply fundamental shift in American education. Certainly in terms of its implications for the body and the arts in higher education, dance's entry into the university proved to be a significant occasion. It made possible alterations in the ways teachers think about the nature of learning and about their actions in the classroom, considerations that Larry Cuban deems hallmarks of "fundamental change" because they are deeply transformative to schooling.[22]

In her dance classes H'Doubler began to look for physical as well as verbal clues to student understanding. Unusually, particularly for a performing arts instructor, she was less interested in technical prowess than in students' connecting emotionally with the movement tasks in which they were engaged. Certainly some of these values had been in place in Progressive Education programs in the elementary grades, but H'Doubler was working specifically with achievement-oriented adults—a very different population. She was also working with an art form, dance, that was only just beginning to value personal sensitivity and physical expression as legitimate subjects for a woman to explore publicly. One of the crucial things H'Doubler did, then, was to fashion a link between these values as educational forces and art forces.

In fact, many of the criteria Cuban uses to distinguish fundamental from incremental change were evident in H'Doubler's dance classes, in-cluding shifting the teacher's role from that of a central source of power and knowledge to that of a coach who guides and helps students find meanings in their own experiences.[23] For H'Doubler this may have begun as a practical necessity; she had a general sense of what kinds of dance movements should be done, but it was up to the students to realize them fully.

Additionally, as in the hallmarks of other Progressive educators' fun-damental changes, student learning became active in H'Doubler's class-room. It included group work toward artistic expression, and instruc-tion was strongly student-centered. So the teacher's understanding about the very nature of knowledge, teaching, and learning in her classroom was also transformed—another marker of fundamental change.[24] While H'Doubler was certainly aware of many of the educational innovations of the nineteenth-century Progressives, her focus was on the *content* of what she was teaching. The methods she would use were dictated by this content and were merely the most effective and authentic means to get what she wanted.

Rather than being part of some grand new Progressive vision of the school, these changes evolved out of classroom necessity. H'Doubler embraced them because they worked; they made possible what she wanted to have happen in her dance classroom. So conceptually H'Doubler was an incremental reformer. Her basic premise was that the structures for teaching women's physical education were sound; she was simply fine-tuning her corner of dance. What would rapidly turn out to need improving by fundamental changes, however, was the way in which H'Doubler delivered the content and understanding of dance to her students and how she shepherded it through administrative barriers as it kept outgrowing containment by standard academic rules, particularly those of physical education.

Ironically, but perhaps not unexpectedly, H'Doubler's reform of the methods of teaching physical education happened as a consequence of her determined focus on offering a new class, which was in fact a new discipline. A radical revision of content in education most assuredly affects the means for delivering that content and vice versa. This is particularly true in the case of dance, which at the outset presented novel challenges for an educational system more comfortable with immobile bodies, mute students, and slumbering spirits.

MAKING THE UNIVERSITY SAFE FOR THE BODY

While H'Doubler accomplished more than she knew in the classroom, her initiation of curricular change was equally dramatic. Within a few years after the institution of that first dance class, other new courses on dance were being added rapidly at the University of Wisconsin in response to burgeoning student interest. For the 1919 summer session, for example, Trilling requested university approval to offer a new course taught by H'Doubler, "Theory of Dancing," in addition to the elementary and advanced levels of "Interpretive Dancing" she was already teaching.[25] During the fall of 1919 approximately twenty-three hundred women were registered in the university, with five to six hundred students in the dance classes alone.[26] By the 1922 summer session there were three levels of "Interpretive Dancing" being offered, elementary through advanced, as well as "Theory and Technique of Dancing," all taught by H'Doubler.[27] Physical education was, of course, required of all women undergraduates at this time, and dance was a means of partially fulfilling that requirement. Initially this expansion took a similar route to that of other sports Trilling added to the curriculum of women's physical education, with skill levels from beginning through advanced gradually being offered and, finally, one overview theory course. However, the dance offerings were also beginning to grow in ways unlike any other sport yet introduced. Within four years the 1926–27 catalogue would list "Rhythmic Form and Analysis," "Dance Composition," and "Philosophy of Dancing," all taught by H'Doubler and all core requirements for the new dance major. The new sport of dancing was rapidly growing into a separate discipline.

Indeed, as much as H'Doubler worked at strategies of academic containment, primarily to play down the theatrical dimensions of this foundling subject, the more her new course offerings began to describe the artistic contours of dance as an art form. *Music, composition,* and *aesthetics* were other words used to describe these three core classes of the new dance major.

Here was another, if unwitting, innovation that H'Doubler's first dance class initiated: movement as a kinetic art form now had a toehold in the university. It might be years before it was fully realized, and it might have gotten in by a back-door route, through athletics, and couched as a sport, but dance was now in the university and growing inevitably toward a new status as an educational art form. H'Doubler had accomplished more than she knew and far more than she intended. One is reminded of Oscar Wilde's quip that there are two great tragedies in life: one is *not* getting what you want, and the other is getting it. H'Doubler got what she wanted—a new course in dance education—and also what she did not—namely, the eventual establishment of dance as a fully theatrical art form in academia. H'Doubler addressed what she considered this "problem" in one of the last sections of *The Dance, and Its Place in Education*:

But as the instructor has probably discovered by this time, it is impossible to go far with any activity, around which so many preconceived ideas and expectations have gathered as the dance, without having to face the demands and expectations of the people outside. *These take their most harassing form in the expectation of some public performance or recital* in which the students may display their skill and grace to an admiring circle of friends and relatives. . . . The average parents find it difficult to understand a theory of dancing which does not include occasional recitals, pageants or exhibitions, and which insists that the raison d'être of the dance should be the pleasure it gives to the individual himself [emphasis added].[28]

While H'Doubler initially deplored dance as a performing art, she later allowed it to sneak into her curriculum. Ironically, this was possible because of the arts' peculiar position in American society. They are always present and always equivocal. Over the past century society as well as academia has continually redefined the various arts as more or less educational or artistic, depending on what is valued and politically safe and expedient at the time. They can be means for political expression or containment, for articulating gender identities, or for addressing cultural difference, to name just a few recent uses of the arts in education.

Dance in higher education would have another big boom period in the late 1960s and early 1970s—not surprisingly, on the wave of this century's second big push for women's rights. The first period of women's suffrage saw dance enter the university, and now, with the second, the field of dance would again expand, along with freedoms for the female, and her body, in society.

For the first several years of H'Doubler's program, her strategy of containment worked well: there were no classes in dance history or criticism at Wisconsin, classes that would have occasioned the full-scale regard of dance as an art form. However, with the addition of Louise Kloepper, the accomplished former professional dancer with Hanya Holm, to the dance teaching staff in 1942, increased technical training and expertise began to creep into the "dancing" classes at Wisconsin. Davidson recalls her as "teaching the technical use of movement in a manner that was informal, demanding, and exciting." Alumnae interviews suggest it was Trilling rather than H'Doubler who invited Kloepper as a professional dancer to join the staff.[29] The style, if not the professionalism, of what Kloepper taught must have pleased H'Doubler, for Kloepper also came from the German tradition of Mary Wigman, the one professional concert modern dancer for whom H'Doubler at least had an affinity.

WHAT DID H'DOUBLER SAY WE LEARN THROUGH DANCE?

In conclusion, the central paradox of H'Doubler's not dancing turned out to be a shrewdly effective strategy in disguise. Her efficacy as a dance education pioneer came in large measure from her *not* being a dancer, from being outside the field. Practitioners of the arts are often not the best educational advocates and theorists for the arts. The situation of not being an artist can give one more credibility with administrators and policy makers. The more neutral vantage point of an engaged outsider can be a powerful perspective from which to affect educational and institutional policy: one tends to frame arguments for academic acceptance from the outside in. Reasoning can be more inclusive of the lay perspective, and recondite truths of the arts can be spelled out and made explicit.

Lacking any real dance training herself, H'Doubler created novel means to help students attend to movement in their bodies. She used skeletons, blindfolds, scarves, hoops, kneepads. She was also free of the taint of "evil" theatrical dance. This was crucial, for even Ruth St. Denis made a big show of renouncing the tawdry side of concert dance when she announced her retirement from vaudeville in July 1919 and formed her Ruth St. Denis Concert Dancers in 1920. She then used a marketing campaign to transform her image from that of a vaudeville performer with artistic leanings to a serious concert artist.[30] This constraint of consciously fashioning dance as *not* a lowly performing art led H'Doubler, much as it led St. Denis in the theater, into an extraordinary new view of dance, one with profound implications for academia. H'Doubler created dance education in part as a hybrid between dance and physical culture, while St. Denis created a new style of ethnically inspired modern dance.

H'Doubler passionately believed that we learn a number of important things through dance. She shaped her curricular innovations to fit her larger view of education, that "education is for living."[31] In this way she argued for, and won, a new conception of dance as a way to prepare students to live creative, productive lives in society—a society they could hope to change someday.

H'Doubler's initial background as a biologist was also crucial in this regard. It led her to see that survival is dependent on an organism's creative use of its resources. She saw the art instinct as having a parallel biological basis where imaginative use of what was available was equally crucial.[32] Thus she viewed this creative use of resources as an innate capacity possessed in some degree by everyone. From the biological necessity of living organisms' imaginative use of resources, H'Doubler extrapolated the belief that everyone has the right to experience dance as a creative art activity.[33]

This generic definition of creativity helped H'Doubler to establish dance in the university. At the same time, it offered a reshaping of dance as a craft, a recreational activity for personal, but not necessarily aesthetic, growth. Early twentieth-century higher education was not the place or time to subject women to an intensely competitive classroom environment based on the professional studio model. Instead, in H'Doubler's classroom students received the message that their movement inventions were interesting and the experiences they had in making them were important. H'Doubler's goal was to develop an integrated, unique individual through exercising each student's creative movement capabilities.

H'Doubler's tacit strategy was also to use the mind as a conduit to the body. Dance and physical education had tended to work in the other direction, addressing the muscles as a way to affect the mind. By reversing the standard path and at times bouncing back and forth between the two methods, H'Doubler spurred her students' own conviction as to their power and efficacy in the world and inspired them with her enthusiasm and faith. This encounter with dance changed their lives.

A final element of H'Doubler's strategy for success was her invention of a vocabulary for dance in education. Her dance studio looked like a stage, but she called it a studio/classroom. Students didn't choreograph, they "made up" dances. Orchesis was a dance club, not a performing ensemble. Programs never listed casts or choreographers. Initially the department correspondence even called H'Doubler a "coach" of dance. As a matter of fact, she was (figure 39).

SIGNIFICANCE AND IMPLICATIONS

H'Doubler's experiment with dance in the university could be seen as one of the first volleys in a radical reconceptualization of the arts as vital educational forces and as disciplines that might be thought about, and taught, as means toward the development of the mind.

The form and shape of the arts in the university reflect society's reshaping and packaging of pieces of its cultural knowledge. The arts can be seen as society's conscience in this regard. The situation becomes more complicated when one considers the arts in education, because educational institutions themselves exert determining and shaping forces on all their disciplines, particularly the extremely malleable arts.

H'Doubler also believed that people have an emotional response to their movements and that emotional material is the central subject matter of all art. This offered a challenge to the Cartesian model of intelligence still holding sway, one that saw human thought existing independently of the body.

In their efforts to place dance in the American university, and on a serious footing, Trilling and H'Doubler offered diverse new images for the American woman, images not realized in the public arena of higher education. These two women dreamed that dance could become a vital part of intellectual and emotional growth, an avenue for understanding oneself that no other discipline could duplicate. H'Doubler initiated a concept of the newly sentient body, a body of which her women students were just gaining self-possession. The implications of this are still being challenged, probed, and realized, not only by dance but by all the visual and performing arts as they continually negotiate their status in the university.

H'Doubler's actions opened the door for a fresh valuing of dance as a means for gaining mediate and immediate understanding of the world. H'Doubler demonstrated that dance could be a means for developing the capacity in students to physicalize experience. She showed that dance could be used as a non-, pre-, and post-verbal medium of expression that made possible kinds of articulation not possible elsewhere.

Figure 39. Margaret H'Doubler in the 1960s (Collection of Louise H'Doubler Nagel)

H'Doubler's reforms endured because they embodied many of the trademarks of educational reforms that last.[34] They were accretions to existing educational structures, they had a constituency, and they were directed toward a specific population of students. H'Doubler's educational reforms also required teachers to change their actual behaviors, rather than trying simply to teach different content in the same old ways. The locale within the university in which H'Doubler worked, physical education, is historically also the one academic arena where students have succeeded in instituting their own educational reforms.[35] H'Doubler's reforms got in on the ground floor.

Indirectly H'Doubler helped initiate, as well as support, a change in the direction of art education. Rather than providing industrial job skill training or moral education, or a route to citizenship or industry, both popular models of the time, her classes offered a glimpse of what art educators would flesh out more fully in the years ahead, that is, art education as an apprenticeship in the changing ideas and vigorous practices that adult artists and audience members pursue.[36] Eventually this would become part of the emergence of a view of human cognition that values imagery, representation, and a capacity for envisioning multiple worlds. The larger view would be that of the arts as powerful ways of knowing, contributing to, and participating in a culture, in life.

Appendixes

Notes

Bibliography

Index

Appendix 1

Granville Stanley Hall

Some of the most remarkable documents concerning dance in education from the late nineteenth and early twentieth centuries are those written by Granville Stanley Hall. An American psychologist who trained in Germany, Hall was among the first Americans to pursue the latest German study in psychology. He returned to the United States determined to use psychology toward a practical end. For Hall and a number of his colleagues, education loomed as a particularly fertile field for this exploration, and as a result the "child-study movement" was launched in the 1880s.[1] Initially, Hall began applying experimental methods to the study of the mind at Clark University, where he established a psychological laboratory that trained students in experimental techniques and sent them out to observe children, recording their data on questionnaires.

Approaching his study with religious zeal, Hall declared that his efforts would "give education what it had long lacked—a truly scientific basis and help to give teachers a really professional status."[2] It was the legacy of this scientific method of collecting enormous quantities of data on students that likely provided the model for collecting facts about women students' bodies in the initial college programs of physical education. It also made the study of children a central part of any serious study of education. By 1894 child-study had been formalized with the National Education Association's creation of a separate Department of Child-Study. Fitting within this, the dance major H'Doubler would initiate at the University of Wisconsin at Madison would initially look toward training dance teachers for children as well as adults.

Hall's educational interests were extremely broad. He saw many opportunities for social betterment through education, particularly through
the right kind of physical activity and controlled performing arts. One of
Hall's earliest formal publications to address the issue of physical activity
in education was a 1902 essay, "Christianity and Physical Culture." It
appeared in the September issue of *Pedagogical Seminary*, which he edited,
and its tone is messianic in linking social salvation to strong muscles. The
theme of this article is summed up in Hall's closing statement: "But there
is one language and one only, of complete manhood, and that is willed
action, and it is to make our lives speak in this language and thus to make
them historic that we train, what psychology now sees to be the chief
power in man, the will, the only organs of which are muscles" (378).³

This linking of "the will," or moral choice, with disciplined muscles would have important repercussions for dance education. A similar
linking of a physically flexible and articulate body with moral rectitude
would underlie higher education's initial valuing of dance. "There is a
sense in which all good conduct and morality may be defined as right
muscle habits," Hall proclaimed. "Rational muscle culture, therefore,
for its moral effects . . . [is] for the young, the very best possible means
of resisting evil and establishing righteousness" (375). Hall went on to
extol the virtue of the system of gymnastics he had witnessed firsthand in
Germany:

The German Turner system, which sometimes brings 5,000 trained men in the
field in this country, exercising in uniform under one command, has been one
of the most potent allies of patriotism in the German Fatherland, and for three
generations has contributed to improve the bodies and increase the national
strength under Jahn's inspiring motto, "only strong muscles can make men great
and nations free." (377)

Writing with surprising prescience, Hall also defined the hybrid that
would become American physical education. At the same time he anticipates the fascistic militaristic bent that would dominate the German use
of physical culture over the next few decades. "We seek to combine the
spontaneity of the Anglo-Saxon body cult; the science of the Swedish; and
the love of country which inspired the Germans, but our loyalty is to a
kingdom invisible, not made with hands. . . . We are soldiers of Christ,
strengthening our muscles not against a foreign foe, but against sin within
and without us" (377).

Hall's 1911 publication, the two-volume *Educational Problems*, continues his examination of a new range of art forms and activities for
their potential educational and moral utility. There seems to be little, if
any, place for idle enjoyment in Hall's social model of the arts. The arts,
like everything else, must be shaped to craft a better person, a more fit

citizen, a stauncher moral advocate for democracy. Hall was not alone in this early twentieth-century drive to make everything as educationally functional as possible. It was only a matter of time until dance, too, properly restructured, would be reconceptualized as the means to an ideal citizen.

Hall's pragmatic approach to the arts is interesting. The theater and "motion pictures" come in for special criticism by Hall because of their potential and their misuse. "School teachers testify with great unanimity that theatre-going makes boys crave excitement, makes them blasé, uninterested, listless, sometimes prone to drop out and earn a little money to indulge this craze; young girls are affected in their ambitions; they assume the mannerisms of the stage and perhaps its dress," he asserts (377). This last comment tacitly confirms the arts' power to both reflect and model social roles and moral values. It also suggests the era's increasing appetite for spiritual and physical redemption. There is a significant shift from earlier times here, for the desire is not to prohibit but to restructure. "The educative force of the theatre is degenerating, and even good theatres introduce vulgar, burlesque features," he concludes. "All this cannot but tend to lower public standards of morality" (377).

In his essay "The Educational Value of Dancing and Pantomime," Hall articulates a clear distinction between desirable and undesirable dance, calling the whole discipline, in fact, "a new type of motor-mindedness" (42).[4] This is a phrase that reflects the long-standing higher regard people in education held for "intellectual" pursuits over physical ones. It also offers important clues as to the aspects of dance that may be emphasized as the most attractive to academics. Indeed, Hall is brutally frank about the dangers of dance that fall outside this realm, particularly ballroom dance:

The dancing here advocated has little to do with the ballroom and finds little more to praise and little less to condemn in it than do Puritan religionists, though on different grounds. The offenses of these dances has [*sic*] usually been against hygiene, involving as they did unreasonable hours, fatigue, excitement, exposure and often too against morality. The types of movement are chiefly confined to the limbs, respiration is restricted, especially facial movements, and expressions are so tabooed that the physiognomy often seems sad and wooden. While the steps are conventionalized so that their athletic value is limited. (61)

It was precisely in recognizing these inherent contradictions in the nineteenth-century American outlook that dance was able to make a case for itself as an educational enterprise. Its staying power in American education, therefore, derives from its having been aligned with the right issues early on. Before H'Doubler's 1917 summer dance class in Madison, a few other prominent educators like Hall had noted the utility of having dance in the curriculum, but they, also like Hall, tended to truncate it into a remedy for well-being or religious health, selling short its capacity for educating the whole person. Hall's following statement would be precisely the starting point for Blanche Trilling and her protégé, H'Doubler, in their reenvisioning of dance:

Dancing I would describe as the liberal, humanistic culture of the emotions by motions. As thus interpreted is it not plain that the new dancing should be taught in every school, even if it has to be open evenings for that purpose. The dances chosen should be simple, rhythmic and allowing great freedom. . . . [They should] cultivate a sense of rhythm, ease, economy and grace of movement. (42)

Dance would not surface as a separate and rigorously legitimate academic discipline until Trilling and H'Doubler reconceived it as such, yet this passage shows Hall anticipating with uncanny accuracy H'Doubler's own recipe for American educational dance.

Appendix 2

Dance Department Memorandum, December 1953

Author's note: This Dance Department memo, written by Margaret H'Doubler, is in the H'Doubler Papers, University of Wisconsin–Madison Archives.

December 11, 1953
M.N.H'D

To create a dance is to produce a new and unique construction out of the existing materials of the physical and psychical natures. The creative and imaginative mind builds new images out of meaningful experience, and with the will and energy the new images are executed motorly and brought into existence thus creating a dance that is an embodiment of emotional experience in expressive movement. The creative act is a building process that constructs out of consciously evaluated experience. Any dance in which the creative mind of the dancer has been permitted to organize and endow its materials with a specific structure and individuality that is its own, is the result of creative effort. Stated another way—a dance is a designed entity—an embodiment of emotional experience transformed by thought and consciously given a movement form upon which the principles of composition have been imposed by the personality which was the subject of the experience.

Subjectively, a dance is an ideal toward which the imaginative mind reaches; a dance is a movement reality so formed that it becomes a symbol of this ideal. It is the observable form of what the mind has created.

A definition sufficiently broad to include the less highly developed forms, such as tap, folk, group, and ballroom dancing, might be stated as follows: A dance is the rhythmic motor expression of feeling states aesthetically valued, whose movement symbols are consciously designed for the pleasure and satisfaction either of expression and communication—or for the delight in experiencing rhythm inherent in the many dance forms.

Notes

INTRODUCTION

1. Suzanne Shelton, *Divine Dancer: A Biography of Ruth St. Denis* (New York: Doubleday, 1981), 182.

2. Ruth St. Denis, "The Creative Impulse and Education," *Denishawn Magazine* 1, no. 4 (summer 1925): 14–16.

3. The genre term *modern dance* is used here to refer to the qualities and structures common to works of dance of early to mid-twentieth-century America. Expression, rather than an established vocabulary, was the key to the identity of this genre. Source: Selma Jeanne Cohen, "Genres of Western Theatrical Dance," in *International Encyclopedia of Dance*, ed. Selma Jeanne Cohen (New York: Oxford University Press, 1998) 3: 130–31.

4. "The dance has suffered too long from the common use made of it as a means of recreation and amusement. Modern civilization has not usually considered it either worthy of serious effort or intellectually profitable. Only recently has progressive education recognized the value of physical education. . . . as more students with a real scholarly interest enter the field of physical education, they are realizing that its program has too long ignored the relation between body and soul as expressed in regulated rhythm." Margaret H'Doubler, *The Dance, and Its Place in Education* (New York: Harcourt, Brace, 1925) 1.

5. St. Denis chides H'Doubler for her remark. "I cannot agree that the stimulus to education by the dance has come, as she says, through a more scholarly interest in physical education," St. Denis writes. "It has come as of old, through the dynamic, creative impulses of the artist." St. Denis, 14.

6. St. Denis, 15.

7. Shelton, 165.

8. Ellen Wiley Todd, *The New Woman Revisited: Painting and Gender Politics on Fourteenth Street* (Berkeley: University of California Press, 1993). Todd writes of New Womanhood in this manner in discussing women painters of the early nineteenth century, but many of her comments can be extended to H'Doubler

and dance with equal validity. H'Doubler remained a single woman until she was forty-five, she never had children, and she always worked outside the home from her early twenties until well into her sixties.

9. Todd, 8.

10. Barbara Miller Solomon, *In the Company of Educated Women: A History of Women and Higher Education in America* (New Haven: Yale University Press, 1985), xvii. Solomon makes a point about the effect of education upon women's life choices at this time.

11. Rosalind Rosenberg, *Beyond Separate Spheres: Intellectual Roots of Modern Feminism* (New Haven: Yale University Press, 1982), xiv.

12. Todd, 260.

13. H'Doubler recounts with amusement that not only did the dean of women not fire her, but she voiced her own private envy of H'Doubler for freeing herself from the burden of long hair. Mary Alice Brennan, interview with Margaret H'Doubler, 1972.

14. Brennan interview.

15. Mary Hinkson, interview with author.

16. H'Doubler's personal files in the University of Wisconsin–Madison Archives contain letters from both the Denishawn and Wigman schools of dance in New York (written in 1931 and 1936, respectively) soliciting her graduates as students in their classes.

17. Solomon, 92.

18. St. Denis, 15.

19. *Dance: A Creative Art Experience* went through five editions from its initial publication in 1940 through its most recent in 1998. More than thirty-six thousand copies of the original edition were sold.

20. Howard Gardner, *Frames of Mind*, 10th ed. (New York: Harper Collins, 1983), 205. Gardner identifies control of one's bodily motions and the capacity to handle objects skillfully as Bodily-Kinesthetic Intelligence.

CHAPTER 1. EARLY TWENTIETH-CENTURY DANCE EDUCATION AND THE FEMALE BODY

1. Mary Lou Remley, "The Wisconsin Idea of Dance: A Decade of Progress, 1917–1926," *Wisconsin Magazine of History* 58, no. 3 (spring 1975): 183.

2. Margaret H'Doubler, *The Dance, and Its Place in Education* (New York: Harcourt, Brace, 1925), 33.

3. H'Doubler's first publication was *A Manual of Dancing*, a student manual that was out of print when she wrote *The Dance, and Its Place in Education*.

4. Matthew S. Hughes, *Dancing and the Public Schools* (Cincinnati: Methodist Book Concern, 1917), 28–29.

5. "The Dance Problem" (1912), "Is Modern Dancing Indecent?" and "The Problem Tango Has Inflicted on the Church." H'Doubler, *Dance, and Its Place,* 261.

6. Richard Powers, interview with author.

7. Isadora Duncan is the best-known American dancer to have derived, in part, her inspiration for a new dance from Greek statues she viewed at the British Museum and at the Louvre in Paris. Isadora Duncan, *My Life* (New York: Liveright, 1927), 67. California painter Arthur F. Mathews made a number of paintings of women costumed like Greek antiquities dancing over the California hills at this time; the most famous is *Youth*, ca. 1917, an oil on canvas in a carved, painted, and gilded wood frame made by Mathews Furniture Shop (Oakland Museum Collection; see figure 6).

8. Stanley Coben, *Rebellion against Victorianism: The Impetus for Cultural Change in 1920s America* (New York: Oxford University Press, 1991), jacket notes.

9. H'Doubler, *Dance, and Its Place*, 9.

10. H'Doubler, *Dance, and Its Place*, 27.

11. H'Doubler, *Dance, and Its Place*, 224.

12. Vivien Gardner and Susan Rutherford, eds., *The New Woman and Her Sisters: Feminism and Theatre, 1850–1914* (Ann Arbor: University of Michigan Press, 1992).

13. H'Doubler, *Dance, and Its Place*, 4.

14. Coben, 74.

15. Ann Daly, *Done into Dance: Isadora Duncan in America* (Bloomington: Indiana University Press, 1995), 9.

16. Daly, 16.

17. H'Doubler, *Dance, and Its Place*, 26–27.

18. Hughes, 25.

19. Daly, 7.

20. Toni Morrison, *Playing in the Dark: Whiteness and the Literary Imagination* (Cambridge: Harvard University Press, 1992), 6. This Africanist presence, Toni Morrison contends, "shaped the body politic, the constitution and the entire history of the [American] culture."

21. See Elaine Showalter, *The Female Malady: Women, Madness, and English Culture, 1830–1980* (New York: Penguin Books, 1985), and Sara Delamont and Lorna Duffin, eds., *The Nineteenth-Century Woman: Her Cultural and Physical World* (London: Croom Helm, 1978).

22. Showalter, 18.

23. Franklin Rosemont, ed., *Isadora Speaks* (San Francisco: City Lights Books, 1981), 48. This speech was originally given in 1922.

24. Rosemont, 48–49.

25. Amy Koritz, *Gendering Bodies/Performing Art: Dance and Literature in Early Twentieth-Century British Culture* (Ann Arbor: University of Michigan Press, 1986), 50.

26. Gertrude Colby entered Teachers College at Columbia University intending to study corrective gymnastics, but her interests switched to dance. In 1917, after teaching children's dance at the Speyer School, the experimental school for Teachers College, Colby returned to Teachers College as an instructor. Colby, in contrast to H'Doubler, championed pantomime, which she called "the essence of

all dancing." Mary P. O'Donnell, "Gertrude Colby," *Dance Observer* (January 1936): 8; Gertrude K. Colby, *The Conflict: A Health Masque in Pantomime* (New York: A. S. Barnes, 1930).

27. Deborah Jowitt, *Time and the Dancing Image* (New York: William Morrow, 1988), 96.

28. Isa Partsch-Bergsohn, *Modern Dance in Germany and the United States: Crosscurrents and Influences*, vol. 5 of *Choreography and Dance Studies*, ed. Robert P. Cohan (Chur, Switzerland: Harwood Academic Publishers, 1994), 5.

29. Koritz, 51.

30. Koritz, 51.

31. H'Doubler's notes to the dancers in her student performance group, Orchesis, contain repeated reminders to always dress modestly and properly when attending receptions associated with student dance concerts and in performance to always wear brassieres—pinned into the costumes—and to scrupulously shave all underarm and leg hair. "Orchesis" (handout, n.d., University of Wisconsin–Madison Archives), 1.

32. There are reports of a series of artful nude photographs of H'Doubler's dancers having been made by a Madison photographer. But the portfolio vanished in the late 1970s, according to Jo Anne Brown in "A Survey of Campus Resources on the History of Dance" (n.d., University of Wisconsin–Madison Archives), 12.

33. Hermine Sauthoff Davidson, interview with author.

34. James C. Whorton, *Crusaders for Fitness: A History of American Health Reformers* (Princeton: Princeton University Press, 1982), 301.

35. Rosemont, 48.

36. Nancy Lee Chalfa Ruyter, "Delsarte System of Expression," in *International Encyclopedia of Dance*, ed. Selma Jeanne Cohen (New York: Oxford University Press, 1998), 2:370.

37. Ruyter, "Delsarte System," 371.

38. Sara Burstall, *The Education of Girls in the United States* (London: Swan Sonnenschein, 1894), 151.

39. Nancy Lee Chalfa Ruyter, "Antique Longings: Genevieve Stebbins and American Delsartean Performance," in *Corporealities*, ed. Susan Leigh Foster (London: Routledge, 1996), 71.

40. Ruyter, "Antique Longings," 71.

41. Selma Landen Odom, "Émile Jaques-Dalcroze," in *International Encyclopedia of Dance*, ed. Selma Jeanne Cohen (New York: Oxford University Press, 1998) 3:594.

42. Partsch-Bergsohn, 6.

43. Jowitt, 80.

44. Mary Alice Brennan, interview with Margaret H'Doubler, 1972.

45. Letter to Professor F. W. Dykema, 1915, Trilling correspondence, University of Wisconsin–Madison Archives.

46. Mary Douglas, *Purity and Danger: An Analysis of Concepts of Pollution and Taboo* (London: Penguin Books, 1966), 4.

47. Ramsay Burt, *The Male Dancer: Bodies, Spectacle, Sexualities* (London: Routledge, 1995), 179.

48. E. Shorter, *Women's Bodies: A Social History of Women's Encounter with Health, Ill-Health and Medicine* (New Brunswick, N.J.: Transaction, 1982), 285.

49. Shorter, 279.

CHAPTER 2. NINETEENTH-CENTURY RESPONSES TO WOMEN'S HEALTH AND SEXUALITY

1. The 1916 University of Wisconsin catalogue lists the title of H'Doubler's first dance class as "Interpretive Dance," and by the 1926 catalogue it is called "Aesthetic."

2. Lois Banner, *American Beauty* (New York: Alfred A. Knopf, 1983), 49.

3. Banner, 53, 56–57.

4. Alexis de Tocqueville, *Democracy in America* (London: Longmans, 1889), 2:81. Cited in Banner, 84.

5. De Tocqueville cited in Graham John Barker-Benfield, "Horrors of the Half-Known Life: Aspects of the Exploitation of Women by Men" (Ph.D. dissertation, UCLA, 1968), 45.

6. Susan Groag Bell and Karen M. Offen, eds., *Women, the Family, and Freedom: The Debate in Documents*, vol. 2, *1880–1950* (Stanford: Stanford University Press, 1983), 1.

7. Bell and Offen, 2.

8. Bell and Offen, 8–9.

9. Bell and Offen, 13.

10. Bell and Offen, 159.

11. Bell and Offen, 137.

12. Jill Conway, "Women Reformers and American Culture, 1870–1930," *Journal of Social History* (winter 1971–72): 164.

13. Bram Dijkstra, *Idols of Perversity* (New York: Oxford University Press, 1986), xiii.

14. Susan R. Bordo, "The Body and the Reproduction of Femininity: A Feminist Appropriation of Foucault," in Susan R. Bordo and Alison M. Jaggar, eds., *Gender/Body/Knowledge* (New Brunswick: Rutgers University Press, 1989), 17.

15. Dijkstra, 8.

16. Dijkstra, 8.

17. Dijkstra, 17, 37.

18. Kathryn Kish Sklar, *Catharine Beecher: A Study in American Domesticity* (New Haven and London: Yale University Press, 1973), 204–7.

19. Sklar, 207.

20. Banner, 54.

21. Dijkstra, 168.

22. See, for example, Herbert Spencer, *Principles of Biology* (London: Williams and Norgate, 1864).

23. Max Nordau, 1893, paraphrased from Dijkstra, 212.

24. Sander L. Gilman, *Difference and Pathology: Stereotypes of Sexuality, Race and Madness* (Ithaca: Cornell University Press, 1985), 54.

25. Dijkstra, 244.

26. Dijkstra, 244, 249.

27. Dijkstra, 25.

28. Dominick Cavallo, *Muscles and Morals: Organized Playgrounds and Urban Reform, 1880–1920* (Philadelphia: University of Pennsylvania Press, 1981), 112.

29. Abba Gould Woolson, *Woman in American Society* (Boston: n.p., 1873).

30. Don Lugi Satori, *Modern Dances* (Collegeville, Ind.: St. Joseph's Printing Office, 1910), 58.

31. E. Lynn Linton, *Modern Women*, 1889, as cited in Dijkstra, 27.

32. Catharine Beecher quoted in Sklar, 210.

33. Elizabeth Kendall, *Where She Danced* (New York: Alfred A. Knopf, 1979), 21–22.

34. Banner, 49.

35. Banner, 48.

36. Sklar, 213.

37. Sklar, 204.

38. Catharine Beecher quoted in Sklar, 204–5.

39. Kathy Peiss, *Cheap Amusements: Working Women and Leisure in Turn-of-the-Century New York* (Philadelphia: Temple University Press, 1986), 4.

40. Peiss, 4.

41. Peiss, 5.

42. Peiss, 178.

43. Peiss, 178.

44. In fact, the leading book about recreational play of the time was titled *Muscles and Morals*. Cavallo, 4.

45. Peiss, 179.

46. Peiss, 181.

47. Peiss, 88.

48. Eric Lott, *Love and Theft: Blackface Minstrelsy and the American Working Class* (New York: Oxford University Press, 1993), 117.

49. Elizabeth Aldrich, *From the Ballroom to Hell: Grace and Folly in Nineteenth-Century Dance* (Evanston: Northwestern University Press, 1991); Aldrich's book borrows its title from T. A. Faulkner's 1894 treatise by the same name.

50. J. Townley Crane, *An Essay on Dancing* (New York: Phillips & Hunt, 1849), 4.

51. T. A. Faulkner, *From the Ball-room to Hell* (Chicago: Henry Brothers & Co., 1894), 3–4.

52. Faulkner, 9–15.

53. David Tyack and Elisabeth Hansot, *Learning Together: A History of Co-Education in American Public Schools* (New York: Russell Sage Foundation, 1990), 147.

54. Rosalind Rosenberg quoted in Tyack and Hansot, 148.

55. Dick Maple, *Palaces of Sin; or, The Devil in Society* (St. Louis: National Book Concern, 1902), 7–8.

56. Ann Wagner, *Adversaries of Dance* (Chicago: University of Illinois Press, 1997), 261.

57. Wagner, 263.

58. Richard Powers, interview with author.

59. Sally Banes, *Terpsichore in Sneakers: Post-Modern Dance* (Boston: Houghton Mifflin, 1977).

60. Peiss, 90.

61. Judith Fryer, *The Faces of Eve: Women in the Nineteenth-Century American Novel* (New York: Oxford University Press, 1976).

62. Faulkner, 22.

63. Faulkner, 22.

64. Faulkner, 22.

65. Fryer, 66.

66. Richard Powers, interview with author.

67. Richard Powers, interview with author.

68. Showalter; Bruce Haley, *The Healthy Body and Victorian Culture* (Cambridge: Harvard University Press, 1978); Patricia A. Vertinsky, *The Eternally Wounded Woman: Women, Doctors and Exercise in the Late Nineteenth Century* (Chicago: University of Chicago Press, 1994).

69. Haley, 255.

70. Crane, 62–63.

71. Tyack and Hansot, 150.

72. Faulkner, 39, 22, 37.

73. Richard Powers, interview with author.

74. Aldrich, jacket notes; Wagner, viii.

75. William Cleaver Wilkinson, *The Dance of Modern Society*, 3d ed. (New York: Funk & Wagnalls, 1884), 25.

76. Haley, 259.

77. Tyack and Hansot, 150.

78. Vertinsky, *Eternally Wounded Woman*, 174.

79. William Blaikie, *How to Get Strong and How to Stay So* (New York: Harper and Brothers, 1899), 36.

80. Michel Foucault, *The History of Sexuality: An Introduction*, vol. 1, trans. Robert Hurley (New York: Random House, 1978).

81. Vertinsky, *Eternally Wounded Woman*, 7.

82. Milan Bertrand Williams, *Where Satan Sows His Seed: Plain Talks on the Amusements of Fashionable Society* (Chicago: Fleming H. Revell, 1896), 121.

83. Martha Banta, *Imaging American Women: Idea and Ideals in Cultural History* (New York: Columbia University Press, 1987), 91.

CHAPTER 3. WOMEN, PHYSICAL ACTIVITY, EDUCATION

1. James C. Whorton, *Crusaders for Fitness: A History of American Health Reformers* (Princeton: Princeton University Press, 1982), 140, 196.

2. For a more complete discussion of these regimens, see Whorton.

3. Ronald Pearsall, *The Worm in the Bud: The World of Victorian Sexuality* (New York: Macmillan, 1969), 423.

4. Pearsall, x.

5. Pearsall, xi.

6. Introduction in Susan R. Bordo and Alison M. Jaggar, eds., *Gender/Body/Knowledge* (New Brunswick: Rutgers University Press, 1989), 40.

7. Paul Atkinson, "Fitness, Feminism and Schooling," in *The Nineteenth-Century Woman: Her Cultural and Physical World,* ed. Sara Delamont and Lorna Duffin (London: Croom Helm, 1978), 92.

8. Whorton, 4.

9. Whorton, 270–71.

10. Whorton, 273.

11. Granville Stanley Hall as quoted in Whorton, 289.

12. Whorton, 289.

13. Betty Spears and Richard Swanson, *History of Sport and Physical Activity in the United States* (Dubuque: William C. Brown, 1978), 273–74.

14. Thomas Wentworth Higginson, "Gymnastics," *Atlantic Monthly* 7 (1861): 301, quoted in Whorton, 273–74.

15. The following discussion of Dio Lewis draws on Whorton, 276–78.

16. Diocesan Lewis, "New Gymnastics," quoted in Whorton, 276.

17. Moses Coit Tyler as quoted in Whorton, 281.

18. Whorton, 282.

19. Whorton, 283.

20. Whorton, 283–84.

21. Whorton, 284.

22. Sheldon Cheney, *The Art of the Dance* (New York: Theatre Arts Books, 1928), 49.

23. Whorton, 293–94.

24. Whorton, 287.

25. Susan R. Bardo, "The Body and the Reproduction of Femininity: A Feminist Appropriation of Foucault," in Bordo and Jaggar, 13.

26. Kathleen E. McCrone, "Play Up! Play Up! And Play the Game: Sport at the Late Victorian Girls' Public Schools," in *From "Fair Sex" to Feminism: Sport and the Socialization of Women in the Industrial and Post-Industrial Eras,* ed. J. A. Mangan and Roberta J. Park (London: Frank Cass, 1987), 130.

27. Mabel Newcomer, *A Century of Higher Education for American Women* (New York: Harper & Brothers, 1959), 28.

28. Patricia A. Vertinsky, "Sexual Equality and the Legacy of Catharine Beecher," *Journal of Sport History* 6, no.1 (spring 1979): 9, 39.

29. Vertinsky, "Sexual Equality," 40.

30. Thomas Woody, *A History of Women's Education in the United States,* vol. 4, book 2, *Science and Education,* ed. J. McKeen Cattell (New York: Science Press, 1929), 122.

31. Woody, 99.

32. Woody, 100.

33. Julia Brown, interview with author; *Etiquette for Ladies: With Hints on*

the Preservation, Improvement and Display of Beauty (Philadelphia: Lindsay and Blakeston, 1848); Vertinsky, "Sexual Equality," 40.

34. Woody, 102.

35. Granville Stanley Hall,"Christianity and Physical Culture," *Pedagogical Seminary* 9, no. 8 (1902): 376.

36. Woody, 109.

37. Catharine Beecher, *Physiology and Calisthenics*, 1856, quoted in Vertinsky, "Sexual Equality," 41.

38. Elaine Showalter, *The Female Malady: Women, Madness, and English Culture, 1830–1980* (New York: Penguin Books, 1985), 41.

39. Vertinsky, "Sexual Equality," 45.

40. Woody, 114.

41. Woody, 114.

42. Woody, 114.

43. Dorothy Ainsworth, *The History of Physical Education in Colleges for Women* (New York: A. S. Barnes, 1930), 10.

44. Ainsworth, 21.

45. J. A. Mangan and Roberta J. Park, eds., *From "Fair Sex" to Feminism: Sport and the Socialization of Women in the Industrial and Post-Industrial Eras* (London: Frank Cass, 1987), 3.

46. Ainsworth, 29. Fencing, too, was frequently listed in women's college catalogues of this time.

47. Ainsworth, 10.

48. Ainsworth, 29.

49. Mangan and Park, 5.

50. Paul Atkinson, "The Feminist Physique: Physical Education and the Medicalization of Women's Education," in Mangan and Park, 50.

51. Atkinson, "Feminist Physique," 51.

52. Atkinson, "Feminist Physique," 53.

53. Atkinson, "Feminist Physique," 51.

54. Mangan and Park, 5.

55. Patricia A. Vertinsky, "Body Shapes: The Role of the Medical Establishment in Informing Female Exercise and Physical Education in Nineteenth-Century North America," in Mangan and Park, 286.

56. McCrone, 131.

57. Mangan and Park, 14.

58. Roberta J. Park, "Sport, Gender and Society in a Transatlantic Victorian Perspective," in Mangan and Park, 59, 61.

59. Park, 74.

60. Vertinsky, "Body Shapes," 273.

61. Park, 74–75.

62. McCrone, 141.

63. Sheila Fletcher, "The Making and Breaking of a Female Tradition: Women's Physical Education in England, 1880–1980," in Mangan and Park, 150.

64. McCrone, 142.

65. Vertinsky, "Body Shapes," 256.

66. Vertinsky, "Body Shapes," 267.

67. David Armstrong, *Political Anatomy of the Body: Medical Knowledge in Britain in the Twentieth Century* (Cambridge: Cambridge University Press, 1983), 160.

68. Carol Ruth Berkin and Mary Beth Norton, *Women of America: A History* (Boston: Houghton Mifflin, 1979), 139.

69. One individual who embodied several contradictory discourses of women, dance, and higher education at the time was Granville Stanley Hall. (appendix 1).

70. Berkin and Norton, 320.

71. Berkin and Norton, 322.

72. Berkin and Norton, 323.

73. Sara Delamont and Lorna Duffin, eds., *The Nineteenth-Century Woman: Her Cultural and Physical World* (London: Croom Helm, 1978), 16.

74. John Morley, "Sex in Mind and in Education," *Fortnightly Review,* n.s., 15 (January 1 to June 1, 1874): 468.

CHAPTER 4. BLANCHE TRILLING

1. Frances Cumbee, interview with author; Blanche M. Trilling, "History of Physical Education for Women at the University of Wisconsin, 1898–1946" (1951, University of Wisconsin–Madison Archives).

2. Lawrence R. Veysey, *The Emergence of the American University* (Chicago: University of Chicago Press, 1965), 15.

3. Frederick Rudolph, *The American College and University* (Athens: University of Georgia Press, 1990), 248.

4. Rudolph, 249.

5. G. G. McBride, *On Wisconsin Women: Working for Their Rights from Settlement to Suffrage* (Madison: University of Wisconsin Press, 1993), 181.

6. McBride, 48.

7. Mabel Newcomer, *A Century of Higher Education for American Women* (New York: Harper & Brothers, 1959), 13.

8. McBride, 4.

9. McBride, 50.

10. Catherine Clinton, *The Other Civil War: American Women in the Nineteenth Century,* ed. Eric Foner (New York: Hill and Wang, 1984), 128–29.

11. Trilling, "History," 5.

12. Clinton, 129.

13. Between the second half of the nineteenth century and the first half of the twentieth, the name for women's physical activities switched from physical education to physical culture to physical training and finally back to physical education, all terms describing the same basic system of physical training and sports. Trilling, "History," 6.

14. Faith Wilcox et al., "History of Physical Education for Women at the University of Wisconsin, 1889–1916" (1916, University of Wisconsin–Madison Archives), 2, 39.

15. Wilcox et al., 2, 40.

16. Wilcox et al., 8.

17. Wilcox et al., 42.

18. Wilcox et al., 43.

19. Trilling, "History," 43.

20. Trilling, "History," 43.

21. Wilcox et al., 4.

22. Trilling, "History," 40.

23. Elliot W. Eisner, *The Educational Imagination: On the Design and Evaluation of School Programs*, 2d ed. (New York: Macmillan, 1985), 98.

24. McBride, 113.

25. Research conducted by author in the files of the State Historical Society of Wisconsin in Madison.

26. F. W Kehl, "Professor Kehl's School for Dancing and Deportment," brochure, 1895.

27. Kehl.

28. All quotations from the University of Wisconsin catalogue in this section are taken from Trilling, "History," 34–38.

29. Dominick Cavallo, *Muscles and Morals: Organized Playgrounds and Urban Reform, 1880–1920* (Philadelphia: University of Pennsylvania Press, 1981), 3–4.

30. Trilling, "History," 12.

31. Wilcox, et al., 6.

32. Wilcox, et al., 7.

33. See Matthew Hughes's antidance book as well as several other antidance treatises published and in use at this time.

34. "Facts Concerning the Department of Physical Education for Women for the First Semester, 1910–1911" (anonymous, n.d.), Trilling files, University of Wisconsin–Madison Archives.

35. Trilling, "History," 6.

36. Trilling, "History," 6.

37. Joan Acocella and David Freedberg, *Dancers* (Boston: Bulfinch Press, 1992), 10.

38. Clarence H. White's 1898 *Triptych* and his 1909 *Nude* are examples of photographs of the period and earlier that capture the physical richness of models comfortable with their bodies. See also Sadakichi Hartmann, *The Valiant Knights of Daguerre: Selected Critical Essays on Photography and Profiles of Photographic Pioneers* (Berkeley: University of California Press, 1978), 182, 185.

39. Hartmann, 2.

40. Trilling, "History," 10.

41. Frances Cumbee, interview with author.

42. Clinton, 127.

43. Clinton, 127.

44. Clinton, 136–37.

45. Louise H'Doubler Nagel, Marion Bigelow, and Edith Boys Enos, interview with author.

46. Clinton, 135.

47. Carol Dyhouse, *No Distinction of Sex? Women in British Universities, 1870–1939* (London: University College London, 1995), 161.

48. Wilcox et al., 30.

49. Trilling, "History," 13.

50. "Feminine" space here implies a building with dark, private, and understated interiors. It seems designed more with an eye toward comfort than for show and as a safe and sheltering environment for the activities within.

51. Trilling, "History," 15.

52. Trilling, "History," 16.

53. The University of Wiscosin–Madison Archives has a postcard, one of many printed at the time, that shows an exterior drawing of the building with a current of women entering and leaving as it sits unencumbered by any adjacent architecture. In the fall of 1998 the building underwent extensive renovation, and the back stairs were replaced with a wheelchair-accessible level entrance.

54. Trilling, "History," 16.

55. Trilling, "History," 66.

56. Roberta J. Park, "Sport, Gender and Society in a Transatlantic Victorian Perspective," in *From "Fair Sex" to Feminism: Sport and the Socialization of Women in the Industrial and Post-Industrial Eras*, ed. J. A. Mangan and Roberta J. Park (London: Frank Cass, 1987), 80.

57. Park, 81.

58. Trilling, "History," 23.

59. Clarke W. Hetherington quoted in Judith Ann Gray and Diane Howe, "Margaret H'Doubler: A Profile of Her Formative Years, 1898–1921," *Research Quarterly for Exercise and Sport* (centennial issue 1985): 95.

60. From an undated and untitled document in the Trilling files, University of Wisconsin–Madison Archives.

61. Helen McKinstry, "The Teacher of Physical Education" (n.p., 1900), 1.

62. Julia Brown, interview with author.

63. Park, 81.

64. Frances Cumbee, interview with author.

65. Edith Boys Enos, letter to author.

66. A letter in Trilling's correspondence files dated September 1915 contains a request from her to her superior in Wisconsin, Professor Dykema, requesting a Dalcroze instructor as soon as funds permit.

67. Julia Brown, interview with author.

68. Outline entry from undated 1922–23 lecture notes headed "For Course 90," Trilling's personal files, University of Wisconsin–Madison Archives.

69. Letter to H. W. Gray Co., 1916, University of Wisconsin–Madison Archives.

70. Lecture II, Seminar I, Course 90, 1923–24, from Trilling's personal files, University of Wisconsin–Madison Archives.

71. "Girls' Olympics Injure Health: Blanche M. Trilling Makes Vigorous

Protest against Strenuous Competition," clipping from unidentified newspaper, October 3, 1929, Women's Physical Education Department scrapbook, University of Wisconsin–Madison Archives.

CHAPTER 5. MARGARET H'DOUBLER AND THE LIBERTY OF THOUGHT

1. Judith Ann Gray and Diane Howe, "Margaret H'Doubler: A Profile of Her Formative Years, 1898–1921," *Research Quarterly for Exercise and Sport* (centennial issue 1985): 95.

2. Carl Gutknecht, interview with Margaret H'Doubler, 1963, historical files, Department of Physical Education for Women, University of Wisconsin–Madison, 4.

3. Louise H'Doubler Nagel, interview with author.

4. Gray and Howe, "Profile," 93; Jay M. Whitham, clipping from *Warren (Illinois) Sentinel-Ledger,* December 14, 1932, from collection of Louis H'Doubler Nagel.

5. Judith Ann Gray, "To Want to Dance: A Biography of Margaret H'Doubler" (Ph.D. dissertation, University of Arizona, 1978), 14.

6. Jo Anne Brown, "A Survey of Campus Resources on the History of Dance" (n.d., University of Wisconsin–Madison, Archives), 12. "According to Professor Herbert Kliebard of the Department of Educational Policy Studies, a local antique dealer (name unknown) had offered for sale last winter the contents of a large album of dance photographs — approximately 100 pages. Most of the photographs were taken on or near Bascom Hill prior to 1930; many depicted nude dancers, enhancing the value of the photographs to various sorts of collectors. Professor Kliebard was unable to persuade the dealer not to break up the collection. After learning of the renewed interest in dance history, Professor Kliebard has been trying to contact the dealer again, thus far unsuccessfully."

7. Hermine Sauthoff Davidson and Ellen Moore, interviews with author.

8. Gray and Howe, "Profile," 93.

9. Gray, 17; Louise H'Doubler Nagel, interview with author.

10. Gutknecht, 1.

11. *Daily Cardinal* article quoted in Gray and Howe, "Profile," 95.

12. *Daily Cardinal* article quoted in Gray and Howe, "Profile," 95.

13. James C. Whorton, *Crusaders for Fitness: A History of American Health Reformers* (Princeton: Princeton University Press, 1982), 283.

14. Gray and Howe, "Profile," 95.

15. Gutknecht, 3.

16. Gutknecht, 4.

17. Catherine Clinton, *The Other Civil War: American Women in the Nineteenth Century,* ed. Eric Foner (New York: Hill and Wang, 1984), 136.

18. Mary Lou Remley, "The Wisconsin Idea of Dance: A Decade of Progress, 1917–1926," *Wisconsin Magazine of History* 58, no. 3 (spring 1975): 180.

19. Gutknecht, 3.

20. Thorstein Veblen quoted in David O. Levine, *The American College and the Culture of Aspiration* (Ithaca: Cornell University Press, 1986), 98.

21. Merle Curti and Vernon Carstensen, *The University of Wisconsin: A History, 1848–1925* (Madison: University of Wisconsin Press, 1949), 2:591.

22. Gutknecht, 3.

23. Gray and Howe, "Profile," 96–97.

24. Gutknecht, 4.

25. Gutknecht, 4.

26. Gutknecht, 4.

27. Mary P. O'Donnell, "Margaret H'Doubler," *Dance Observer* (November 1936): 99.

28. O'Donnell, "Margaret H'Doubler."

29. O'Donnell, "Margaret H'Doubler."

30. Gertrude K. Colby, *The Conflict: A Health Masque in Pantomime* (New York: A. S. Barnes, 1930), 5.

31. M. P. O'Donnell, "Gertrude Colby," *Dance Observer* (January 1936): 8.

32. Robert D. Moulton, "Bird Larson, the Legend," *Dance Observer* (April 1959): 53.

33. Moulton, 54.

34. Moulton, 54.

35. Gray and Howe, "Profile," 97.

36. Gray and Howe, "Profile," 97.

37. Gutknecht, 4.

38. Gutknecht, 2.

39. Gutknecht, 5.

40. Remley, 181.

41. Mary Alice Brennan, interview with Margaret H'Doubler, 1972.

42. Brennan interview.

43. Gutknecht, 2.

44. Brennan interview.

45. Alys Bentley quoted in Remley, 179–95.

46. Brennan interview.

47. Brennan interview.

48. Brennan interview.

49. Alys Bentley, *The Dance of the Mind* (New York: Shemin Printing, 1933).

50. Louise H'Doubler Nagel, interview with author. Francis H'Doubler was doing his internship in general surgery at Brigham Hospital from 1915 to 1918.

51. Brennan interview.

52. Brennan interview.

53. Brennan interview.

54. Gutknecht, 3.

CHAPTER 6. MARGARET H'DOUBLER AND THE PHILOSOPHY OF JOHN DEWEY

1. Barnes received special permission to enroll as a student in one of Dewey's

seminars at Columbia during the 1917–18 academic year and thus began his lifelong friendship with Dewey.

2. Carl Gutknecht, interview with H'Doubler, 1963, historical files, Department of Physical Education for Women, University of Wisconsin–Madison, 3.

3. George Dykhuizen, *The Life and Mind of John Dewey* (Carbondale: Southern Illinois University Press, 1973), 123.

4. Dykhuizen, 127.

5. Dykhuizen, 123.

6. Dykhuizen, 128.

7. John Dewey, *Democracy and Education* (New York: Macmillan, 1916), 141.

8. Margaret H'Doubler, *Dance: A Creative Art Experience*, 2d ed. (Madison: University of Wisconsin Press, 1940), 72.

9. Quoted in Judith B. Alter, "Dance-Based Dance Theory," in *New Studies in Aesthetics*, ed. Robert Ginsberg (New York: Peter Lang, 1991), 87.

10. Dewey, *Democracy and Education,* 163.

11. Dykhuizen, 114.

12. Undated page from a special issue of *Impulse* dedicated to H'Doubler, supplied by Louise H'Doubler Nagel.

13. John Dewey, *Art as Experience* (New York: Capricorn Books, 1934), 19.

14. Dewey quoted in Dykhuizen, 180.

15. John Dewey, "Three Prefaces to Books by Alexander," in *John Dewey and F. M. Alexander*, ed. Frank Pierce Jones (Champaign, Ill.: North American Society of Teachers of the Alexander Technique, n.d.), 1.

16. Dewey, "Three Prefaces," 19.

17. Katherine Camp Mayhew and Anna Camp Edwards, *The Dewey School: The Laboratory School of the University of Chicago, 1896–1903* (New York: Appleton-Century, 1936), 256, 260.

18. C. C. Turbayne, *John Dewey and F. Matthias Alexander* (Champaign, Ill.: North American Society of Teachers of the Alexander Technique, 1948), 6.

19. Dykhuizen, 213.

20. Dewey, *Democracy and Education*, 159.

21. Dewey, *Democracy and Education*, 159.

22. Dykhuizen, 30.

23. A. A. Leath, interview with author. Early Women's Physical Education Department files and reports gave no indication that men students attended classes in the initial years of H'Doubler's program. However, in 1922 a local newspaper article said that "a peeping Tom" had climbed onto a window ledge at Lathrop Hall and discovered fifteen men in Grecian costumes "tripping the light fantastic." H'Doubler explained that these dancing classes for men had been organized at the request of several male students and were kept secret with consent of university deans. *Wisconsin State Journal*, February 23, 1922, as quoted in Mary Lou Remley, "The Wisconsin Idea of Dance: A Decade of Progress, 1917–1926," *Wisconsin Magazine of History* 58, no. 3 (spring 1975): 179–95.

24. D. Cavallo, *Muscles and Morals: Organized Playgrounds and Urban Reform, 1880–1920* (Philadelphia: University of Pennsylvania Press, 1981), 5.

25. Dewey, *Democracy and Education*, 336.

26. Dewey, *Democracy and Education*, 160, 161.

27. Mayhew and Edwards, 260.

28. Margaret H'Doubler, *The Dance, and Its Place in Education* (New York: Harcourt, Brace, 1925), xi, 31.

29. Dewey quoted in Dykhuizen, 260.

30. Dewey, *Democracy and Education*, 135.

31. Gutknecht, 4.

32. Judith Ann Gray, "To Want to Dance: A Biography of Margaret H'Doubler," (Ph.D. dissertation, University of Arizona, 1978), 157.

33. H'Doubler, *Dance: A Creative Art Experience*, ix, x.

34. H'Doubler, *Dance: A Creative Art Experience*, 177.

35. Margaret Jewell Mullen, Hermine Sauthoff Davidson, and Ellen Moore, interviews with author.

36. Robert Roth, *John Dewey and Self-Realization* (Englewood Cliffs, N.J.: Prentice-Hall, 1962), 5.

37. Alter, 38.

38. H'Doubler, *Dance: A Creative Art Experience*, 37.

39. Philip M. Zeltner, *John Dewey's Aesthetic Philosophy* (Amsterdam: B. V. Gruner, 1975).

40. Dewey, *Art as Experience*, 135, 54.

41. H'Doubler, *Dance: A Creative Art Experience*, 82, 62.

42. Dewey, *Art as Experience*, 84.

43. Dewey, *Art as Experience*, 147.

44. Margaret Jewell Mullen, interview with author.

45. Nancy Lee Chalfa Ruyter, *Reformers and Visionaries: The Americanization of the Art of Dance* (New York: Dance Horizons, 1979), 102.

46. Charles Beard and Mary R. Beard, *America in Middle Passage*, vol. 3, *The Rise of American Civilization* (New York: Macmillan, 1939), 781, 764.

47. Dykhuizen, 181.

48. Dewey, "Three Prefaces," 6–19.

49. Dewey quoted in Dykhuizen, 121.

50. Dykhuizen, i.

51. F. Matthias Alexander, *Man's Supreme Inheritance* (New York: Dutton, 1912), xvii.

52. John Dewey, "Comment on the Foregoing Criticisms (of Benedetto Croce)," *Journal of Aesthetics and Art Criticism* 6, no. 3 (1943): 207–9, 203.

53. Laurel N. Tanner, *Dewey's Laboratory School Lessons for Today* (New York: Teachers College Press, 1997), 16–17.

54. Margaret Lloyd, *The Borzoi Book of Modern Dance* (New York: Dance Horizons, 1949), 79–80.

55. "Proceedings of a Symposium on John Dewey's *Art as Experience*," *Journal of Aesthetic Education* 23, no. 3 (fall 1989): 49–67.

56. Dykhuizen, 213.

57. Roth, 3.

58. Mayhew and Edwards, vi.

59. Philip Jackson, "If We Took Dewey's Aesthetics Seriously, How Would the Arts Be Taught?" in *The New Scholarship on Dewey*, ed. Jim Garrison (Dordrecht: Kulwer Academic Publishers, 1995), 26.

60. Beard and Beard, 781.

61. Jackson, 28.

62. Mayhew and Edwards, 262.

CHAPTER 7. STRUCTURING EXPERIENCE IN THE CLASSROOM

1. Duncan never permitted herself to be filmed. The only known film footage of her dancing comes from an outdoor garden party, when a photographer hidden behind a tree recorded a fragment of her dancing and acknowledging the crowd.

2. Philip W. Jackson, *Untaught Lessons* (New York: Teachers College Press, 1992), 19.

3. Elliot W. Eisner, *The Educational Imagination: On the Design and Evaluation of School Programs,* 2d ed. (New York: Macmillan, 1985), 45–44.

4. Ellen A. Moore, interview with author.

5. Ellen A. Moore, "A Recollection of Margaret H'Doubler's Class Procedure: An Environment for the Learning of Dance," *Dance Research Journal* 8, no. 1 (1975): 14.

6. Mary Lou Remley, "The Wisconsin Idea of Dance: A Decade of Progress, 1917–1926," *Wisconsin Magazine of History* 58, no. 3 (spring 1975): 178.

7. Remley, 189.

8. Anna Halprin, video interview/demonstration about H'Doubler's dance class, April 14, 1999. Classes in anatomy, including the dissection of a human cadaver by groups of four students, were a required part of the dance major, Hermine Sauthoff Davidson recalled (interview with author).

9. Moore, 14.

10. Anna Halprin, interview with author.

11. Moore, 13.

12. Anna Halprin, interview with author.

13. William Blake once observed that the quest of an artist was "having started at innocence, gone through experience and, in doing so, being able to return to a higher, informed innocence."

14. Isadora Duncan, Merce Cunningham, and the Judson Church choreographers all to some degree stripped back to movement basics.

15. Hermine Sauthoff Davidson, interview with author; Billie Frances Lepczyk, "Margaret H'Doubler's Classification of Movement Qualities Viewed through Laban Analysis," *Dance Notation Journal* 14, no. 1 (spring 1986): 5.

16. Margaret H'Doubler, "Movement and Its Rhythmic Structure: An Educational Theory of Motor Learning" (1946, University of Wisconsin–Madison Archives), 2.

17. Margaret H'Doubler, paper prepared for Gulick Award (1973, University of Wisconsin–Madison Archives), 17.

18. Hermine Sauthoff Davidson, interview with author.

19. Moore, 14.

20. Halprin, video interview/demonstration.

21. Hermine Sauthoff Davidson, interview with author.

22. Moore, 14.

23. Moore, 14.

24. Moore, 14.

25. Moore, 15.

26. Helen M. Niehoff, letter to author.

27. Jane Eastham, interview with author.

28. Edith Boys Enos, interview with author.

29. Hermine Sauthoff Davidson, interview with author. Davidson recounted how H'Doubler cultivated the wealthy society women in town; consequently, in the 1930s one of them donated a grand piano that became a fixture in the dance studio.

30. Moore, 15.

31. Moore, 15.

32. Moore, 16.

33. Ellen A. Moore, interview with author.

34. Hermine Sauthoff Davidson, interview with author. Mary Burchenal was a leading early educator in folk dance and published numerous dance description and sheet music sets.

35. Halprin, video interview/demonstration.

36. Moore, 16.

37. Edith Boys Enos, interview with author.

38. Margaret Jewell Mullen, interview with author.

39. Margaret Jewell Mullen, interview with author.

40. Hermine Sauthoff Davidson, interview with author.

41. Hermine Sauthoff Davidson, interview with author.

42. Marion Bigelow says that in addition to her, the class of 1931–32 included nineteen other graduate students in dance; interview with author.

43. Anna Halprin, interview with author. Halprin's 1965 and 1966 summer dance workshops on her outdoor dance deck in Kentfield, California, numbered among their students Simone Forti, Trisha Brown, Yvonne Rainer, Meredith Monk, and musician LaMonte Young, all of whom went on to major careers in avant-garde performance.

44. Mary Hinkson, interview with author.

45. Mary Hinkson, interview with author.

46. Mary Hinkson, interview with author.

47. Anna Halprin, interview with author.

48. Mary Hinkson, interview with author.

49. Hermine Sauthoff Davidson, letter to author.

50. Margaret H'Doubler, *The Dance, and Its Place in Education* (New York: Harcourt, Brace, 1925), 49, 55, 211.

51. H'Doubler, *Dance, and Its Place*, 212.

52. H'Doubler, *Dance, and Its Place*, 208.

53. Edith Boys Enos, letter to author.

54. Mary Hinkson, interview with author.

55. Hermine Sauthoff Davidson, interview with author.

56. Margaret Jewell Mullen, interview with author.

57. Margaret Jewell Mullen, interview with author.

58. Judith Ann Gray, "To Want To Dance: A Biography of Margaret H'Doubler" (Ph.D. dissertation, University of Arizona, 1978), 52.

59. H'Doubler, *Dance, and Its Place*, 59.

60. Margaret Jewell Mullen, interview with author.

61. Mary Hinkson, interview with author.

62. Moore, 17, and interview with author.

63. Ellen Moore, interview with author.

64. Hermine Sauthoff Davidson says that well into the 1930s *all* of H'Doubler's classes took place in the fifth-floor dance studio regardless of whether they were 100 percent activity classes or not. In fact, Davidson notes that none of H'Doubler's classes in these initial decades were either exclusively movement or lecture; they were always a blend of both.

65. Gray, 76.

66. H'Doubler, *Dance, and Its Place*, 37.

67. Gray, 157.

68. H'Doubler visited the American Southwest and observed Native American dance rituals during the summers of 1922, 1923, and 1924. It was there that she purchased two Navajo drums, one of which she sold to dance major Edith Boys Enos, who used it for decades in her own teaching. Ellen A. Moore, Julia Brown, and Hermine Sauthoff Davidson, interviews with author.

69. Mary Hinkson, interview with author.

70. Hermine Sauthoff Davidson, interview with author.

71. H'Doubler, *Dance, and Its Place*, 232.

72. Lynn Conner, *Spreading the Gospel of the Modern Dance* (Pittsburgh: University of Pittsburgh Press, 1997), 1.

73. Much about this image—the style of the photograph, the women's hairstyles and the post–World War I subject matter—suggests it dates from 1919 or 1920. Mygdal was a physical education major at the University of Wisconsin, class of 1926. She returned as an instructor in dance for several years in the 1930s and 1940s.

74. Franklin Rosemont, ed., *Isadora Speaks* (San Francisco: City Lights Books, 1981), 43.

75. Edith Boys Enos, interview with author.

76. Hermine Sauthoff Davidson, interview with author.

77. Edith Boys Enos, interview with author.

78. Mary Alice Brennan, interview with Margaret H'Doubler, 1972, 7.

79. Margaret H'Doubler, letter to Ellen A. Moore, 1949–1951.

80. Isadora Duncan also abhorred classical ballet. She quipped that in watching a ballet dancer one saw a deformed skeleton dancing before them. It is important to keep these remarks in context, however, for with the exception of Diaghilev's Ballets Russes de Monte Carlo, which was essentially unknown in

Madison, ballet at this time in America was in tawdry form. Mary O'Donnell, who later directed the dance program at Barnard, once wrote about "remembering the usually cheerful Miss H'Doubler in ballet slippers performing the five positions with no manifestation of joy." Mary P. O'Donnell, "Margaret H'Doubler," *Dance Observer* (November 1936): 99.

81. Edith Boys Enos and Ellen A. Moore, interviews with author.

82. Brennan interview.

83. Edith Boys Enos, interview with author.

84. This information is also contained in an undated two-page document by H'Doubler titled "Outline of Paper on Dance and Personality," H'Doubler papers, University of Wisconsin–Madison Archives.

85. Brennan interview.

86. H'Doubler, *Dance, and Its Place*, 209, 207.

87. H'Doubler, *Dance, and Its Place*, 48.

88. Orchesis programs, 1928, 1929, 1930, 1931, 1932, 1946, 1947, 1951, University of Wisconsin–Madison Archives.

89. Hermine Sauthoff Davidson, interview with author.

90. H'Doubler, *Dance, and Its Place*, 219.

91. Margaret H'Doubler, "Orchesis" (n.d., University of Wisconsin–Madison Archives). Hermine Sauthoff Davidson reports (interview with author) that in 1931 Orchesis shared a program with guest artist Berta Ochsner, and the full cast was invited to a family reception afterward; H'Doubler instructed all her dancers that they had to wear formals to this reception. With regard to wearing bras while dancing, she told her students: "I don't want to see a bunch of little cows!"

92. Judith Ann Gray and Diane Howe, "Margaret H'Doubler: A Profile of Her Formative Years, 1898–1921," *Research Quarterly for Exercise and Sport* (centennial issue 1985): 100.

93. Margaret H'Doubler, "A Question of Values and Terms," *Dance Observer* 12, no. 7 (August/September 1945): 83.

94. David O. Levine, *The American College and the Culture of Aspiration* (Ithaca: Cornell University Press, 1986), 97.

95. Hermine Sauthoff Davidson, interview with author.

96. Edith Boys Enos, interview with author.

97. Judith Ann Gray and Diane Howe, "Margaret H'Doubler and the First Dance Major," Committee on Research in Dance Souvenir Program (1987, University of Wisconsin–Madison Archives), 5.

98. Brennan interview, 9.

99. Frederick Rudolph, *The American College and University* (Athens: University of Georgia Press, 1990), 435.

100. Merle Curti and Vernon Carstensen, *The University of Wisconsin: A History, 1848–1925* (Madison: University of Wisconsin Press, 1949), 2:144.

101. Gray and Howe, "Margaret H'Doubler and the First Dance Major," 6. In the fall of 1932 H'Doubler was invited to give a lecture-demonstration at the New School for Social Research in New York City. She took ten or fifteen of her

students to work with her in this performance during the Thanksgiving break.

102. Edith Boys Enos, interview with author.

103. Seen in this context, the Orchesis club becomes an important consistent weekly dance class, which those interested in dance could attend for several semesters consecutively. Dance technique lessons were taken for "o" credits, according to Hermine Sauthoff Davidson (interview with author).

104. Margaret H'Doubler, "Letters and Sciences Document" (1926, University of Wisconsin–Madison Archives).

105. Remley, 194.

106. Margaret H'Doubler, "Report on Dancing" (1927–28, University of Wisconsin–Madison Archives), 47. Also cited in Remley.

107. Marion Bigelow, interview with author.

108. Edith Boys Enos, interview with author.

109. Mary Hinkson, interview with author.

110. Margaret H'Doubler, "Educational Basis of Dance and Dance as Education" (n.d., University of Wisconsin–Madison Archives, reproduced January 1975), 1, 10.

111. Carl Gutknecht, interview with Margaret H'Doubler, 1963, historical files, Department of Physical Education for Women, University of Wisconsin–Madison, 4.

112. Edith Boys Enos, letter to author, enclosing a copy of her course material, including the final exam questions, from H'Doubler's "Theory and Philosophy of Dance" class.

113. Jonathan C. Matthews, "Mindful Body, Embodied Mind: Somatic Knowing and Education" (Ph.D. dissertation, Stanford University, 1994), 3.

114. John Dewey, *The School and Society*, ed. Jo Ann Boydston (Carbondale: Southern Illinois University Press, 1976), 5.

CHAPTER 8. MARGARET H'DOUBLER'S CLASSROOM

1. Lawrence Cremin, *The Transformation of the School: Progressivism in American Education, 1876–1957* (New York: Vintage, 1964), vii.

2. Stuart Macdonald, *The History and Philosophy of Art Education* (London: University of London Press, 1970), 348.

3. Arthur Wesley Dow quoted in Macdonald, 349.

4. Macdonald, 146.

5. Arthur Efland, *A History of Art Education: Intellectual and Social Currents in Teaching the Visual Arts* (New York: Teachers College Press, 1990), 133.

6. William Blaikie, *How to Get Strong and How to Stay So* (New York: Harper and Brothers, 1899).

7. Lest we dismiss the linking of morality to the artist as naive, this same association has been prevalent in the late twentieth century, particularly in the instance of the photographs of Robert Mapplethorpe, whose work has been condemned as immoral in part because of his own illness from AIDS and his personal practices as a homosexual, both of which form a subtext of his photographs. Andreas Serrano

also had his work denounced in the late 1980s because some felt it was an example of immorality.

8. Efland, 146.

9. Margaret H'Doubler, "Educational Basis of Dance and Dance as Education" (n.d., University of Wisconsin–Madison Archives, reproduced January 1975), 9. H'Doubler quotes John Dewey, without citing the context, as saying, "Kinesthesia is as important to a well rounded education as education is to a good life" (11).

10. Margaret Jewell Mullen, interview with author. This notion of movement being linked to emotions applied to H'Doubler's whole philosophy.

11. Edith Boys Enos, interview with author.

12. Anna Halprin, interview with author.

13. Merle Curti and Vernon Carstensen, *The University of Wisconsin: A History, 1848–1925* (Madison: University of Wisconsin Press, 1949), 2:132.

14. Margaret H'Doubler, *The Dance, and Its Place in Education* (New York: Harcourt, Brace, 1925), 32–33.

15. H'Doubler, *Dance, and Its Place*, 32–33.

16. H'Doubler, *Dance, and Its Place*, 33–34.

17. H'Doubler, *Dance, and Its Place*, xiii.

18. Margaret H'Doubler, *Dance: A Creative Art Experience*, 2d ed. (Madison: The University of Wisconsin Press, 1940), 39.

CHAPTER 9. MARGARET H'DOUBLER'S LEGACY

1. Blanche Trilling, university correspondence, 1917, and letter to George Ehler, 1915, University of Wisconsin–Madison Archives.

2. William James Lawson, ed., *Dance Magazine College Guide* (New York: Dance Magazine, 1988–89), 11.

3. Sali Ann Kriegsman, *Modern Dance in America: The Bennington Years* (Boston: G. K. Hall, 1981), 6.

4. Kriegsman, 6.

5. Mary P. O'Donnell, "Martha Hill," *Dance Observer* (April 1936): 43–44.

6. Martha Hill, "Martha Hill Reminisces about Bennington," videotape of lecture delivered at Bennington College, July 25, 1985, Dance Collection, New York Public Library, MGZHA 4–375: 1985.

7. Marian Van Tuyl, personal recollection from her personal historical files, n.d., 5. Courtesy of Gayle Van Tuyl Campbell, Marian Van Tuyl's daughter.

8. Van Tuyl, 5.

9. Janice Ross, "Marian Van Tuyl," in *American National Biography*, ed. John A. Garraty (Cary, N.C.: Oxford University Press, 1995).

10. Elizabeth Goode, "The Dance at Mills College," *Dance Observer* (August/September 1939): 252.

11. Van Tuyl, 5.

12. Alma Hawkins, interview with author.

13. Elizabeth Dunkel, "Put Dancing in Its Place," *Journal of Health and Physical Education* 9 (September 1938): 419.

14. Dunkel, 419.

15. Allen E. McCormack, ed., *Dance Magazine College Guide* (New York: Dance Magazine, 1996–97), 3.

16. Kriegsman, 15.

17. Kriegsman, 328.

18. Alma M. Hawkins, *Modern Dance in Higher Education* (New York: Teachers College Press, 1954), 14.

19. Patricia J. Gumport, "Curricula as Signposts of Cultural Change," *Review of Higher Education* 12, no. 1 (autumn 1988): 49–61; quoted below, 49, 55.

20. See, for example, E. Fox Keller, "The Anomaly of a Woman in Physics," in *Working It Out*, ed. S. Daniels and P. Ruddick (New York: Pantheon, 1977), and W. Luttrel, "Working-Class Women's Ways of Knowing: Effects of Gender, Race and Class," *Sociology of Education* 62, no. 1 (January 1989): 33–46.

21. Carol S. Vance, "The War on Culture," *Art in America* (September 1989), in Richard Bolton, ed., *Culture Wars: Documents from the Recent Controversies in the Arts* (New York: New Press, 1992), 111.

22. Larry Cuban, *How Teachers Taught: Constancy and Change in American Classrooms, 1880–1990*, 2d ed. (New York: Teachers College Press, 1993).

23. Cuban, 4.

24. Cuban, 4.

25. Blanche Trilling, "Suggestions for Summer Session 1919," Physical Education Department memo, University of Wisconsin–Madison Archives. Interestingly, Trilling's draft of the course description for "Interpretive Dancing—Elementary, P.E. 46aS" contains the explanation "Fundamentals are based on the Bentley method," a rare reference to Alys Bentley, H'Doubler's inspiration in New York, as having a dance "method."

26. Mary Lou Remley, "The Wisconsin Idea of Dance: A Decade of Progress, 1917–1926." *Wisconsin Magazine of History* 58, no. 3 (spring 1975): 187.

27. Blanche Trilling, "Schedule of the Courses to Be Given in the Summer Session by the Women's Division" (1922, University of Wisconsin–Madison Archives).

28. Margaret H'Doubler, *The Dance, and Its Place in Education* (New York: Harcourt, Brace, 1925), 207.

29. Hermine Sauthoff Davidson, interview with author.

30. Lynn Conner, *Spreading the Gospel of the Modern Dance* (Pittsburgh: University of Pittsburgh Press, 1997), 85.

31. Margaret H'Doubler, "Educational Basis of Dance and Dance as Education" (n.d., University of Wisconsin–Madison Archives, reproduced January 1975), 1.

32. H'Doubler, "Educational Basis of Dance," 2.

33. Some of these ideas almost anticipate Jerome Bruner's later observation that the curriculum of a subject should be determined by the most fundamental understanding that can be achieved of the underlying principles that give structure to the subject. From H'Doubler's vantage point the simple physical pleasure of bodily explorations was the starting point of dance and of her classes.

34. See David Tyack and Larry Cuban, *Tinkering toward Utopia* (Cambridge: Harvard University Press, 1995), 57–58.

35. See D. Tyack and E. Hansot, *Learning Together: A History of Co-Education in American Public Schools* (New York: Russell Sage Foundation, 1990), 193.

36. See Dennie Palmer Wolf, introduction to Arts Education Assessment Framework, prepared for the National Assessment Governing Board (Washington: College Board, 1994 prepublication edition), 9.

APPENDIX 1: GRANVILLE STANLEY HALL

1. Jason R. Robarts, "The Century of Hope: The Quest for a Science of Education in the Nineteenth Century," *History of Education Quarterly* 8, no. 4 (winter 1968): 431–47; 440 quoted.

2. Robarts, 441.

3. Granville Stanley Hall, "Christianity and Physical Culture," *Pedagogical Seminary* 9, no. 8 (1902). Page numbers follow each quotation in the text.

4. Granville Stanley Hall, "The Educational Value of Dancing and Pantomine," in *Educational Problems*, vol. 1 (New York: D. Appleton, 1911). Page numbers follow each quotation in the text.

Bibliography

Acocella, Joan, and David Freedberg. *Dancers.* Boston: Bulfinch Press, 1992.

Ainsworth, Dorothy. *The History of Physical Education in Colleges for Women.* New York: A. S. Barnes, 1930.

Aldrich, Elizabeth. *From the Ballroom to Hell: Grace and Folly in Nineteenth-Century Dance.* Evanston: Northwestern University Press, 1991.

Alexander, F. Matthias. *Man's Supreme Inheritance.* New York: Dutton, 1912.

Alter, Judith B. "Dance-Based Dance Theory." In *New Studies in Aesthetics,* ed. Robert Ginsberg. New York: Peter Lang, 1991.

Armstrong, David. *Political Anatomy of the Body: Medical Knowledge in Britain in the Twentieth Century.* Cambridge: Cambridge University Press, 1983.

Atkinson, Paul. "The Feminist Physique: Physical Education and the Medicalization of Women's Education." In *From "Fair Sex" to Feminism: Sport and the Socialization of Women in the Industrial and Post-Industrial Eras,* ed. J. A. Mangan and Roberta J. Park. London: Frank Cass, 1987.

Atkinson, Paul. "Fitness, Feminism and Schooling." In *The Nineteenth-Century Woman: Her Cultural and Physical World,* ed. Sara Delamont and Lorna Duffin. London: Croom Helm, 1978.

Banner, Lois. *American Beauty.* New York: Alfred A. Knopf, 1983.

Banta, Martha. *Imaging American Women: Idea and Ideals in Cultural History.* New York: Columbia University Press, 1987.

Barker-Benfield, Graham John. "Horrors of the Half-Known Life: Aspects of the Exploitation of Women by Men." Ph.D. dissertation, University of California, Los Angeles, 1968.

Bassett, Gladys B. "Co-eds Find New Atmosphere in Lathrop Hall." *Wisconsin Alumni Magazine,* 34, no. 4 (January 1933): 102–7.

Beard, Charles, and Mary R. Beard. *America in Middle Passage,* vol. 3, *The Rise of American Civilization.* New York: Macmillan, 1939.

Becher, Tony. "The Cultural View." In *Perspectives on Higher Education,* ed. Burton R. Clark. Berkeley: University of California Press, 1984.

Bell, Susan Groag, and Karen M. Offen, eds. *Women, the Family, and Freedom:*

Bibliography

The Debate in Documents, vol. 2, *1880–1950*. Stanford: Stanford University Press, 1983.

Bennie, (n.f.n.) de. "Fashionable Academy." Madison: Rare Books, State Historical Society of Wisconsin, 1889.

Bentley, Alys. *The Dance of the Mind*. New York: Shemin Printing, 1933.

Berkin, Carol Ruth, and Mary Beth Norton. *Women of America: A History.* Boston: Houghton Mifflin, 1979.

Blaikie, William. *How to Get Strong and How to Stay So*. New York: Harper and Brothers, 1899.

Blanchard, Jean W. "The Role of Blanche M. Trilling in the Development of the Women's Sports Program at the University of Wisconsin, Madison, 1912–1946." Master's thesis, University of Wisconsin–Madison, 1986. Collection of Julia M. Brown.

Bolton, Richard, ed. *Culture Wars: Documents from the Recent Controversies in the Arts*. New York: New Press, 1992.

Bordo, Susan R. "The Body and the Reproduction of Femininity: A Feminist Appropriation of Foucault." In *Gender/Body/Knowledge*, ed. Susan R. Bordo and Alison M. Jaggar. New Brunswick: Rutgers University Press, 1989.

Brehm, Mary Ann. "Margaret H'Doubler's Approach to Dance Education and Her Influence on Two Dance Educators." Ph.D. dissertation, University of Wisconsin–Madison, 1988.

Brehm, Mary Ann. "Working Topology for H'Doubler Research." 1987. University of Wisconsin–Madison Archives.

Brennan, Mary Alice. Interview with Margaret H'Doubler, 1972. Dance Collection, New York Public Library.

Brinson, Peter. *Dance as Education: Towards a National Dance Culture*. Basingstoke: Falmer Press, 1991.

Brookes, Jason H. *The Modern Dance*. Chicago: Church Press, 1890.

Brown, Jo Anne. "A Survey of Campus Resources on the History of Dance." Undated. University of Wisconsin–Madison Archives.

Burstall, Sara. *The Education of Girls in the United States*. London: Swan Sonnenschein, 1894.

Burt, Ramsay. *The Male Dancer: Bodies, Spectacle, Sexualities*. London: Routledge, 1995.

Butler, Judith. *Gender Trouble: Feminism and the Subversion of Identity*. London: Routledge, 1990.

Cavallo, Dominick. *Muscles and Morals: Organized Playgrounds and Urban Reform, 1880–1920*. Philadelphia: University of Pennsylvania Press, 1981.

Cheney, Sheldon. *The Art of the Dance*. New York: Theatre Arts Books, 1928.

Clark, Burton R. "The Organizational Conception." In *Perspectives on Higher Education*, ed. Burton R. Clark. Los Angeles: University of California Press, 1984.

Clinton, Catherine. *The Other Civil War: American Women in the Nineteenth Century*. Ed. Eric Foner. New York: Hill and Wang, 1984.

Coben, Stanley. *Rebellion against Victorianism: The Impetus for Cultural Change in 1920s America*. New York: Oxford University Press, 1991.

Colby, Gertrude K. *The Conflict: A Health Masque in Pantomime.* New York: A. S. Barnes, 1930. Dance Collection, New York Public Library.

Colby, Joy H. "Colleagues Plan Claxton Tribute." *Detroit News,* July 7, 1983.

Cole, Arthur C. "The Puritan and Fair Terpsichore." Reprinted by Dance Horizons from *Mississippi Valley Historical Review* 29, no. 1 (June 1972).

Conner, Lynn. *Spreading the Gospel of the Modern Dance.* Pittsburgh: University of Pittsburgh Press, 1997.

Conway, Jill. "Women Reformers and American Culture, 1870–1930." *Journal of Social History* (winter 1971–72): 164–82.

Coughlan, Neil. *Young John Dewey.* Chicago: University of Chicago Press, 1975.

Crane, J. Townley. *An Essay on Dancing.* New York: Phillips & Hunt, 1849.

Cremin, Lawrence. *The Transformation of the School: Progressivism in American Education, 1876–1957.* New York: Vintage, 1964.

Cremin, Lawrence, and Richard Freeman Butts. *The History of Education in American Culture.* New York: Teachers College Press, 1953.

Cuban, Larry. *How Teachers Taught: Constancy and Change in American Classrooms, 1880–1990.* 2d ed. New York: Teachers College Press, 1993.

Curti, Merle, and Vernon Carstensen. *The University of Wisconsin: A History, 1848–1925,* vol. 2. Madison: University of Wisconsin Press, 1949.

Daly, Ann. *Done into Dance: Isadora Duncan in America.* Bloomington: Indiana University Press, 1995.

Dearborn, Mary. *Love in the Promised Land: The Story of Anzia Yezierska and John Dewey.* New York: Free Press, 1988.

Delamont, Sara, and Lorna Duffin, eds. *The Nineteenth-Century Woman: Her Cultural and Physical World.* London: Croom Helm, 1978.

Dewey, John. *Art as Experience.* New York: Capricorn Books, 1934.

Dewey, John. "Comment on the Foregoing Criticisms (of Benedetto Croce)." *Journal of Aesthetics and Art Criticism* 6, no. 3 (1943): 203–9.

Dewey, John. *Democracy and Education.* New York: Macmillan, 1916.

Dewey, John. *The School and Society.* Ed. Jo Ann Boydston. Carbondale: Southern Illinois University Press, 1976.

Dewey, John. "Three Prefaces to Books by Alexander." In *John Dewey and F. M. Alexander,* ed. Frank Pierce Jones. Champaign, Ill.: North American Society of Teachers of the Alexander Technique, n.d.

Dijkstra, Bram. *Idols of Perversity.* New York: Oxford University Press, 1986.

Dodworth, Allen. *Dancing and Its Relations to Education and Social Dance.* New York: Harper and Brothers, 1885.

Douglas, Ann. *The Feminization of American Culture.* New York: Alfred A. Knopf, 1977.

Douglas, Mary. *Implicit Meanings and National Symbols.* London: Routledge and Kegan Paul, 1975.

Douglas, Mary. "Jokes." In *Rethinking Popular Culture,* ed. Chandra Mukerji and Michael Schudson. Berkeley: University of California Press, 1991.

Douglas, Mary. *Purity and Danger: An Analysis of Concepts of Pollution and Taboo.* London: Penguin Books, 1966.

Duncan, Isadora. *My Life.* New York: Liveright, 1927.

Dunkel, Elizabeth. "Put Dancing in Its Place." *Journal of Health and Physical Education* 9 (September 1938): 419.

Dyhouse, Carol. *No Distinction of Sex? Women in British Universities, 1870–1939*. London: University College London, 1995.

Dykhuizen, George. *The Life and Mind of John Dewey*. Carbondale: Southern Illinois University Press, 1973.

Efland, Arthur. *A History of Art Education: Intellectual and Social Currents in Teaching the Visual Arts*. New York: Teachers College Press, 1990.

Eisner, Elliot W. *The Art of Educational Evaluation*. Philadelphia: Falmer Press, 1985.

Eisner, Elliot W. *The Educational Imagination: On the Design and Evaluation of School Programs*. 2d ed. New York: Macmillan, 1985.

Eisner, Elliot W. "The Efflorescence of the History of Art Education: Advance into the Past or Retreat from the Present?" Keynote address, Pennsylvania State University, 1989. Unpublished; private collection of Elliot W. Eisner.

Eisner, Elliot W. *The Enlightened Eye: Qualitative Inquiry and the Enhancement of Educational Practice*. New York: Macmillan, 1991.

Eisner, Elliot W. "Reshaping Assessment in Education: Some Criteria in Search of Practice." *Journal of Curriculum Studies* 25, no. 3 (1993): 219–33.

Eisner, Elliot W., and Alan Pehskin, eds. *Qualitative Inquiry in Education: The Continuing Debate*. New York: Teachers College Press, 1990.

Eliot, T. S. "The Ballet." *Criterion* 3 (April 1925): 441–43.

Ellfeldt, Lois. *Dance from Magic to Art*. Dubuque: William C. Brown, 1976.

Faulkner, T. A. *From the Ball-room to Hell*. Chicago: Henry Brothers & Co., 1894.

Fletcher, Sheila. "The Making and Breaking of a Female Tradition: Women's Physical Education in England, 1880–1980." In *From "Fair Sex" to Feminism: Sport and the Socialization of Women in the Industrial and Post-Industrial Eras*, ed. J. A. Mangan and Roberta J. Park. London: Frank Cass, 1987.

Foucault, Michel. *The History of Sexuality: An Introduction*, vol. 1. Trans. Robert Hurley. New York: Random House, 1978.

Fryer, Judith. *The Faces of Eve: Women in the Nineteenth-Century American Novel*. New York: Oxford University Press, 1976.

Fryer, Judith. *Felicitous Space: Imaginative Structures of Edith Wharton and Willa Cather*. Chapel Hill: University of North Carolina Press, 1986.

Gardner, David P. "Issues Confronting American Higher Education." *Higher Education Quarterly* 42, no. 3 (summer 1988): 230–37.

Gardner, Howard. *Frames of Mind*. 10th ed. New York: Harper Collins, 1983.

Gardner, Vivien, and Susan Rutherford, eds. *The New Woman and Her Sisters: Feminism and Theatre, 1850–1914*. Ann Arbor: University of Michigan Press, 1992.

Geertz, Clifford. *The Interpretation of Cultures*. New York: Basic Books, 1973.

Gilman, Sander L. *Difference and Pathology: Sterotypes of Sexuality, Race and Madness*. Ithaca: Cornell University Press, 1985.

Glassow, Ruth B. "Building a Splendid Reputation." *Wisconsin Alumni Magazine* 34, no. 4 (January 1933): 102–7.

Goode, Elizabeth. "The Dance at Mills College." *Dance Observer* (August/September 1939): 252.

Gray, Judith Ann. "To Want to Dance: A Biography of Margaret H'Doubler." Ph.D. dissertation, University of Arizona, 1978.

Gray, Judith Ann, and Diane Howe. "Margaret H'Doubler: A Profile of Her Formative Years, 1898–1921." *Research Quarterly for Exercise and Sport* (centennial issue 1985): 93–101.

Gray, Judith Ann, and Diane Howe. "Margaret H'Doubler and the First Dance Major." Committee on Research in Dance Souvenir Program, 1987. University of Wisconsin–Madison Archives.

Griffith, Betty Rose. "Theoretical Foundations of Dance in Higher Education in the United States, 1933–1965." Ph.D. dissertation, University of Southern California, 1975.

Gross, J. B. *Parsons on Dancing*. Boston: n.p., 1879.

Gumport, Patricia J. "The Contested Terrain of Academic Program Reduction." *Journal of Higher Education* 64, no. 3 (May/June 1993): 284–311.

Gumport, Patricia J. "Curricula as Signposts of Cultural Change." *Review of Higher Education* 12, no. 1 (autumn 1988): 49–61.

Gutknecht, Carl. Interview with Margaret H'Doubler, 1963. Historical files, Department of Physical Education for Women, University of Wisconsin–Madison.

Haley, Bruce. *The Healthy Body and Victorian Culture*. Cambridge: Harvard University Press, 1978.

Hall, Granville Stanley. "Christianity and Physical Culture." *Pedagogical Seminary* 9, no. 8 (1902): 374–79.

Hall, Granville Stanley. *Educational Problems*, vols. 1 and 2. New York: Appleton, 1911.

Halprin, Anna. Videotape of interview and demonstration about Margaret H'Doubler, April 14, 1999. Anna Halprin Collection, San Francisco Performing Arts Library and Museum, San Francisco, California.

Hammond, Sandra. "Dance in Universities." *Arts in Society* 13, no. 20 (1976): 336.

Hawkins, Alma M. *Modern Dance in Higher Education*. New York: Teachers College Press, 1954.

H'Doubler, Margaret. *Dance: A Creative Art Experience*. 2d ed. Madison: University of Wisconsin Press, 1940.

H'Doubler, Margaret. *The Dance, and Its Place in Education*. New York: Harcourt, Brace, 1925.

H'Doubler, Margaret. "Dance as an Educational Force." *Arts in Society* 13, no. 2 (summer–fall 1976): 324–35.

H'Doubler, Margaret. *A Manual of Dancing*. Madison: [s.n.], 1921. University of Wisconsin–Madison Memorial Library.

H'Doubler, Margaret. "A Question of Values and Terms." *Dance Observer* 12, no. 7 (August/September 1945): 83.

Hill, Martha. "Martha Hill Reminisces about Bennington." Videotape of lecture delivered at Bennington College, July 25, 1985. Dance Collection, New York

Public Library, MGZHA 4–375: 1985.

Howe, Daniel Walker. "Victorian Culture in America." In *Victorian America*, ed. Daniel Walker Howe. Philadelphia: University of Pennsylvania Press, 1976.

Hughes, Matthew S. *Dancing and the Public Schools*. Cincinnati: Methodist Book Concern, 1917.

Jackson, Philip. "If We Took Dewey's Aesthetics Seriously, How Would the Arts Be Taught?" In *The New Scholarship on Dewey*, ed. Jim Garrison. Dordrecht: Kulwer Academic Publishers, 1995.

Jackson, Philip. *Untaught Lessons*. New York: Teachers College Press, 1992.

Jones, Margaret DeHaan, and Ruth Whitney. *Modern Dance in Education*. New York: Teachers College Press, 1947.

Jowitt, Deborah. *Time and the Dancing Image*. New York: William Morrow, 1988.

Katznelson, Ira, and Margaret Weir. *Schooling for All: Class, Race and the Decline of the Democratic Ideal*. New York: Basic Books, 1985.

Kehl, F. W. "Professor Kehl's School for Dancing and Deportment." Brochure, 1895. State Historical Society of Wisconsin.

Keller, E. Fox. "The Anomaly of a Woman in Physics." In *Working It Out*, ed. S. Daniels and P. Ruddick. New York: Pantheon, 1977.

Kendall, Elizabeth. *Where She Danced*. New York: Alfred A. Knopf, 1979.

Koritz, Amy. *Gendering Bodies/Performing Art: Dance and Literature in Early Twentieth-Century British Culture*. Ann Arbor: University of Michigan Press, 1986.

Kramer, Lawrence. *Music as Cultural Practice, 1800–1900*. Berkeley: University of California Press, 1990.

Kraus, Richard. *History of the Dance*. Englewood Cliffs, N.J.: Prentice-Hall, 1969.

Kriegsman, Sali Ann. *Modern Dance in America: The Bennington Years*. Boston: G. K. Hall, 1981.

Langer, Susanne. *Feeling and Form: A Theory of Art*. New York: Scribner, 1953.

Laundauer, Bella Clara. "Terpsichorean Ephemera." Madison: Rare Books, State Historical Society of Wisconsin, 1880s.

Lawson, William James, ed. *Dance Magazine College Guide*. New York: Dance Magazine, 1988–89.

Lepczyk, Billie Frances. "Margaret H'Doubler's Classification of Movement Qualities Viewed through Laban Analysis." *Dance Notation Journal* 14, no. 1 (spring 1986): 5–11.

Levine, David O. *The American College and the Culture of Aspiration*. Ithaca: Cornell University Press, 1986.

Levine, Lawrence W. *Highbrow Lowbrow: The Emergence of Cultural Hierarchy in America*. Cambridge: Harvard University Press, 1988.

Levine, Mindy. "Widening the Circle: Towards a New Vision for Dance Education." In *National Task Force on Dance Education in Washington, D.C.*, ed. Mindy Levine. Washington: Dance/USA, Washington, 1994.

Lloyd, Margaret. *The Borzoi Book of Modern Dance*. New York: Dance Horizons, 1949.

Bibliography

Logan, Olive. *Apropos Women and Theatre with a Paper or Two on Parisian Topics.* New York: Carleton, 1869.

Logan, Olive. *Before the Footlights and behind the Scenes.* Philadelphia: Parmelee, 1870.

Lott, Eric. *Love and Theft: Blackface Minstrelsy and the American Working Class.* New York: Oxford University Press, 1993.

Luttrel, W. "Working-Class Women's Ways of Knowing: Effects of Gender, Race and Class." *Sociology of Education* 62, no. 1 (January 1989): 33–46.

Macdonald, Stuart. *The History and Philosophy of Art Education.* London: University of London Press, 1970.

Madenfort, Duke. "The Aesthetic as Immediately Sensuous: An Historical Perspective." *Studies in Art Education* 16, no. 1 (1974–75): 5–17.

Mangan, J. A., and Roberta J. Park, eds. *From "Fair Sex" to Feminism: Sport and the Socialization of Women in the Industrial and Post-Industrial Eras.* London: Frank Cass, 1987.

Maple, Dick. *Palaces of Sin; or, The Devil in Society.* St. Louis: National Book Concern, 1902.

Marks, Joseph E., III. *America Learns to Dance.* New York: Exposition Press, 1957.

Marks, Joseph E., III. *The Mathers on Dancing.* New York: Dance Horizons, 1971.

Mather, Increase. "An Arrow against Profane and Promiscuous Dancing Drawn from the Quiver of the Scriptures," 1685. New York: Dance Horizons, 1975.

Matthews, Jonathan C. "Mindful Body, Embodied Mind: Somatic Knowing and Education." Ph.D. dissertation, Stanford University, 1994.

Mayhew, Katherine Camp, and Anna Camp Edwards. *The Dewey School: The Laboratory School of the University of Chicago, 1896–1903.* New York: Appleton-Century, 1936.

McBride, Genevieve G. *On Wisconsin Women: Working for Their Rights from Settlement to Suffrage.* Madison: University of Wisconsin Press, 1993.

McCormack, Allen E. *Dance Magazine College Guide: A Directory of Dance in North American Colleges and Universities.* New York: Dance Magazine, 1994.

McCrone, Kathleen E. "Play Up! Play Up! And Play the Game: Sport at the Late Victorian Girls' Public Schools." In *From "Fair Sex" to Feminism: Sport and the Socialization of Women in the Industrial and Post-Industrial Eras,* ed. J. A. Mangan and Roberta J. Park. London: Frank Cass, 1987.

McKinstry, Helen. "The Teacher of Physical Education." N.p., 1900. Dance Collection, New York Public Library.

"Memorial Resolution of the Death of Emeritus Professor Blanche M. Trilling." Faculty Document 6, December 7, 1964. 3 pages. University of Wisconsin–Madison Alumni Office.

Meyer, Leonard B. *Music, the Arts and Ideas.* Chicago: University of Chicago Press, 1967.

Milam, John H., Jr. "The Presence of Paradigms in the Core Higher Education Journal Literature." *Research in Higher Education* 32 (1991): 651–68.

Moore, Ellen A. "A Recollection of Margaret H'Doubler's Class Procedure: An Environment for the Learning of Dance." *Dance Research Journal* 8, no. 1 (1975): 12–17.

Morley, John. "Sex in Mind and in Education." *Fortnightly Review*, n. s., 15 (January 1 to June 1, 1874): 466–83.

Moulton, Robert D. "Bird Larson, the Legend." *Dance Observer* (April 1959): 53–54.

Newcomer, Mabel. *A Century of Higher Education for American Women*. New York: Harper & Brothers, 1959.

O'Brien, Dorothy Adella. "Theoretical Foundations of Dance in American Higher Education, 1885–1932." Ph.D. dissertation, University of Southern California, 1966.

Odom, Selma Landen. "Émile Jaques-Dalcroze." In *International Encyclopedia of Dance*, vol. 3, ed. Selma Jeanne Cohen. New York: Oxford University Press, 1998.

O'Donnell, Mary P. "Gertrude Colby." *Dance Observer* (January 1936): 8.

O'Donnell, Mary P. "Margaret H'Doubler." *Dance Observer* (November 1936): 99.

O'Donnell, Mary P. "Martha Hill." *Dance Observer* (April 1936): 43–44.

Park, Roberta J. "Sport, Gender and Society in a Transatlantic Victorian Perspective." In *From "Fair Sex" to Feminism: Sport and the Socialization of Women in the Industrial and Post-Industrial Eras.*, ed. J. A. Mangan and Roberta J. Park. London: Frank Cass, 1987.

Partsch-Bergsohn, Isa. *Modern Dance in Germany and the United States: Crosscurrents and Influences*. Vol. 5 of *Choreography and Dance Studies*, ed. Robert P. Cohan. Chur, Switzerland: Harwood Academic Publishers, 1994.

Pearsall, Ronald. *The Worm in the Bud: The World of Victorian Sexuality*. New York: Macmillan, 1969.

Peiss, Kathy. *Cheap Amusements: Working Women and Leisure in Turn-of-the-Century New York*. Philadelphia: Temple University Press, 1986.

Peshkin, Alan. "In Search of One's Own Subjectivity." *Educational Researcher* 17, no. 7 (1988): 17–21.

"Proceedings of a Symposium on John Dewey's *Art as Experience*." *Journal of Aesthetic Education* 23, no. 3 (fall 1989): 49–67.

Remley, Mary Lou. "The Wisconsin Idea of Dance: A Decade of Progress, 1917–1926." *Wisconsin Magazine of History* 58, no. 3 (spring 1975): 179–95.

Rice, Emmett A., John L. Hutchinson, and Mabel Lee. *A Brief History of Physical Education*. New York: Ronald Press, 1958.

Robarts, Jason R. "The Century of Hope: The Quest for a Science of Education in the Nineteenth Century." *History of Education Quarterly* 8, no. 4 (winter 1968): 431–47.

Rosemont, Franklin, ed. *Isadora Speaks*. San Francisco: City Lights Books, 1981.

Rosenberg, Rosalind. *Beyond Separate Spheres: Intellectual Roots of Modern Feminism*. New Haven: Yale University Press, 1982.

Ross, Janice. "Marian Van Tuyl." In *American National Biography*, ed. John A. Garraty. Cary, N.C.: Oxford University Press, 1995.

Bibliography

Roth, Robert. *John Dewey and Self-Realization*. Englewood Cliffs, N.J.: Prentice-Hall, 1962.

Rudolph, Frederick. *The American College and University*. Athens: University of Georgia Press, 1990.

Ruyter, Nancy Lee Chalfa. "Antique Longings: Genevieve Stebbins and American Delsartean Performance." In *Corporealities*, ed. Susan Leigh Foster. London: Routledge, 1996.

Ruyter, Nancy Lee Chalfa. "Delsarte System of Expression." In *International Encyclopedia of Dance*, vol. 2, ed. Selma Jeanne Cohen. New York: Oxford University Press, 1998.

Ruyter, Nancy Lee Chalfa. *Reformers and Visionaries: The Americanization of the Art of Dance*. New York: Dance Horizons, 1979.

Ryan, Mary P. *Women in Public: Between Banners and Ballots, 1825–1880*. Baltimore: Johns Hopkins University Press, 1990.

Satori, Don Lugi. *Modern Dances*. Collegeville, Ind.: St. Joseph's Printing Office, 1910. Collection of Richard Powers.

Scholes, Percy. *The Puritans and Music*. London: Oxford University Press, 1934.

Shelton, Suzanne. *Divine Dancer: A Biography of Ruth St. Denis*. New York: Doubleday, 1981.

Shorter, Edward. *Women's Bodies: A Social History of Women's Encounter with Health, Ill-Health and Medicine*. New Brunswick, N.J.: Transaction, 1982.

Showalter, Elaine. *The Female Malady: Women, Madness, and English Culture, 1830–1980*. New York: Penguin Books, 1985.

Sklar, Kathryn Kish. *Catharine Beecher: A Study in American Domesticity*. New Haven and London: Yale University Press, 1973.

Slosson, Edwin. *Great American Universities*. New York: Macmillan, 1910.

Smith-Autard, Jacqueline M. *The Art of Dance in Education*. London: A. & C. Black, 1994.

Solomon, Barbara Miller. *In the Company of Educated Women: A History of Women and Higher Education in America*. New Haven: Yale University Press, 1985.

Sparshott, Francis. *Off the Ground: First Steps to a Philosophical Consideration of the Dance*. Princeton: Princeton University Press, 1988.

Spears, Betty, and Richard Swanson. *History of Sport and Physical Activity in the United States*. Dubuque: William C. Brown, 1978.

Staley, S. C., and D. M. Lowery. *Gymnastic Dancing*. New York: Association Press, 1920.

St. Denis, Ruth. "The Creative Impulse and Education." *Denishawn Magazine* 1, no. 4 (summer 1925): 14–16.

Storey, John. *An Introductory Guide to Cultural Theory and Popular Culture*. Athens: University of Georgia Press, 1993.

Suleiman, Susan Rubin. *The Female Body in Western Culture*. Cambridge: Harvard University Press, 1986.

"Symposium on John Dewey's *Art as Experience*." *Journal of Aesthetic Education* 23, no. 3 (1989): 49–67.

Tanner, Laurel N. *Dewey's Laboratory School Lessons for Today*. New York:

Teachers College Press, 1997.

Thwaites, Ruben Gold. *The University of Wisconsin: Its History and Its Alumni with Historical and Descriptive Sketches of Madison.* Madison: J. N. Purcell, 1900.

Todd, Ellen Wiley. *The New Woman Revisited: Painting and Gender Politics on Fourteenth Street.* Berkeley: University of California Press, 1993.

Trilling, Blanche. "History of Physical Education for Women at the University of Wisconsin, 1898–1946." 1951. University of Wisconsin–Madison Archives.

Tyack, David B. "The Spread of Public Schooling in Victorian America: In Search of a Reinterpretation." *History of Education* 7, no. 3 (1978): 173–82.

Tyack, David B., and Larry Cuban. *Tinkering toward Utopia.* Cambridge: Harvard University Press, 1995.

Tyack, David B., and Elisabeth Hansot. *Learning Together: A History of Co-Education in American Public Schools.* New York: Russell Sage Foundation, 1990.

Vance, Carol S. "The War on Culture." *Art in America* (September 1989). In *Culture Wars: Documents from the Recent Controversies in the Arts,* ed. Richard Bolton. New York: New Press, 1992.

Veeser, H. Aram, ed. *The New Historicism.* New York: Routledge, 1989.

Vertinsky, Patricia A. "Body Shapes: The Role of the Medical Establishment in Informing Female Exercise and Physical Education in Nineteenth-Century North America." In *From "Fair Sex" to Feminism: Sport and the Socialization of Women in the Industrial and Post-Industrial Eras,* ed. J. A. Mangan and Roberta J. Park. London: Frank Cass, 1987.

Vertinsky, Patricia A. *The Eternally Wounded Woman: Women, Doctors and Exercise in the Late Nineteenth Century.* Chicago: University of Chicago Press, 1994.

Vertinsky, Patricia A. "Sexual Equality and the Legacy of Catharine Beecher." *Journal of Sport History* 6, no. 1 (spring 1979): 38–49.

Veysey, Lawrence R. *The Emergence of the American University.* Chicago: University of Chicago Press, 1965.

Wagner, Ann. *Adversaries of Dance.* Chicago: University of Illinois Press, 1997.

Whorton, James C. *Crusaders for Fitness: A History of American Health Reformers.* Princeton: Princeton University Press, 1982.

Wilcox, Faith, et al. "History of Physical Education for Women at the University of Wisconsin, 1889–1916." 1916. University of Wisconsin–Madison Archives.

Wilkinson, William Cleaver. *The Dance of Modern Society.* 3d ed. New York: Funk & Wagnalls, 1884.

Williams, Milan Bertrand. *Where Satan Sows His Seed: Plain Talks on the Amusements of Modern Society.* Chicago: Fleming H. Revell, 1896.

Williams, Robert Bruce. *John Dewey, Recollections.* Washington: University Press of America, 1982.

Wolf, Dennie Palmer. Introduction to Arts Education Assessment Framework, prepared for the National Assessment Governing Board. Washington: College Board, 1994 prepublication edition.

Woody, Thomas. *A History of Women's Education in the United States,* vol. 4, book 2, *Science and Education,* ed. J. McKeen Cattell. New York: Science Press, 1929.

Woolson, Abba Gould. *Woman in American Society.* Boston: Roberts Brothers, 1873.

Zeltner, Philip. *John Dewey's Aesthetic Philosophy.* Amsterdam: B. V. Gruner, 1975.

INTERVIEWS AND CORRESPONDENCE WITH AUTHOR

Bigelow, Marion. Fresno, California. Interview with author, May 25, 1996.

Brown, Julia. Madison, Wisconsin. Telephone interview with author, May 25, 1999.

Cumbee, Frances. Madison, Wisconsin. Telephone interview with author, April 26, 1999.

Davidson, Hermine Sauthoff. Madison, Wisconsin. Letter to author, May 10, 1996. Interviews with author: March 17, 1996; January 19, 1997; March 26, 1999. Telephone interviews with author: March 25, 1996; June 12, 1997; May 5, 1998.

Eastham, Jane. Madison, Wisconsin. Interview with author, March 27, 1999.

Enos, Edith Boys. Upper Montclaire, New Jersey. Interview with author, July 27, 1996. Letters to author: August 1, November 19, 1996; January 3, 1997.

Halprin, Anna. Kentfield, California. Interview with author, July 19, 1999.

Harper, Nancy. Madison, Wisconsin. Telephone interview with author, March 28, 1999.

Hawkins, Alma. Los Angeles, California. Interview with author, May 13, 1997.

Hinkson, Mary. New York, New York. Telephone interview with author, March 3, 1997.

Leath, A. A. Madison, Wisconsin. Interview with author, August 28, 1992.

Moore, Ellen A. Madison, Wisconsin. Interviews with author: March 23, 1996; March 27, 1999. Telephone interview with author, April 13, 1998.

Mullen, Margaret Jewell. Menlo Park, California. Interview with author, October 17, 1992.

Nagel, Louise H'Doubler. Piedmont, California. Interview with author, May 9, 1998.

Neihoff, Helen M. Letter to author, July 1996.

Powers, Richard. Stanford, California. Interview with author, April 20, 1996.

Index

Index

Maple, Colonel Dick, 43
marriage: of H'Doubler, 90–91, 112;
as "legalized prostitution," 90; and
professionalism, 90–91; and teaching,
90–91
Marsh, Lucille, 207
Martin, John, 207
masculinity: and antidance treatises,
41–42; and images of women, 33–34
master of fine arts degree, in dance, 189
Mathews, Arthur, 31
May Fêtes, 84–91, 110, 125
Mayhew, Abby Shaw, 82, 83, 95, 133
McCrone, Kathleen, 67, 68
McIver, Charles, 24
McKenzie, R. Tait, 58
McMartin, Elizabeth C., 62
Mead, Margaret, 11
media, dance criticism in, 173, 207
medical profession, 46, 52, 57, 61, 66, 76
men: and antidance treatises, 39–41,
49; feminization of boys and, 33;
good dancers as emulating, 169; and
"gymnastic dancing," 111; and ideals
of manhood, 67; and "male gaze," 171.
See also masculinity
Methodist Episcopal Church, 10
Metropolitan Opera House (New York,
N.Y.), 116, 167
Midwest, isolation of, 206–7
military drills, 57, 78, 85
Mills College (Oakland, Calif.), 65, 203,
204–5, 207
mind: dance as means for developing,
199–200; German philosophers' views
of, 194. *See also* mind-body issues
mind-body issues: and affective domain in
physical education, 126; and Alexander
Technique, 139–41; and antidance
treatises, 47, 48–49; and benefits
of dance, 59; and dance in higher
education, 214; Dewey's views about,
125, 132–33; and exercise as means of
attaining perfection, 59; and experience
in H'Doubler's classroom, 154, 157,
160, 182; and functions of dance, 7;
and gender, 27, 28, 72; and goals of
education, 190; H'Doubler's views
about, 127–28, 190, 195, 198, 199–
200, 213, 214; and movement training,
139–41; and physical education, 54, 59,

79, 213; and "proper" physical activity,
64; Trilling's views about, 100–101,
214; and University of Wisconsin dance
program, 213; and Victorianism, 47; and
women's access to higher education, 53
mirrors, in dance studios, 171, 172
modern dance, 3–4, 10, 11, 86, 89, 139,
203, 207
Moore, Ellen, 108, 147, 150, 151, 155,
156–57, 160, 161, 169–70, 179, 181
morality: and antidance treatises, 38,
39, 41, 46, 48, 49; and arts, 194–95;
and body, 49; and dance, 19, 20,
26, 68, 84, 194, 206; and dance in
higher education, 138; Delsarte's views
about art and, 21–22; and emergence
of physical education, 57, 59; and
foreign influences on America, 46; in
France, 46; and functions of sport,
60; and goals of physical education,
81; H'Doubler's views about, 194,
195; and health, 51; and hygiene, 54;
and images of women, 29, 34; and
immigrants, 49; and performing arts,
84; and physical exercise, 38; and
"proper" physical activity, 64, 65, 67,
68; and redefinition of women's roles,
63; and social dancing, 38, 39, 84; and
theatrical dance, 138; and Trilling's
goals for physical education program,
78; and Victorianism, 25, 26; women as
arbiters of, 26
Morley, John, 71
Morrill Federal Land Grant Act (1862),
74, 75
Moscow, Russia, Duncan's dance school
in, 17–18
motherhood, 55, 56, 63, 68
Mount Holyoke College, 63–64
"Movement and Its Rhythmic Structure"
(course), 147
movement training: of Alexander, 128,
139–41; and dance performance,
130–33; of Delsarte, 20–22; and
Dewey, 139–41; and Dewey's influence
on H'Doubler, 138; and dualism,
130–33; "follow-the-demonstrator,"
151; H'Doubler's interest in, 7; health
through, 14; Larson's system of, 117–18;
and mind-body issues, 139–41; and
physical education, 65

269